Modern English Literature

W. W. ROBSON

Modern English Literature

000879
820

Oxford New York Toronto Melbourne
OXFORD UNIVERSITY PRESS

Oxford University Press, Walton Street, Oxford OX2 6DP

OXFORD LONDON GLASGOW
NEW YORK TORONTO MELBOURNE WELLINGTON
NAIROBI DAR ES SALAAM CAPE TOWN
KUALA LUMPUR SINGAPORE JAKARTA HONG KONG TOKYO
DELHI BOMBAY CALCUTTA MADRAS KARACHI

ISBN 0 19 888051 0

© *Oxford University Press 1970*

First published 1970
Fourth impression 1979

PRINTED IN GREAT BRITAIN
BY RICHARD CLAY (THE CHAUCER PRESS) LTD
BUNGAY SUFFOLK

In Memory of my Father and Mother

Preface

THIS BOOK IS not a comprehensive account of modern English literature. It discusses only a selection of the writers of the period whom I have
read and enjoyed. For this selection I take sole responsibility, as I do for
the opinions expressed. These, in so concise a book, cannot be supported
by evidence. But I have usually mentioned by name the specific works
on which I have based them.

I have accepted the common convention that by literature is meant the
imaginative exploration of human possibilities; that is, prose fiction, poetry,
and plays. But from time to time I have included brief discussions of non-
fictional writers, so as to suggest, however sketchily, the general movement
of thought in this country. The scope of this book excludes writers outside
the British Isles. But Henry James, T. S. Eliot, and Ezra Pound are so
crucial to the understanding of modern English literature that no book on
this period could omit them. And it will be remembered that the first two
of these writers lived in England and became British subjects.

Modern writers, by definition, have not stood the 'test of time', that
steady scrutiny of many generations, that gradual process of sifting, without which literary history is impossible. But those whose main work
was done before 1950 can be seen in some sort of historical perspective,
however limited and temporary this may be; and it is on a selection of
their work that I have based my most substantial discussions. My brief
references in the Epilogue to the work of more recent writers must be
regarded only as offering suggestions and pointers, not as representing any
widespread critical agreement.

I have tried throughout this book to keep my general standards as broad
and humane as possible. No writer should be condemned merely because
we dislike his point of view. One of the great pleasures of literature, after
all, is to escape from ourselves and see the world through other eyes.

I am grateful to Mr. J. C. Maxwell, to the staff of the Clarendon
Press, and to my wife, for their invaluable help with the manuscript.

W.W.R.

Contents

Contents

Introduction

ONE OF THE masterpieces of European art is *La Grande Jatte*, painted by the French artist Georges Seurat in 1886. The art-critic must explain, if he can, how this picture of people fishing and boating, or sitting quietly with their children, achieves its extraordinary beauty. To the social historian the sunny calm of this scene has another significance. It is a reminder that middle-class life in Western Europe, so uncomfortable at the beginning of the nineteenth century, had reached by its end the greatest comfort that had ever been known, or perhaps ever will be, for real comfort is impossible without abundant domestic service. The new twentieth century seemed to promise to more and more people more and more of this peace and prosperity. The tenor of thought in the age was optimistic, liberal, and progressive. This last word, like its opposite 'reactionary', needs an explanation. What progressives affirm, and what reactionaries deny, is that human improvement—not necessarily perfectibility—is possible; that the only tolerable inequalities among men and women are either those imposed by physical nature, or those which are rationally defensible; and that the instrument for carrying out social and political changes is reason. Until 1914 the number of thinking people who affirmed these convictions, and of unthinking people who took them for granted, was very large. And they seemed to have good grounds for their confidence.

England shared the general European serenity. And there were special reasons why English life was so peaceful. George Lichtheim has pointed out the most important of these. England, the pioneer industrial nation, had its industrial revolution without a political revolution. The class war has remained a metaphor. There is nothing in English history like the June days of 1848, when the working class and the bourgeoisie fought out their quarrel on the streets of Paris. The English socialist tradition has never been revolutionary. The English labour movement grew up in the bosom of the Liberal party. In English history political events have seldom quickened the slow processes of social change. Some thinkers at the beginning of the century wondered whether this would always be so. G. K. Chesterton in his poem 'The Secret People' surmised that the wrath of the English people might one day surpass 'Russia's wrath' of 1905. It is interesting to place this poem beside Kipling's castigation of the governing class in 'The Islanders'. Both poems read like auguries of a revolution in England. But it has never come.

Real and deep changes, however, did occur in the first decade of the twentieth century. This was the period which George Dangerfield has described as 'the strange death of Liberal England'. The great Liberal party, the party of Gladstone, had emerged from the nineteenth century with its dominant element, the landowning grandees, gradually losing control. But they had transmitted their philosophy of government and their aristocratic Whig outlook to the well-to-do patricians and able professional men who provided the Liberal party, in its last phase of power, with leaders. It was the Haldanes and Asquiths and Greys who were to conduct England into the modern period. But the rank and file of their party were very different. Lower-middle class, Nonconformist, and provincial, they were opposed with almost equal intensity to war and to strong drink. These Radicals, as they were called, produced one great man, Lloyd George. But he was to desert them, to become (in 1916) the ablest Prime Minister of the century, but, in the end, a leader who had lost his following.

Contemporaries may not have anticipated the death of Liberal England. But they did find an extraordinary significance in the death of Queen Victoria in 1901. What men felt at her passing is evoked in the famous last paragraph of Lytton Strachey's *Queen Victoria*. This feeling was not confined to the educated. Thousands of popular elegies were written to commemorate the departed mother of her people. The accession of her son Edward VII was felt in contrast to be an anticlimax. The stout, florid, sociable king personified for W. B. Yeats 'new commonness upon the throne', and Henry James was not alone in regretting the supersession of 'little mysterious Victoria' by 'dreadful fat vulgar Edward'. James's disciple Max Beerbohm caricatured the King savagely. A flavour of cigar-smoke and baccarat, financiers and race-meetings, pervaded the new reign. Yet King Edward was widely popular, and he had a genuine dignity and attractiveness which Max's caricatures do not convey. And the brief phase of English civilization to which his name has been given has something mellow about it. There is good reason why people nowadays dwell wistfully on the golden afternoon of the Edwardian age.

But this mellowness should not be over-emphasized. There was a darker, harsher side to English life. The grim facts were to be found in sociological studies like those of Mr. and Mrs. Webb. They underlie the efforts of imaginative writers to stimulate the social conscience, like

Kipling in 'The Record of Badalia Herodsfoot', or Shaw in his propaganda plays, or the early work of Galsworthy. Speaking after the advent of a new school of writers which had no use for him, Galsworthy described his own literary period, ending, he thought, about 1910, as characterized by 'a passionate or ironic perception of inequalities and injustice'. A younger novelist, E. M. Forster, wrote an optimistic parable of Edwardian England in *Howards End*. This book, with all its absurdities, is one of the few English novels to make a successful use of deliberate symbolism. And through his symbolism Forster hints at a happy future for England in the emergence of a new ruling class, through the alliance of the traditional liberal culture (the Schlegels) with the new, pushing, business people (the Wilcoxes). But it is notable that the lower-middle classes (the Basts) appear as pathetic victims. Across the golden afternoon there loomed the ominous shadow of the exploited poor.

So progressives could not feel complacent. Much remained to be done. But the modernization of England was proceeding rapidly. That there might be loss as well as gain in this process worried few. It did worry George Sturt (1863–1927), who wrote as 'George Bourne' about that close-knit village life of England which is still not quite extinct. In *The Wheelwright's Shop* (1923) George Bourne reminded his readers of what has been lost since the arrival of the motor-car and the techniques of mass-production. But to the Edwardian progressive, this would have seemed mere sentimentality. Urban civilization was 'here to stay'. Urgent problems like the relief of poverty bulked larger than wistfulness about the rural past. And modernization was happening everywhere. Samuel Hynes has remarked that nearly everything we think of as characteristically modern already existed in England by 1914: aircraft, radio telegraphy, cinemas, the sculpture of Epstein, the physics of Rutherford. (To this list Mr. Hynes adds, rather surprisingly, the Labour party.)

Literary culture was being penetrated by the moderns. D. H. Lawrence, Joyce, Pound, Virginia Woolf, Forster were all Edwardian authors. In art, a complacent provincialism still flourished. The Tate Gallery (opened 1897) had made a dreary start. But the first exhibition of Post-Impressionist paintings was held in London in 1910. It was in that year, said Mrs. Woolf, that human nature changed. Her friend Roger Fry was the chief English backer of the Post-Impressionists. English culture was being Europeanized. There was Russian opera and ballet. There were Russian novels, particularly those of Dostoevsky, becoming known through the translations of Constance Garnett. The Edwardian censorship still barred any serious treatment of sex or politics or religion, but it was being challenged. Dramatists like Shaw and Granville

Barker fought it. Novelists like Bennett questioned the rigidity of the divorce laws. Havelock Ellis and Edward Carpenter campaigned for more tolerant attitudes towards sex. The feeling of a new stir in the world was not confined to England. Jacques Rivière, the French critic, wrote in 1913: 'A sharp little wind is being blown suddenly through the darkness and boredom of the dying nineteenth century. Once more it is morning. Everything is beginning again.'

All was not well with Edwardian England. There was still widespread poverty and disease among the people. There were signs of hysteria and violence, as in the movement for Woman Suffrage and the reaction of the authorities to it. The tragic problem of Ireland still smouldered. But the disaster that was finally to demoralize the rational humanists came not from within but from outside. England had begun the century as still a great imperial power, but insecure after the South African War, in which world opinion was against her. As so often, England's rôle was disputed. Some favoured 'splendid isolation'; some Continental alliances. Some still put their faith in imperialism. But it was plain to all that the high confidence of the Victorian age was no more. It is for historians to discuss what brought about England's war with the Germany of Wilhelm II. Its outbreak came as a shattering surprise to most English people: what Lowes Dickinson lamented as 'the international anarchy' had kept the general European peace since 1871. The war's length and cost, material and spiritual, was to be even more shattering. To us it has become a miserable truism that high technological efficiency can accompany barbarism. But to many in 1914 this was a painful novelty. War seemed obsolete. The Great War was a triumph of unreason. To many, it seemed like lightning from the clear sky of rational humanism. But one spacious mind had already responded sensitively to the temper of the age that led to it. The American–Spanish philosopher George Santayana wrote in 1913: 'The world is obviously the sport of cruder powers—vested interests, tribal passions, stock sentiments, and chance majorities. Having no responsibility laid upon it, reason has become irresponsible.'

In literature, as in other things, the Edwardian age was the epilogue of the Victorian age. Meredith and Swinburne died. Yeats had paused in his development. If he had died in 1910 he would not now be regarded as a great poet. Hardy lived on, but wrote no more novels. Henry James, after his failure with the theatre, had entered his curious last phase. The general public ignored him. Compared with James, the most publicized writers of the age—Shaw, Wells, Kipling, Chesterton, Belloc—have something of the journalist about them. Their best work is still alive, but it is dated as James's or Hardy's is not. Galsworthy,

Bennett, and Maugham continued the novel in its post-French and post-Russian phase. They were genuine artists, if not great ones. Conrad is the only great artist in Edwardian fiction.

There was a feeling of optimism in the period, typified by Shaw and Wells, but also by Forster's early novels, with their faith, reminiscent of Meredith's, in the power of nature to restore health and sanity to civilized man. Even the most tragic writer of the age, Thomas Hardy, ended *The Dynasts* on a note of hope. We detect little uneasiness in the characteristic art of the period, in the music of Elgar, the novels of Galsworthy, or the paintings of Orpen. Even satirists like Beerbohm or 'Saki' do not seem radically disturbed. Since the Aesthetic movement had suffered its setback, with the fall of Oscar Wilde, there had been a new practical spirit in the literature of the age. Pound's *Hugh Selwyn Mauberley*, a sequence of poems written after the war, suggests that it had a tinge of vulgar materialism. But even in Aesthetic circles there was a feeling that this was no time for poses and posturing. Yeats conveyed it vividly when he wrote, years later: 'In 1900 everyone got down off his stilts; henceforth nobody drank absinthe with his black coffee; nobody went mad; nobody committed suicide; nobody joined the Catholic Church; or if they did I have forgotten.' It is doubtful whether Yeats himself ever got down off his stilts. But his words recall the widespread sense, at the beginning of this century, that a new literary period was about to dawn.

1

The Age of Shaw and Wells

Shaw—Wells—Kipling—Chesterton—Belloc

BERNARD SHAW (1856–1950), like his fellow-Irishmen Wilde and Yeats, believed that 'processions that lack high stilts have nothing that catches the eye'. He had a talent for publicity and showmanship. He enjoyed his rôle as national jester. Yet in his secretary's reminiscences he seems a shy, colourless man. Readers have been reminded of the great actor after the theatre has closed and the grease-paint is off. The public figure of 'G.B.S.' was merely another of his dramatic creations. The real Shaw remains a mystery; only to be fathomed, if at all, in his creative work.

When Shaw left Dublin for London, at the age of twenty, he took up socialist politics. He became an effective public speaker. But he soon realized that his true ambition was to be 'king in the realm of the English language'. The novels he wrote were slow to find a publisher. But as he wrote them he developed a witty prose style, sharpened by debate. 'Effectiveness of assertion,' he said, 'is the alpha and omega of style.' 'My method is to take the utmost trouble to find the right thing to say, and then to say it with the utmost levity.'

Shaw began as a book-reviewer, art-critic, music-critic—the best music-critic we have ever had. He did not write plays till he was middle-aged. When he was over forty, after a serious illness, he married an Irish lady of good family, advanced views, and private fortune. His plays began to succeed and make money. He gave up his bohemian manner of life. He remained high in the progressive ranks of the Fabian Society. But he now gave less time to public speaking and more to playwriting.

Shaw did not win easy success in the theatre. The English managers were shy of his work. He wanted his plays to be read and discussed. So he wrote long prefaces which have little to do with the plays they introduce, but expatiate on many topics. Like his contemporary J. M. Barrie, he wrote elaborate stage directions, so that his plays could be read like novels. He enlivened the plays with topicalities. His comedy made Englishmen laugh at themselves. 'An Englishman thinks he is moral when he is only uncomfortable'—this kind of satire wins friends among the satirized. Shaw writes with an air of saying something scandalous and shocking. But this is only a stylistic device. His views were the advanced commonplaces of the time. He preached that the ordering of society should be in the hands of educated, reasonable men. His ideal was ordered progress in a democracy. What hampers this is not evil and selfishness, as moralists thought, but stupidity and inefficiency. The emotional basis of Shaw's progressivism was his hatred of the narrow-minded religious bigotry he had known in his boyhood, just as his austere mode of life, his Jaeger suits, his abstention from strong drink and flesh-meat, were a reaction against the seedy, shabby, *louche* background of his youth. But Shaw professed to be appealing to reason, not emotion. He professed a belief in argument. He used rhetoric; but he cultivated a clear, lucid manner of writing.

Shaw invites his audience to laugh with him at the sentimental absurdities of the conventional theatre. He proclaims that he is showing life as it is. But this is all part of the joke. Shaw's plays are wild romances like Molière's. His characters are familiar theatrical types. His plays abound in traditional tricks of the theatre, absurd or spectacular costumes, uproarious dénouements, horse-play. Though he ridiculed Victorian melodramas and 'well-made plays' for their false sentiment, his own plays are full of corny pathos and stagey rhetoric. Often these are used ironically. But sometimes, to our discomfort, they are used straightforwardly.

Shaw's humour always tends towards the farcical. Unlike the authors of classic comedy, he does not combine making fun of people with moral disapproval. As a serious dramatist Shaw was at a disadvantage compared with Molière or Ben Jonson. Living in the twentieth century, he could not take for granted the standards by which conduct is condemned as eccentric. He had to put forward his own standards. This makes the author himself seem another eccentric. Hence the atmosphere of irresponsibility and farce.

But Shaw's master in drama was not primarily a writer of comedy. His chosen medium for enforcing his ideas was the new European theatre of Ibsen. Ibsen's main theme is the tyranny and inhumanity of social convention, which denies to human beings their need to express their unique and peculiar natures. Ibsen's plays fall short of the tragic. Social convention, dramatically speaking, is a poor substitute for Fate. It can be altered; whereas in tragedy the hero is confronted with something unchangeable and ultimate. However, Ibsen's plays, if not tragic, are gloomy. Shaw avoided gloom. Even in his 'unpleasant' or propaganda plays, where he is a didactic dramatist like Ibsen or Brecht or Arthur Miller, farce is always breaking in. The material is like Ibsen's, but Shaw evades its gloomy implications. Shaw's comedy flowers in the 'pleasant' plays. The exposition scene of *Arms and the Man* (1894) is enough to show his skill, with its surprises, its suspense, its touches of fancy. *Arms and the Man* seems to us a light comedy. Yet at the time it was thought shocking because of its unromantic treatment of war and soldiering. Yeats admired and hated it. 'It seemed to me,' he said, 'inorganic, logical straightness, and not the crooked path of life.' Shaw for Yeats was a smiling sewing-machine. The Irish dramatist he backed was J. M. Synge, who was 'by nature unfitted to think a political thought'. Synge was essentially a poet: Shaw was not. This is clear in *Candida* (1894), where the poet Marchbanks belongs in a farce. The play as a whole, though amusing, is serious. Candida herself is one of the types in whom Shaw is interested: the self-sufficient character. It is her simple confidence in the power of her own virtue which gives her strength. She anticipates the strong-minded women of Shaw's later plays. Her 'manly' husband turns out to be a grown-up baby, ludicrous and pathetic.

Shaw achieved a better balance between farce and seriousness in *Caesar and Cleopatra* (1901). Caesar is the first of his portraits of the great man. Shaw adopted Nietzsche's term, the Superman. *Man and Superman* (1903) was the most ambitious play he had yet written. It is still a popular favourite. But the best part of it, the third act, is rarely performed. This is a long dream sequence in which Mendoza, who represents the Devil, presides over a debate in hell. The debt to Mozart is obvious. Shaw had a lifelong interest in opera. He tells us how it taught him to shape his plays into recitatives, arias, duets, trios, ensembles, finales, and bravura pieces to display the technical accomplishments of the executants. But *Man and Superman* has lessons to teach. The play has a voluminous introduction in which Shaw expounds them. Tanner, his spokesman, goes on talking after the play in 'The Revolutionist's Handbook' and 'Maxims for Revolutionaries'. Shaw expounds his belief in God, but a God who is not transcendent. Shaw prefers the phrase 'Life Force'. To serve the purposes of the Life Force, the Superman must be bred by eugenics. Such is Tanner's gospel. But in the play as we normally see it, without dream sequence or preface or handbooks, the honours go not to him but to his captor Ann. This is not in accordance with Shaw's intentions. But popular theatrical instinct may be sounder.

John Bull's Other Island (1907) reveals unexpected aspects of Shaw. He shows that he can enter imaginatively, like Yeats, into the Irishman's feeling for Ireland, the 'endless dreaming'. But what for Yeats was a mode of insight into a higher reality was for Shaw a horrible temptation, like drugs. Another theme of *John Bull's Other Island* is interesting. For the first time Shaw draws a religious character, Father Keegan. It has been said that though Shaw may be remembered as an artist rather than a prophet, his best-drawn characters are religious people, not artists. From Father Keegan to Saint Joan, religious characters are among his most memorable.

Major Barbara (1905) is also concerned with religion: the attraction of the Salvation Army for the educated, idealistic Barbara. But the main theme of this play is power. The mystique of power is embodied in the entrepreneur, Undershaft. The play's lesson is a grim *Realpolitik*. Shaw, like Carlyle, was fascinated by power. The twentieth century had begun with widespread optimism about progress, democracy, and socialism. Belief in them has foundered because their supporters failed to understand that all require the use of power: and power corrupts. Shaw saw the need for power, but averted his eyes from the corruption. Beatrice Webb, Shaw's old friend and the leading spirit of the Fabian Society, was shocked by *Major Barbara*. Shaw, she said, was 'gambling with ideas and emotions'. The play was 'a dance of devils'. Shaw's appeal to the intellect was by now obviously secondary. His most powerful work came out of latent, unconscious material. His ideological choreography, like his buffoonery and clowning, seems to have been a device to enable him to evade its tragic implications.

Tragic material—jealousy, untimely death, the place of beauty among other values—is evaded in *The Doctor's Dilemma* (1906). Critics agree that Dubedat, the amoral painter, is boring and a failure as a character. What we enjoy is the satire on doctors. As usual with Shaw, we like the people satirized. *Getting Married* (1908) and *Misalliance* (1914) bring up the question of Shaw's treatment of sex. D. H. Lawrence condemned it for flippancy and irreverence. Shaw in his younger days was rumoured to be a great pursuer of women. He conducted a long and ardent correspondence with two actresses, Ellen Terry and Mrs. Patrick Campbell. He constantly talks of love and passion, but he cannot convey it. A striking thing in these plays is Shaw's repugnance to the idea of family. His own early background was in some ways like Joyce's, but in one vital respect it was different. The Joyces quarrelled incessantly, but there was a warm feeling among them. There was not among the Shaws.

Shaw's finest comedy, *Pygmalion* (1913), has deep roots in his own psychology. Everyone knows, if only from the musical play *My Fair Lady*, the story of the eccentric phonetician who makes a lady out of a flower-girl. It is the legend of Galatea. But Eliza is the opposite of Galatea, the statue who came to life. She is turned from a living person into an object—Bergson's definition of comedy. Few scenes in drama are funnier than Eliza's social début as a talking doll. The fourth act of the play is profound. It shows the immorality of using a person as a *means* to anything. The fifth act is a failure. Shaw, the anti-romantic, refused to let Higgins marry Eliza. Popular instinct demands it. But Shaw weakened the structure of his play (there has to be an epilogue to tell us how Eliza married another man) rather than bring them together. The reason may be that *Pygmalion* is full of personal material. The relation between Higgins and Eliza reminds us of the relation between Shaw and Ellen Terry or Mrs. Patrick Campbell, his attempts to manipulate them, to make them dolls.

Heartbreak House (1919) shows more obviously the stresses and conflicts in Shaw. The façade of rational humanism is very thin in this play. Most of it is farce; but its culminating mood is King Lear's 'Off, off you lendings!' The play was planned before the Great War, although the closing incident was suggested to Shaw by a Zeppelin raid near his home in 1915. Its dominant feeling is captured in the recurrent image of England as a drifting ship. What unity it has is provided by the old mad mystic Captain Shotover. Shaw had turned in this play from Ibsen to a greater dramatist, Chekhov. But what is touching in Chekhov's *Cherry Orchard* is hysterical in Shaw: what is gentle humour in the one is wild farce in the other.

Up to 1914 Shaw's influence had spread over the whole civilized world. But his fame did not come in the way he had hoped. He did not carry conviction as a constructive thinker. Iconoclasm had become an obsession with him. His clowning obscured his serious purposes. A critic called him a mixture of prophet and playboy. It seemed that he could not reconcile the two. After the war he tried to do this in the enormous four-part play *Back to Methuselah* (1921). He took up the idea which histologists were suggesting, that human tissue could be preserved indefinitely. Aldous Huxley uses this idea in *After Many a Summer* (1944). He uses it to arouse horror and disgust. Shaw's purpose is different. He hails the prospect of an endless future for humanity. But, as in most utopias, it is a humanity which has been stripped of everything recognizably human. This is a grisly dream, only made bearable by the rattle of Shaw's levity.

Back to Methuselah seemed to show that spiritually Shaw had not survived the war. But in *Saint Joan* (1924) he wrote the greatest of his plays. For the first time he reconciles his comedy with his serious convictions. Shaw's historical plays—*Saint Joan, Caesar and Cleopatra, Androcles and the Lion*—are among his best. He is freed from the lure of the topical. But *Saint Joan* shows little concern for actual history. Warwick and the Bishop of Beauvais interpret medieval problems in a modern way. All the same, the historical setting, and above all the character of Joan, give dignity to Shaw's theme. The profound question which he raises, in making her the expression of the Life Force, is why Joan failed. Her faith in her voice, means for him the conviction that imagination is the voice of God. Yet the medieval church was an impressive institution, and Shaw makes it seem so. It gives Joan a fair trial. The Inquisitor's long speech is the finest in Shaw. But Shaw's sympathies are with Joan, the inspired individual. For once Shaw has not avoided strong drama. The forces opposed to Joan are impressive, and taken seriously. The play is Shaw's version of Dostoevsky's 'Grand Inquisitor'. Can we afford a saint? Do we want one? Shaw does not give an unambiguous answer.

Saint Joan restored Shaw to critical favour. Critics said that he had given up teasing, and was showing sympathy with the simple and the good. But he had always done so—in *The Devil's Disciple*, in *Candida*, in Father Keegan of *John Bull's Other Island*. What the critics did not notice is that Shaw's admiration for Joan, the inspired individual, was bound up with his admiration for dictators. Shaw's socialist friends were uneasy about this, but they excused it. After all, Shaw admired Stalin as well as Mussolini.

After *Saint Joan* Shaw's powers as a dramatist declined. His later plays are mostly political extravaganzas. Their wit and their powers of exposition are astonishing in a man so old. But Shaw's capacity to stage *debates* had gone. After *The Apple Cart* (1930) what he offers is a monologue, still entertaining, but predictable. Years before, he had said that 'a man is like a phonograph with half-a-dozen records. You soon get tired of them all; and yet you have to sit at table while he reels them off to every new victim.' This was to be his own fate.

It is hard to judge Shaw. In some ways he is too near to us, and in some ways too remote. What is most enjoyable in Shaw is his style. Some people prefer the prefaces to the plays, because there they can sample it without dramatic disguise. The basis of all Shaw's writing is the soapbox. He writes a brisk debater's prose. There is no drivel. Every sentence carries a punch; yet they are flowing and musical. It is the best kind of English prose, in the tradition from Swift to George Orwell.

What is least enjoyable in Shaw is his subordination of the individual to the collective. When Eve in *Back to Methuselah* finds out about generation she says to Adam: 'You may die when I have made a new Adam. Not before. But then, as soon as you like.' This contempt for the individual is pernicious. And it contradicts Shaw's own insights as a dramatist. His best plays, *Pygmalion* and *Saint Joan*, both affirm the priceless value of the individual.

What was Shaw's dramatic achievement? He will live in stage history. He abolished the 'curtain', the 'aside', the 'one-man play'. All these have come back again : but such is the theatre. He tried to take away the 'star' appeal from drama and replace it by the theatre of ideas. This too has been ephemeral, because few dramatists have any ideas. Shaw carried on a battle with Shakespeare throughout his career. In a late playlet, *Shakes versus Shav*, he lets 'Shakes' have the last word. This seems right. Shaw was the best English dramatist since Shakespeare. But this is not such a compliment as it sounds : English drama since Shakespeare has been a minor art. Great poetic drama, with its charged brevity and imaginative concentration, is the highest achievement of the human mind. *Macbeth*, *Phèdre*, the *Oresteia*, are unsurpassed. Shaw did not surpass them. But he stands high above most of his English predecessors and all his successors. Most dramatists before and after Shaw have been either unliterary or unplayable. Shaw was neither.

The Scottish dramatist J. M. BARRIE (1860–1937) was the only serious rival to the Irish dramatist Shaw. He too had genius, though of a limited and peculiar kind. Barrie came to London and began as a journalist. He made his name with stories of bachelor life in England and village life in Scotland. His first outstanding play is *The Admirable Crichton* (1902). It is a drawing-room comedy with a new twist : the hero is the butler. But it is more than that. In contrasting the life on the island where the characters are shipwrecked with the day-to-day comedy of London life, Barrie is quietly asking social and political questions. Is the set-up on the island, where Crichton the butler dominates as a natural superior, preferable to the set-up in London, where he 'knows his place'? Progressivists would say yes, reactionaries no. The play does not answer. It reveals rather than tells.

Barrie's most powerful work goes deeper. His theme was the wish to remain a child. This theme had personal origins. Barrie seems to have had a relationship with his mother, when he was young, which was similar to D. H. Lawrence's. (Lawrence was interested in Barrie's work, and Barrie admired *Sons and Lovers*.) Out of this material Barrie created *Peter Pan* (1904). The god Pan frequently appears in Edwardian writers, but this is his only successful incarnation. Barrie belongs to a late phase in the tradition going back to Rousseau and *The Prelude* and *David Copperfield* : the discovery of the importance of childhood, the survival of the child in the man. With Barrie's work we may compare *Le Grand Meaulnes* of the French writer Alain-Fournier, the children's classic *The Wind in the Willows* (1908) by Kenneth Grahame (1859–1932), and the songs and stories of A. A. Milne (1882–1956). There are displeasing things in *Peter Pan*, such as the mawkishness about Wendy. But there are also the romance and comedy that children enjoy. And, however softened and whimsicalized, there is a real conflict between Peter and Hook. Barrie's later play, *The Boy David* (1936), is not successful. But its theme, David against Goliath, was the theme of *Peter Pan*: the image of youth, at once poignantly vulnerable and terribly menacing. The play has remained a children's classic. But it appeals to adults too. We are not surprised to hear of Rupert Brooke's love for it. He was a Peter Pan in real life.

Mary Rose (1920) is Barrie's other important play. It too is about the wish to remain always a child. But it also looks squarely at a problem which Tennyson had raised but evaded in *In Memoriam*. We treasure the beloved memory of our dead: but do we really want them back? *Mary Rose* is an uncomfortable and disturbing play. The sentimentality is in the stage-directions rather than the play itself.

Just as flippancy is the usual charge against Shaw, sentimentality is the usual charge against Barrie. Some readers may be afraid of losing control of their response to his work. At any rate, sentimentality seems to occur when an author tries to make us feel a tender emotion which we do not want to feel at the moment. We are contemptuous when he fails, and angry when he succeeds. Barrie has perhaps angered as many people as he has pleased.

Barrie and Shaw were not Englishmen. Some of the peculiarities of their work may be traced to their national heritage. With Wells we come to a writer whose work is quintessentially English.

H. G. WELLS (1866–1946) may not be the greatest English writer of the twentieth century. But he has a high claim to be considered the most characteristic. If a reader ignorant of English literature was confined to one author, to give him an idea of the trend of English life in this century, Wells would be the best choice.

In his *Experiment in Autobiography* (1934) Wells has given an amusing account of his early life. His background of gardening and professional cricket, shopkeeping and domestic service, is essential to understanding him. His thought was always related to his class-consciousness. We have a self-portrait of Wells as a young schoolmaster in *Love and Mr. Lewisham* (1900): 'a passable-looking youngster of eighteen, fair-haired, indifferently barbered. He wore ready-made clothes. His black jacket of rigid line was dusted about the front and sleeves with scholastic chalk, and his face was downy and his moustache incipient.' In 1884 Wells became a student in what was to be the Royal College of Science. He left without taking a degree and supported himself by teaching and journalism.

Wells was to become the most famous popularizer of progressive thought in the world. The driving-force in his thought was his dislike of the English governing class. He grew up when thinkers like Darwin and Marx were altering the whole outlook of educated men. But their ideas made little impression on the traditional humanism of the English upper class. All his life Wells was impatient with the old classical education. This, he kept reiterating, was the age of science. He made his name as the prophet of a large class of men who were beginning to think in this way. Wells himself was neither a scientist nor a man of scientific temperament. He was impatient, impulsive, inaccurate. He was often superficial. But he had grasped imaginatively the possibilities of modern science. The dominant myth of the nineteenth century was evolution. Nineteenth-century thinkers tended to interpret this myth optimistically. They averted their eyes from the grim fact that what we regard as improvement in Nature is the exception to the general rule of degeneration. To the optimistic evolutionist, science was giving us the means to better our fellow-men. The progressivism of Shaw and Samuel Butler was stimulated by their hatred of narrow religious bigotry. Wells's was stimulated by the stagnant, muddled, lower-middle-class life he had known. Time and again his books insist on its waste of human possibilities. Below Wells's class lay the proletariat, the Morlocks of *The Time Machine*, inarticulate, potentially menacing. Above it the well-to-do, ignorant of science, were sunk inertly in their vested interests and fossilized traditions. It was time for the new educated class to find its prophet. They found him in Wells.

Wells won his early fame not as a prophet but as an entertainer. In Tennyson's phrase, he wrote 'fairy-tales of science'. Sometimes the fairy-tale is better than the science, as in *The Time Machine* (1895). The Machine itself is ridiculous. Wells worked harder on this story than on his later books. The aesthetic nineties lie behind his careful revisions. But Wells's main effort in his early work was frankly directed towards commercial success. He achieved it because he wrote on a topical subject: the practical applications of science. Jules Verne had led the way. Like Verne, Wells was often inspired in his stories by current scientific speculation. But Wells was less interested than Verne in the practical side. Verne was concerned with how men could actually get to the moon, and he made an astonishingly accurate prediction. Wells simply has his inventor make a substance which defeats gravitation. His real interest is in the romantic wonder of the unknown, the icy vacancy of space, and, at the end, the opportunity for satire, when Cavor expounds European civilization to the Grand Lunar.

But Wells was often a true prophet. He shows foresight as well as insight. In a novel published in 1914, *The World Set Free*, he was writing of the atomic bomb. It has sometimes been thought that Wells was optimistic about the possibilities of science, till the end of his life, when he despaired. But this is wrong. As early as *The Island of Dr. Moreau* (1896) we have a story of scientific outrage to human nature. Wells as usual was ahead of his time: we think of contemporary misgivings about transplants. A pessimistic strain is common in his work. 'The Country of the Blind' (1911), one of his best stories, is a gloomy version of Plato's allegory of the Cave. His 'man who could work miracles' is at the point of destroying the world when he gives up his power. Wells, like his successor William Golding, is pessimistic about human nature.

Wells came to feel his responsibility as a writer of what were then called 'scientific romances' (nowadays 'science fiction'). The people were ignorant. In scientific research there was no co-ordination, no leadership. Hence there were great dangers. Wells, who foresaw air warfare and poison gas, came to see human history as 'a race between education and catastrophe'. He flung himself into a campaign for improved scientific education. He continued to write novels, but his subject-matter had changed. From imagining scientific marvels he turned to consider people as they are. He wrote a series of novels in which the hero, an inventor or reformer, is let loose with his ideas in typical settings of English life. His hero is a friendly treatment of the kind of character Virginia Woolf depicts with hostility as Charles Tansley in *To the Lighthouse*. Wells's hero is based on himself. He comes to grief not because of his opponents' malice, but because of their stupidity. Wells sides with his hero, but keeps his own sense of humour. These books are not dull. But they are journalism rather than literature.

The truth is that Wells had little artistic conscience. His method of writing fiction had always been old-fashioned. He combines episodes and links them by lightly sketched figures. He has no real central character. The reader's interest lies in what will happen next, not in the book as a whole. All this could not satisfy the aesthetic purist Henry James. He wrote to Wells about *The New Machiavelli* (1911) that it showed 'your capacity for chewing up the sickness of the world in such enormous mouthfuls'. He spoke of 'the accursed autobiographical form which puts a premium on the loose, the improvised, the cheap'. He complained that there was no detachment in Wells's novels. They had not gone through the crucible of the imagination. This artistic quarrel was to have repercussions later, at the end of James's life, when Wells satirized the older novelist in *Boon* (1915) and provoked a final rupture. Who came off best in the famous quarrel? Surely Henry James did. James's best work is as fresh as it ever was. Wells's social and political novels read like old newspapers. But, in fairness to Wells, more of the truth comes out in his correspondence with a novelist with whom he did not quarrel, Arnold Bennett. Wells thought Bennett an excellent craftsman but no genius. Bennett thought Wells a genius who did not take enough pains. Probably both were right.

What is best in Wells's later novels is their comedy. Kipps in 1905, the Ponderevo circle in *Tono-Bungay* in 1909, Mr. Polly in 1910, have taken their place with Dickens's characters. The living figures in Wells's novels are all comic. As always with the best comedy, Wells's rests on something serious: the absurd pathos of the misfit. His humour is sometimes irascible; in this he resembles writers of our own day like Kingsley Amis or John Wain. But often it is indulgent. The beautiful *rallentando* at the end of *Mr. Polly* shows its closeness to poetry.

From *The New Machiavelli* (1911) onwards there is little but a documentary interest in Wells's fiction. His books discuss politics, education, and (in and out of season) free love. But it is all discussion. And it is very self-centred. D. H. Lawrence was a harsh critic of his contemporaries, and he himself, like Wells, was apt to serve up autobiography as the art of fiction. But he had a point when he complained of the egocentricity of *The World of William Clissold* (1926). The truth is that Wells's heart was not in fiction. The Great War was followed by 'the petty peace'. The war, which killed so many young men in the flesh, killed many older men in the spirit. Wells seemed to be one of them. His last good novel, *Mr. Blettsworthy on Rampole Island* (1928), is suffused with pessimism. Another war seemed likely. Wells's message had not been heeded. He had preached the need for drastic adaptations of society, but people lacked the knowledge to carry them out.

In his later work Wells set himself to do something constructive about this. After the Great War he produced a great body of non-fictional work, *The Outline of History* (1919–20), *The Science of Life* (1929), in which he had collaborators, and *The Work, Wealth and Happiness of Mankind* (1932). *The Outline of History* may be Wells's greatest book. It is his answer to Uncle Ponderevo's wish for something better than 'drum and trumpet history'. It has its place in the great myth of Man which pervades the whole of Wells's work. Man emerges from darkness, survives against incredible odds, and rises to a dazzling summit of achievement, before the final darkness descends again. This is the supreme imaginative myth of the modern world, and it is accepted by countless people as the truth. Wells did not invent it: but he gave it unforgettable expression.

Wells was a clever man with many ideas. But his genius was in his imagination. Sometimes he is merely fanciful. *The Invisible Man* is an entertaining story, but Wells realizes only the comic and thrilling possibilities of the idea. Higher in his work come the serious fables or allegories, like 'The Pearl of Love'. 'The Country of the Blind' is the best of these. It is one of the stories in which Wells comes nearest to uniting intellect and imagination. Highest of all come stories like 'The Door in the Wall', which seem to hint at another dimension of meaning, like myths. Wells at his best, like Plato, was a myth-making genius.

But even in his lesser work Wells could make any subject interesting. He was a humorist who could describe the lower-middle-class world of his youth without exaggeration or false pathos. Even his later and inferior books are enlivened by vivid sketches of people he had met. In all his work his own personality comes through: the lively host and companion, with his rapid mind, his high-pitched voice, his quick and very blue eyes; a readily amused, mischievous, irritable man, a raconteur, an improviser, a lover of games—not cricket, which for Wells was a game for the hated upper class, but croquet, though not as the upper class played it. Wells's playfulness brightens the drearier stretches of his work. Like Shaw, he was a great popularizer of the thoughts of other men. And like Shaw he has dated. Shaw's daring sallies no longer raise an eyebrow in any modern country. Most of Wells's non-fictional work is dead. Science changes so quickly that his expositions are out of date. His historical predictions so far have been mostly wrong. His plans for the betterment of the world are forgotten. But nothing can rob Wells of his greatest gift: the ancient art of the story-teller.

There are three ways in which RUDYARD KIPLING (1865–1936) is unique among modern writers. First, his power rests on something even more primitive than Shaw's or Wells's. If Shaw is a jester and Wells a story-teller, Kipling is a witch-doctor. In his heyday he had an almost hypnotic hold over his public. Yet he combined with this primitive power an essentially modern technique of writing, sophisticated, allusive, economical. Secondly, Kipling's point of view is unusual. Although he is famous as the pre-eminently nationalistic English writer, he remained in some ways a foreigner, looking at England from the outside. He called it jokingly 'the most marvellous of all the foreign countries I have ever been in'. Compared with the work of a writer like Hardy, there is something a little artificial about Kipling's cult of the English past. What is worse is the embarrassment he causes when he acclaims the virtues of his English contemporaries. It is true that he also castigated their vices. But there is still something incongruous about an English writer stridently proclaiming to the world the value of English modesty and reserve. Too often he himself fell into the tones of the visiting M.P. in *Stalky and Co.*, 'the Jelly-Bellied Flag-Flapper'. Finally, Kipling's subject-matter is unusual. He was to win his fame as the writer who identified himself with the British Empire, and especially with British India. And he is the only writer who has written anything of lasting value about that phase of our history. But India was only for a time, and incidentally, his subject. All his characteristic work is devoted to the human qualities that are needed to make any modern society a going concern. He writes about tough, dedicated, not very imaginative men, in various walks of life, who combine a strong sense of duty with a command of technique, tricks of the trade, and 'know-how'. These men are not usually at the top of the administration. They are often undermined and frustrated by the men at the top. Kipling espoused their cause. That he happened first to encounter such people in India was merely an accident. Kipling was concerned with qualities that transcend ideology, or class, or race. These qualities are often unamiable, and Kipling does not make them seem less so. But he rubs in, more than any other writer, how indispensable they are.

Kipling had his first literary success in India. He wrote about, and for, the society of Anglo-India that he knew. When he came to London, the Aesthetic movement was still powerful. Kipling's colourful, emphatic writing, which had been greatly enjoyed in Anglo-India, seemed crude and vulgar to the Aesthetes. And their dislike of Kipling was reciprocated. Yet Kipling's own background was not philistine. His father was a museum curator and an artist and scholar. And through relatives on his mother's side he came early into contact with people distinguished in art and literature. The painter Burne-Jones was his uncle. The poet William Morris was an intimate friend of his family. But Kipling chose to sing the praises of men of action, the rank and file of the soldiers and the civilians who ran the Empire. At a time when sayings like 'Living? Our servants will do that for us' were popular in literary London, Kipling extolled hard, practical people. He stirred emotions on behalf of a code of obedience, discipline, patriotism. He insisted on the importance of training, of authority, of 'licking into shape'.

In real life, as in Kipling's stories, such things often mean bullying. Those who dislike Kipling say that he admires bullies. It has been suggested that his early sufferings as a child, which underlie one of his best stories, 'Baa Baa Black Sheep', had a curious psychological effect on him. Instead of identifying himself with the underdog, as many benefactors of humanity have done after such childhoods, Kipling identified himself with the oppressors. Whether that is so or not, Kipling is certainly preoccupied with cruelty. He is quite detached and candid about his interest in it, in his otherwise reticent autobiography *Something of Myself* (1937). His early sufferings may or may not have made him a cruel writer. They certainly gave him a great insight into cruelty, and made him more aware of men's need for compassion.

Kipling's convictions, and the emphasis with which he expounded them, made a forceful impact in the literature of the nineties. The Aesthetes and the progressives, for different reasons, were affronted.

But Kipling became widely popular. His verse, as well as his prose, was read eagerly. He was perhaps the last widely popular English poet. Kipling's fellow-writers recognized his genius. Henry James was an early admirer, and so was Wells. But their admiration dwindled. Wells had no use for Kipling's cult of obedience and the Law, which he satirized in *The Island of Dr. Moreau*. And James became dissatisfied and bored with the growing inhumanity of Kipling's work. By the beginning of the century Kipling had few literary friends left. His kind of patriotism did not seem the best kind. G. K. Chesterton remarked that Kipling loved England not because she was England but because she was great. During the South African War, Kipling's imperialism made him ideologically hateful to many. Imperialism was not so obnoxious as it later became. Joseph Conrad supported it. There were Liberal imperialists, of whom Winston Churchill was to become the most famous. Many Fabians were on their side. But Kipling's brand of imperialism resembled that of his friend, the adventurer Cecil Rhodes. It sounded crude and bellicose. Its insistence on duties and responsibilities towards subject peoples seemed to many a mere screen for greed and exploitation. On his side, Kipling had come to feel that the cultivated classes were politically irresponsible. There was an irritable, paranoid streak in his conservatism. He muttered darkly about 'foreign influence' behind strikes. He attacked progressive causes like Lloyd George's 'People's Budget', Irish Home Rule, Woman Suffrage. He denounced the national passion for sport, the 'flannelled fools' and the 'muddied oafs'. Developments in India and South Africa displeased him. The Great War brought personal tragedy as well as national catastrophe. His only son was killed at Loos in 1915. He was cut off by his strong-minded, socially ambitious wife from the ordinary people he had mixed with in his most creative days. We hear of him at dinner-parties, silent and withdrawn. His wife did the talking.

Political passions left their mark on Kipling as a man and an artist. And they still obstruct the fair judgement of his work. Only one thing need be said here about Kipling's politics. He was not a Fascist. The word as applied to him is both anachronistic and inaccurate. Fascism, or Nazism, represented to Kipling the extreme perversion of the insubordinate democracy which he hated. Kipling was an old-fashioned conservative, a Victorian moralist who believed in duty and responsibility. But he had an excitable, hysterical streak which broke out when his convictions were challenged. It was then that he was betrayed into his worst fault as a writer, over-emphasis.

In his prose fiction Kipling excelled in the short story. His novel, *The Light that Failed* (1890), is inferior, and his best book, *Kim* (1901), is a *nouvelle* rather than a novel. In his short stories Kipling, like Maupassant, and unlike Joyce, was not a 'pure' artist. He wrote for a magazine-reading public. He made products for consumers. He wished to instruct his readers as well as entertain them, but he knew that to do this he must first entertain them. This means that certain kinds of beauty are not to be found in his work. A story like Joyce's 'The Dead' has a quality of feeling that Kipling never achieved. But most writers have taken the tastes and capacities and inclinations of their readers into account. These, after all, are part of the 'medium' of writing. And Kipling wrote about subjects that matter. He wrote about things that men and women care about and have died for. The name of art cannot be denied to his best work. 'The Man who would be King' and 'On Greenhow Hill', 'Without Benefit of Clergy' and 'The Wish House' and 'The Gardener'—these are not pot-boilers.

Kipling, like Wells, had a long career, and wrote a great deal. But unlike Wells he always wrote with care. Every word is painstakingly selected for its flavour and cadence. Every touch tells. Indeed, Kipling's chief failing is that he over-wrote. His is not an art that conceals art. His style shows that his vision of life owes more to the will than the imagination. Only occasionally does his art become subtle and gentle: when he deals with the sufferings of the poor, or of women or children.

His programme is always varied. But certain preoccupations, or obsessions, constantly recur. One is the ordeal. As with Conrad, the ordeal is Kipling's favourite way of examining and testing a man's character. Military discipline is his cherished metaphor. And discipline is closely connected with ritual. 'Ritual is fortifying,' said Kipling. That is why he likes secrets, cryptograms, esoteric jargon, 'little languages'; that is why he likes totems, symbols, and Masonic signs. In nothing is Kipling so English as in his love of ritual.

But Kipling knew that men need a holiday from discipline and ritual. He likes to write farces in which things get completely out of hand, and order collapses amid helpless laughter. He thought of laughter primarily as a release from the strained posture of the will. But some readers have found Kipling's farces not joyous but hysterical. They often turn on elaborate practical jokes, or hoaxes. Some of these stories are less farces than tales of revenge. 'The Village that Voted the Earth was Flat' is an example. 'Dayspring Mishandled', one of the later stories, is a strange cryptic study of a vindictive hoaxer.

In such stories Kipling shows an interest in psychological abnormality. This sometimes overlaps with an interest in the paranormal. 'They' and 'The House Surgeon' and 'The Dog Hervey' explore this region. They are subtler than more famous stories like 'At the End of the Passage' or 'The Mark of the Beast'. Indeed, 'The Dog Hervey' is so subtle as to be obscure. So is 'Mrs. Bathurst'. Kipling's economy of technique sometimes leads to obscurity. In the stories written after the Great War, Kipling is especially preoccupied with mental abnormality. But it is notable that in these stories he is even more preoccupied with healing.

Stories like those in *Many Inventions* (1893) show another side to Kipling's mind. He is the only important writer in our century who responded positively to the machine age. Most writers have found it uninteresting or repugnant. They use 'mechanical' as a pejorative term. But Kipling evolved real poetry from machinery. Much more than the Marxian romantics, Mayakovsky for example, or the Left writers of the 1930s, Kipling was at home with modern machines. True, his treatment of them is fanciful and anthropomorphic. He writes about a ship that found herself, or talking railway engines. But in his interest in machines he does not usually desert humanity. He is interested in them largely because they give him an opportunity to write about the men who operate them: hard, practical, competent men who share a common jargon and common activities. He was fascinated by cliques, fraternities, in-groups.

Kipling is rarely successful when he deals with sex. Only in a few stories, like 'On Greenhow Hill' or 'Without Benefit of Clergy' or 'The Wish House', does he deal tenderly and unsentimentally with the relations between men and women. Usually he is perfunctory on this topic. Sometimes he conveys a fear and dislike of women. This may be the explanation of the notorious war-time story 'Mary Postgate', which centres on a repressed spinster's vindictiveness. Kipling likes to dwell on manliness, what Latin-Americans call *machismo*. Like his successor Ernest Hemingway he is concerned with 'proving' manliness. But unlike Hemingway he is not a 'loner'. He yearns for brotherhood and freemasonry. This is his panacea for mental sickness and loneliness.

The oddities of Kipling's art invite psychological exploration. But it resists deep analysis, because his manipulations of his themes are so deliberate and conscious. His complexity lies on the surface. It is like an artificially made jewel rather than a flower. He is not always so relentlessly didactic as in fables like 'A Walking Delegate' or 'The Mother Hive', but he is fond of lessons. Even his excursions into fantasy are firmly controlled.

Apart from a few stories, Kipling's most secure work is what he wrote for children or boys. Like other great Victorians, he is at his most natural and spontaneous when he writes for them. He can avoid troublesome material while releasing his imagination. Kipling's less likeable qualities can emerge in this kind of writing too. The school in *Stalky and Co.* (1899) is an awful place, but Kipling likes the awfulness. It is a study of savage life which we cannot enjoy as much as he does.

We have read E. M. Forster. The *Jungle Books* (1894, 1895) need no defending. They recreate the world of childhood. And they contain implicitly everything that Kipling wanted to say. *Puck of Pook's Hill* (1906) and *Rewards and Fairies* (1910), fabulous evocations of the English past, may be too sophisticated. Some young readers have felt that they were being got at. Kipling's greatest story is written from a boy's point of view. *Kim* is his *Huckleberry Finn*. But *Huckleberry Finn* deals with tragic issues: *Kim* does not. The ugly problems of imperialism are not ignored in this enchanting panorama of India, but they are not grappled with. The charm of *Kim* is its boyishness, its adventurousness, its optimism. Kim is not a pathetic outcast like Huckleberry Finn. He has his 'Great Game'. It is rather chilling to discover that the Great Game is espionage. All the same, *Kim* is a good book. Above all it is humane and tolerant. Rarely did Kipling achieve again that warm kindliness towards people of other races and creeds. The spirit of the gentle Lama pervades the book. Gentleness and sweetness are not the whole of goodness; but in a writer who was so often harsh and shrill, they do something to mitigate and atone.

Kipling won fame in poetry as well as in prose. He did not claim to be a poet. Yet all his best critics agree that, whatever his limitations, Kipling *was* a poet. Robert Bridges praised *Barrack-Room Ballads* (1892) for doing what the Wordsworth of *Lyrical Ballads* had claimed but failed to do: Kipling had really used the language of common men for poetry. Nothing could be easier than to denounce these ballads of army life as crude and vulgar. But Kipling was a wonderful technician. And there is reason to think that the common men he claimed to speak for did feel that he spoke for them. His poems can be dismissed as journalistic only if we are prepared to dismiss anything of direct everyday interest as unfit for poetry. To call a poem like 'The Broken Men' journalism is either unfair, or a compliment to journalism. Ballads like 'Gentlemen-Rankers' or 'Danny Deever' not only show a command of common responses: they show a real understanding of the ancient tradition in which Kipling is writing. He can also rise to grand occasions, as in 'For all we have and are' and 'Recessional'. 'Recessional' is particularly impressive. Writing at a moment of national self-congratulation, Victoria's Diamond Jubilee of 1897, Kipling gave a timeless warning to a great nation. Much later in 'The Storm Cone' (1932) he was to speak again in that strain to his countrymen.

T. S. Eliot called Kipling a great hymn writer, and much of his verse is congregational and communal. His patriotic verse is no more xenophobic than that of his predecessors Tennyson and Swinburne, and it has a foundation in common sense which they lack. Kipling is at his best when he admonishes, at his worst when he hectors. People will always disagree whether 'If' does one or the other. But no one will deny that it shows Kipling's love of preaching. Preaching was in his blood. And, like many great preachers, he was a master of invective. 'Gehazi' is one of the most powerful poems of scorn ever written.

A typical poem of Kipling acts upon the will. He wrote poems that could raise subscriptions, like 'The Absent-Minded Beggar'. But his best work has a deeper appeal. His soldier poems are notorious for their brutality, but they are full of imagination. 'Mandalay' may be despised, but it can never be forgotten. Poems like 'A Tree Song' or 'A Charm' or 'The Land' appeal more subtly. When people say that Kipling is not a poet, they may mean that his poems lack the sensuous-associative dimension of poetry. This is not true of 'Cities and Thrones and Powers' or 'The Way through the Woods'. But these are exceptions. As a rule Kipling's verse lacks suggestion and depth. He is a phrase-maker: many of his phrases have become household words. But this is because they are economical and telling, not suggestive and evocative. Kipling can be equally effective in prose. (A phrase he lent his cousin Stanley Baldwin helped Baldwin to destroy Lord Beaverbrook as a political force.) It has often been remarked that Kipling's verse shows no development. There is no early and late Kipling as there is an early and late Yeats. Verse for him was functional and instrumental, not the expression of his inner life.

Was Kipling a great writer in verse or prose? He was a *tremendous* writer in both. He cannot be ignored. The formidable little man with his gleaming spectacles, his beetling brow, his huge moustache, still broods over twentieth-century England. But much in his work may not outlive his time. To the end he was something of a journalist. Kipling was content to be judged so. There is an ironic significance in the motto he wrote for a society of journalists: 'We have served our day.'

G. K. Chesterton (1874–1936) will always be associated with his fellow-writer Belloc. Both were lively, pugnacious polemicists in an age of polemics. Kipling, Shaw, Wells, Belloc, Chesterton all took part. All opponents had a kindness for Chesterton: none had a kindness for Belloc. Chesterton was a picturesque figure, with his vast size, his bandit moustache, his opera cloak, his sword stick. But, despite his flamboyant appearance, he was a humble man. At the height of his fame he was asked by an American journalist which of his works he considered the greatest. He replied that he did not consider any of his works at all great. Humility was the secret of his genius. In an age of rampant progressivism, he tried to recall men to a sense of proportion. Questions of *scale* always preoccupied him. This may have been because of his own bulk. But it was more probably because he refused to forget or disparage the childish response to the world. He retained a child's power to see familiar things with the freshness of first vision.

Chesterton says of a young politician: 'When he thought of a joke he made it, and was called brilliant; when he could not think of a joke he said that this was no time for trifling, and was called able.' Chesterton himself could always think of a joke. He was a witty writer, whose wit throve on controversy. His beginnings as a writer were in the Aesthetic movement. Wit and paradox and epigram were cultivated there, and Chesterton delighted in them. In his prose as well as his poetry it is clear that Swinburne, one of the founders of the Aesthetic movement, had captivated his imagination. But he is a more visual writer than Swinburne. We must remember that he began as a painter. A story like 'The Wrong Shape' stays in the mind like a picture. The spiritual meaning of wrongness of shape is what interests Chesterton, but as always he has visualized it. Chesterton's sensibility was formed in the age of Swinburne. But his point of view and outlook, after his youth, were antithetical to Swinburne's. He disagreed with the Aesthetes, who either ruled out moral and religious considerations from art, or adopted an immoral or anti-moral position. Chesterton invoked against them the Catholic tradition of Christianity, and a Victorian moral seriousness like Ruskin's. But he did so gaily, not solemnly.

Chesterton first made his name as a critic and biographer. He wrote on Browning, on Stevenson, on Shaw, on Dickens. He was an excellent critic, with an inspired eye for verbal detail, rather like William Empson's in our own day. *The Victorian Age in Literature* (1913) abounds in quotable sayings. He is one of our best critics of fiction.

Chesterton himself wrote much fiction. But his novels suffer from a fatal fault: long-windedness. They are really blown-up short stories. The exception is *The Man who was Thursday* (1908). This strange book resembles the work of Franz Kafka, in that it has the effect of an allegory, and yet does not disclose its literal significance. Like some of Kafka's stories, it resembles a dream much more than most work which aims at the dream-like. Apart from this novel, Chesterton's best fiction is in the 'Father Brown' stories. Father Brown made his first appearance in 1911, and became the successor of Sherlock Holmes for the next generation. He does not belong to folk-lore as Holmes does. On the other hand, Chesterton's stories are much more ingenious than Conan Doyle's. The style is better, the poetry is much richer. And these tales are unique among detective stories for their insight into sin and guilt.

As a poet, Chesterton belongs to the period which was to become unfashionable after the rise of T. S. Eliot and his school. He belongs to the last phase of the Victorian romantic tradition. His most ambitious poem, *The Ballad of the White Horse* (1911), is an epic done in ballad style. It is remarkable that its most famous and grim lines, those beginning 'I tell you naught for your comfort', come from a writer who is often thought to be hearty and jolly. Chesterton's rhythms are too uniform, like Kipling's and Sir Henry Newbolt's. But some of his light verse has become familiar currency. As a writer of light verse he shares with Belloc and with Kipling the advantage of a serious point of view. The best of his poems, 'The Secret People', combines wit and seriousness. It sums up his version of English history.

This version is somewhat doctrinaire. And one element in it is disagreeable. Chesterton had taken over from his brother, Cecil Chesterton, and from Belloc, a belief that the English Liberal régime was thoroughly corrupt. With them, he regarded the Marconi scandal, in which Lloyd George and others were involved, as the most important event in English history. Though he was not personally anti-Semitic, he shared their dark thoughts about a conspiracy of Jewish financiers. The worst aspect of Chesterton's and Belloc's work is their fostering of sterile hatreds. But the kindliest of men can be led astray by wrong ideas. And not all Chesterton's ideas were wrong.

Chesterton was mainly a controversialist. He was better at opposition, as in *Heretics* (1905), than positive apology, as in *Orthodoxy* (1908). But Chesterton's religious beliefs were real and serious. He was a rationalist. He inquired of any belief or opinion, not whether it was in accordance with the presumed needs of 'modern man', but whether it was sound and reasonable. Chesterton shares the advantage with his admirers, C. S. Lewis and Ronald Knox, of being a thoughtful man contending with the thoughtless. Once thoughtless men were thoughtlessly religious; now they are thoughtlessly irreligious. Chesterton showed them that it was possible to be witty and provocative at the expense of the conventionally unorthodox.

Chesterton took his arguments to the market-place. He was a journalist who wrote rapidly. His aphorisms came to seem manufactured. He became an expert in surprises and paradoxes rather than arguments. The spice of his style could not hide the poor meat. He had a serious illness during the war, which reduced his vitality. His post-war work lacks sparkle. He was essentially a pre-war writer.

Chesterton is now completely in eclipse, except in old-fashioned Roman Catholic circles. Yet he was as witty as Shaw and as imaginative, in his own way, as Wells. Perhaps his eclipse is due to anti-Catholicism. But it may be due to the fact that Chesterton did not excel in any of the big literary genres. He was at his best in essays and short stories, and these are not taken very seriously by English critics. Furthermore, all his works are on the borderline between literature and journalism. But this is also true of Swift and Samuel Johnson, and yet they are in very good standing with critics. Perhaps Chesterton's day may come round again.

If it does, he must be clearly distinguished from HILAIRE BELLOC (1870–1953). Shaw, their friendly enemy, christened their alliance 'the Chesterbelloc'. But they are very different. Chesterton was fundamentally a liberal writer. Belloc was fundamentally illiberal: that is, he felt and encouraged contempt for *categories* of people. But Belloc was a better poet than Chesterton, and arguably a better prose stylist and a more powerful thinker. We may not like him so much, but he deserves to be taken seriously.

Belloc was the son of a French father. He was born in Paris. And though his education was in England, he retained in all his work a certain French quality. His satirical novels about political life have a 'brutality of the intellect' (to use a phrase of Chesterton's) which is commoner in French literature than in English. *Mr. Clutterbuck's Election* (1908) is one of the best political novels in our language. With all its deliberate exaggerations, it has a ring of reality.

Belloc was absorbed in English political life and controversy. In *The Servile State* (1912) he wrote what still remains an impressive study of the tendencies of modern collectivism. At the centre of his controversial battles was his propaganda for the Catholic Church and for 'Latin' civilization—he hardly separated the two. His defence of the Catholic Church may be summed up in two lines from one of his comic poems: 'And always keep a hold of Nurse, For fear of finding something worse.' Through biographies, essays, and pamphlets he laboured to overthrow what later came to be called the Whig interpretation of history. Whether Belloc's story is more convincing than the Whig story, or the Marxist story, or any other, must be left to historians. His historical works are always highly readable, though often repetitious. He had a particular interest in what used to be called, in pre-nuclear times, 'the art of war'. All his life Belloc was proud of having once served as a French soldier. It is above all as a fighter that we remember him.

Belloc fought with words. His battles with H. G. Wells have a vigour that we miss today. But his most lasting work may be in his poetry. His fifteenth and twenty-fifth sonnets are good examples of his grave, limpid manner. They suggest the predominance of judgement over emotion. He cultivated a lapidary style, like Landor. His best work is in his serio-comic verse. He wrote many memorable epigrams. The content is sharp and scathing, but the verse laughs and sings. Critics do not usually regard serio-comic poems like 'Mrs. Roebeck' as important. But some great poets of the past have excelled in it. So has a leading poet of our own day, W. H. Auden. Serious light verse derives from a poet's immediate interest in the world around him and his desire to communicate it to the reader. Belloc was the best writer of light verse in this century, and the best political satirist since Dryden. This suggests that it is an advantage for a satirist to have a conservative point of view. But Belloc's tone is anti-liberal rather than conservative. It is engaging in the youthful travel-diary *The Path to Rome* (1902), but cantankerous in the later *Cruise of the Nona* (1925).

Belloc's strong points as a writer are his vigorous and elegant style, and his gift for the picturesque. He had a particular liking for the French Revolutionary period, where great dramatic moments are frequent. Drier historians may disparage him. But many of the Revolutionary figures were themselves rather theatrical people, and Belloc conveys this. Belloc's most repulsive quality is his habit of suggesting that Catholicism is the only possible creed for superior people, and conveying this not by argument but by innuendo. In this respect his work resembles some of T. S. Eliot's more precious essays. Belloc knew what he was doing, which is a point in his favour. If what you are opposing is not an argument but a tone of voice, a tone of voice may be the only answer. But arguments should be met by arguments, and Belloc knew that the other side had arguments too.

Shaw, Wells, Kipling, Chesterton, and Belloc were all great journalists. The species is almost extinct today. Some will not regret this. To the young iconoclasts of the nineteen-twenties, it seemed obvious that the pre-war writers were inferior to Lytton Strachey and Aldous Huxley and Edith Sitwell and Virginia Woolf. Today it is not so obvious.

2

The Novel: Edwardian Realists

James—Conrad—Bennett—Maugham—
Galsworthy—other fiction

HENRY JAMES (1843–1916) is today at the pinnacle of critical favour. He is more acclaimed in America than in England. This is natural. For though James spent most of his writing life in England, and died a British subject, he is essentially an American writer. But he has his cult in England too. It flourishes especially in academic circles. However, James does not appeal to the ordinary reader, except in one or two of his stories, like *The Turn of the Screw*. His admirers might say this is because the ordinary reader lacks the intelligence to appreciate him. But other great novelists—Jane Austen and George Eliot, Thomas Hardy and D. H. Lawrence—have ordinary readers. The position of James is anomalous. At present he is invoked by writers who have little or nothing in common with him. One day they may realize this. Then he may be dismissed, as he was in his lifetime, as a mere literary curiosity. We must try to imagine how he will be judged when the critical pendulum has come to rest.

Henry James was born in New York City. His father had inherited a fortune from commercial sources and lived a life detached from practical affairs. He had evolved a religion of his own, partly based on the mystical writings of Swedenborg, which some critics believe to have had a lasting influence on his son's work. Henry James senior educated his children by a succession of governesses and tutors, and by prolonged European travel. The young Henry James spent a great part of his life in hotels.

This unusual family background, and restless mode of life, may have something to do with James's oddities. Of all twentieth-century writers in English, he is the strangest. The ordinary reader finds it hard to see what he is getting at. James's style, especially in his later work, is complicated and oblique. The stories he tells are sometimes incredible, from a matter-of-fact point of view. And when they are not incredible they seem rather trivial. A typical story by James is at the opposite extreme from a folk-tale. The manifest meaning of a folk-tale is simple, though the latent meaning may not be. In James the manifest meaning is not simple. Some of his hostile critics have suggested that there is no latent meaning. It is all much ado about nothing. But this is not so. A story of James like 'The Jolly Corner' owes its power to its latent meaning quite as much as a folk-tale like 'Rapunzel'. What puzzles the plain reader is that the story is not simply told.

Quite apart from the mystery of its deeper meaning, James's favourite subject is unusual. He seems early to have formed an idea of civilization which was not straightforwardly based on the observed behaviour of civilized people. It was based on a contrast between what he thought of as European and what he thought of as American. But just what he meant by this contrast is not clear. Of course his 'international' theme does have some direct reference to the actual world. James had a keen eye for manners. He is a master of social comedy. The misunderstandings and tensions between Americans and Europeans—especially English people—have, of course, a 'period' character in James's books. But in one form or another they are still with us. His early portraits of the charming, innocent but unconventional American girl—'Daisy Miller' is the most famous—would not have won him popularity if they had not been recognizable. What James admires in Europeans is their sophistication, ease, and urbanity. What he deplores in Americans is their rawness, crudity, and provinciality. He had told us in his autobiography, *A Small Boy and Others* (1913), of his nostalgia for the culture and the social forms of the Old World. He envied schoolfellows who enjoyed the 'pre-eminence' of being European. Later he was to envy the 'deep rich English tone' of George Eliot's novels and the 'density' of Balzac's France. In comparison, he found American civilization arid and immature. In a famous passage in his book on Hawthorne he lists the items of high civilization which were missing from American life.

But the contrast between European and American for James was not simply a contrast of sophistication with provinciality. It was complicated by a moral element. From another point of view, America stood in his mind for innocence and Europe for corruption—something deeply attractive but morally dubious. This may explain why his stories so often involve deception, betrayal, and conspiracy.

From the time when he left America as a young man, James was preoccupied with the problems of the expatriate. He recognized good qualities in the America he had left. He spoke of Turgenev as having 'a poet's quarrel with his native land'. This applies to himself. In particular, he admired much in the tradition of New England. Though he himself was not a New Englander, he had many personal connections with that culture. He admired its moral uprightness, its sincerity and straightforwardness, its freedom from snobbery, its democratic spirit and manners. On the other hand, he thought New England life limited, uncultivated, and unimaginative. Stories like *Roderick Hudson* (1875) and *The Europeans* (1879) dramatize the good and bad points of this culture by bringing contrasting figures into contact with it: Europeans, or Americans from other parts of America. In *The Bostonians* (1886) James investigates further weaknesses in New England culture. Provincial and lacking in worldly wisdom, it was an easy prey for charlatans. His satire in *The Bostonians* is sharp.

Here James was doing, in his chosen art, what Matthew Arnold had done in his critical essays. James himself was a fine literary critic, especially in a field which Arnold had rather neglected, the new European art of prose fiction. For James the novel was a major form of art, which challenged the traditional pre-eminence of drama and poetry. He deplored the absence of serious criticism of fiction. He regretted the indifference of American writers to the new potentialities which French and Russian novelists were developing. So when, in 1875, he migrated to Europe to live by literature, his first choice of residence was Paris. But within a year he left for London. He remained a lifelong admirer of the French masters. But there were elements in French high culture that he found distasteful. He found, to his distress, a coarseness and ill-breeding among the French writers. And in their own way they too were somewhat provincial. They were ignorantly indifferent to English literature. Still, James envied them their sophistication, their freedom to treat any subject they wanted. Fiction for them was a completely adult art. James came to the conclusion that English high culture and high society might supply what he desired: a blend of polite sophistication with the respect for moral conventions which his ancestral puritanism demanded. He was, in fact, to encounter much philistinism, and some immorality, in England. But henceforth England was to remain his home, and English life was to provide much of the stimulus for his art.

James's stories may be called social criticism. But this does not suggest their actual effect. They are queer psychological tales, written in a growingly indirect and oblique style. Imagery, metaphor, and simile convey a constant sinister undercurrent. This strange art may have had a private origin in James's own personal history. In a clever and talkative family, he was shy and silent. This may have increased his sense of isolation. And there may have been deeper causes. In 1861 he had a mysterious accident which, whatever it was, confirmed his belief that he was destined for a purely contemplative rôle in life. He was a lifelong celibate. And, though he enjoyed society and dining out, he was essentially a solitary man. His emotions found their outlet more and more in a passionate dedication to his art. In his notebooks we hear his long intimate communings with his own genius. His art became increasingly esoteric. He derived hints for his stories from anecdotes he heard: but he was impatient to remove them as soon as possible from the shape-lessness and clumsiness of real life. Real life provided only *données* for manipulation. He wished his materials to be under the absolute control of his art. 'Art *makes* life,' he fervently told H. G. Wells in their final quarrel.

James's art extends the possibilities of fiction. He set himself to per-fect a kind of novel in which there is little external action. Nearly everything is carried out in conversation. His stories are narrated through dialogue and social contacts, against a background of polite-ness and comfort. James disliked Oscar Wilde and his work, but he shared with Wilde a love of the worldly and urbane and brilliant. He is as witty as Wilde. But his wit is less extractable from its context: it is woven into the action of the book.

Like Wilde, and like Shaw, James wrote plays. He strove for many years to win popular success in the theatre. But he never did. And his efforts reached a sad anti-climax with the failure of *Guy Domville* (1895). Why did James fail in the drama? Strife and conflict lay at the basis of his art. But he could not project them on the stage in a con-vincing, gripping form. His technical originality was confined to the novel. He did not attempt to compete with the new drama of Ibsen or Shaw. He remained in the French tradition of 'the well made play'.

Whatever the reasons for James's failure in the theatre, his years of playwriting were not wasted. Later novels like *The Spoils of Poynton* (1897) and *What Maisie Knew* (1897) and *The Awkward Age* (1899) show how much the stage had influenced him. He used dialogue to reflect subtle nuances of character and mood. He took pains with the setting of the scene, the dovetailing of one episode into another, the balance and construction of his plot. Perhaps the most valuable by-product of his years in the theatre is his novel *The Tragic Muse* (1890). It reflects James's lifelong interest in the art of acting.

The best introduction to James's work is his first masterpiece, *The Portrait of a Lady* (1881). Its title reminds us of James's love of paint-ings. He always spoke of novels in the studio way. He talks of 'form' and 'rhythm' and 'composition'. Henry James was the child of the Aesthetic movement, which was dominated by painters. The story in *The Portrait of a Lady* seems quite simple. A charming American girl is in Europe, choosing among her suitors. She is trapped by a cunning pair into a bad marriage. At the end her noble nature compels her to re-nounce the opportunity to escape from her hateful husband, and accept the consequences of her choice, even though it was not the free choice she imagined. 'There was a very straight path.' But the story is not as

simple as it seems. The crucial problem is just *why* Isabel Archer
allowed herself to be snared into marrying Osmond. Her decision is
wrapped in mystery. The story as James treats it, through the consciousness of his central character Isabel, seems to cover an inner action
of quite different meaning. James's brilliant social comedy, his finely
observed English and American types, his wit and humour, can be enjoyed by any intelligent reader. They have made this novel popular. It is
in the treatment of his tragic material that James leaves us uncertain of
his purpose. In another of James's stories, *Washington Square* (1881),
we catch ourselves wondering whether the story, as it is told, is credible.
Could a father break a daughter's life in the way he does here? All
James's work uses the motivations of traditional fiction, love or money
or self-respect. But in his books they may be a sort of code which
disguises different meanings. If so, we may ask: is a novelist entitled to
play with human behaviour and motivations, for his own private purposes?

This question has occurred to readers of the late group of James's
novels, *The Wings of the Dove* (1902), *The Ambassadors* (1903), *The
Golden Bowl* (1904). On the face of it, these stories describe a set of idle
rich people who spend their time in trying to ferret out each other's
hidden thoughts from their conversation. They are not only inquisitive
but predatory. Yet on the face of it, James finds these people attractive.
But some readers think that his intention is to expose the decadence of
this society. For all its polish and grace, it is only a parody of true
aristocracy. Beneath the polite surface lurk monsters of vice and cruelty.
The American critic Newton Arvin wrote an article called 'Henry
James and the Almighty Dollar'. He points out James's preoccupation,
throughout his career, with this theme. 'Have they nothing golden but
their *ton*? Are there no symptoms of wealth?' a European aristocrat
asks about her American hosts in the early story, *The Europeans*. In a
late story, *The Ivory Tower* (1917), the dying American millionaire, Mr.
Betterman, says of his contemporaries: 'Money is their life.' We know
that James came to regret his romanticizing of the aristocratic Belle-
gardes, in his early book *The American* (1877). He had discovered that
aristocrats were capable of 'accommodation' of their 'noble indifference'
to 'deep avidities'. We remember characters such as the fortune-hunter
Townsend in *Washington Square*, the predatory aesthete Osmond in
The Portrait of a Lady, the aristocratic sponger Prince Amerigo in *The
Golden Bowl*. In 'Lady Barberina' the noble English heroine 'wants a
definite income'. 'She wants to be safe.' This phrase might be used to
sum up the moral tragedy of girls like Kate Croy in *The Wings of the
Dove* or Charlotte Stant in *The Golden Bowl*, who commit treason to
themselves and those they love for 'a settlement'.

Other critics have agreed to see James as much more socially respons-ible than he appears to be. Lionel Trilling has noted his forebodings of social and political revolution in *The Princess Casamassima* (1886). James had an ominous feeling that 'much of English life is grossly materialistic, and wants some blood-letting'. He had a sense of some-thing going on 'irreconcilably, subversively, beneath the smug surface'. *The Princess Casamassima* is not one of James's best novels. But his intentions may have been what Trilling says. And we might well see a moral concern, for the fate of children and young people, in the fahionable society shown in *What Maisie Knew* and *The Awkward Age*.

The trouble is that any confident interpretation of James's later work is difficult. His style, especially in the stories written after 1900, is tortuous and oblique. His brother William's explanation was that Henry had changed his stenographer, and the new one took down all his hesi-tations and ellipses. However that may be, the elaborations of James's later style serve as much to conceal as to reveal his attitude towards his characters. If we prosaically extricate the story of *The Golden Bowl*, the most extraordinary of the later novels, it seems to be about adultery, treachery, hypocrisy, and, strangest of all, an American millionaire buy-ing people as if they were *objets d'art*. But the novelist's attitude to-wards all this is enigmatic. Some have suggested that he was morally confused. Others have thought that his moral sense was in abeyance. On the other hand, it might be urged that James is dealing with a very unusual set of people, whose moral sensibilities belong to a peculiar cultural tradition. We must try to understand them on their own terms. A polished society, by definition, is one in which moral questions have become questions of manners.

Whatever James meant, readers in the new century were baffled. James's popularity dwindled. He was never to repeat the success of *Daisy Miller*. Even his admirers were discouraged by the etiolation of his later style, 'gold to airy thinness beat'. Even those who were pre-pared to take him on his own terms had to admit that he seemed to be presenting a static society. His art reflected its inner contradictions: but these seemed to produce only perplexity in James. There was no hint of any positive solution. To many in the new age he seemed a stranded Victorian. Shaw complained that he did not 'thrust us forward into the invigorating strife raised by Wagner and Ibsen'. Wells cruelly satirized him in *Boon*. James was to die feeling that his art had not been intel-ligently appreciated. The death-bed award of the Order of Merit may have been for his support of England's cause in the Great War, rather than for his literary eminence. After his death his repute as a writer sank very low.

But half a century later it has never been higher. This turn of fashion is welcome. James is a brilliant writer. His concern to extract the last drop of significance from his material is unequalled in fiction. Short stories like 'The Pupil' or 'The Abasement of the Northmores' or 'The Lesson of the Master'—many others might be mentioned—can be read again and again, and yield something new at each reading. Every stroke tells. The style is far from terse, yet no sentence, no word could be improved. Nothing is out of place. James was right to feel pride in his art, and sorrow that it was so little noticed. This may have been because he shows us contacts rather than direct conflicts. His highly bred sophisticates treat polite refinements as sacred. His art is largely an art of exclusion.

James paid a heavy price for his exclusiveness. His conviction that highly civilized people never speak out became an obsession. He became oblique and obscure. The limitations of his art became apparent. Compared with other great novelists—Stendhal, for example, or Dostoevsky, or Hardy—he seems to have no general ideas. The atmosphere of his work is enclosed and a little sickly. Our minds are opened and our imaginations freed if we turn from any of James's novels to *War and Peace*, and read how Prince Andrew listens to Natasha singing, or, wounded on the field at Borodino, looks up at the figure of Napoleon dwarfed by the starry sky.

Perhaps Henry James's most admirable quality as an artist—his passion for formal perfection—is the very thing that rules him out from the ranks of the greatest writers. It was Flaubert, of all people, who said that 'the very great men often write quite badly, and so much the better for them'. They are not so obsessed with perfection as Flaubert and James were. None the less, James's achievement was a great one. He was right to feel that he had created a new aspect of beauty. His art concentrates the light on a single human consciousness, a quality of mind, which he conveys perfectly to the reader who is prepared to share in his labour of distillation. He composed subtle portraits of men and women who try to maintain their inner ideal of refined decency in an uncertain, ambiguous world. In dramatizing their speech and conduct, he added something unique to the art of fiction.

JOSEPH CONRAD (1857–1924), like Henry James, was an exile. His mother country was Poland. But he loved England and chose it as his home. He chose the English language as the medium of his art; and he placed his idea of English temperament and character at the centre of his work.

Conrad's real name was Josef Teodor Konrad Korzeniowski. He was born in southern Poland and died in Kent. He is buried at Canterbury.

His father was a small landowner in Poland, a minor literary man, and a Polish patriot whom the Russian Czarist authorities eventually exiled to Vologda in Russia. His wife shared his exile till her death in 1865. For the next four years Conrad led a lonely dismal life with his father. He began to form the ambition to be a writer. But at first another career attracted him. After his father died Conrad demanded to be allowed to go to sea. His family opposed his wish, but eventually gave way. Before he was seventeen Conrad was in the Mediterranean. He later gave conflicting accounts of his life and adventures. It seems that he was engaged in gun-running for the Spanish Carlists. In an obscure episode he was wounded, as the result either of a duel, or of attempted suicide.

Even this brief sketch shows the connection between Conrad's art and his early life. Themes of exile and expatriation and loneliness, life at sea, adventure and violence, dominate his work. Many of his characters, like many of Ibsen's, commit suicide. Other Edwardian novelists, in comparison with Conrad, seem insular and sedentary. We see why Conrad is in higher favour with modern critics. He seems to belong spiritually to our own time, when many people who are not actual expatriates feel uprooted. His interest in violence and conflict, in isolation and guilt, link him with Malraux and Koestler and Silone, with Hemingway and Sartre, rather than with his English contemporaries.

Conrad was to become one of the greatest English writers. But he did not set foot in England or speak a word of English till he was twenty-three. He joined an English ship in 1878 and made England his home. In 1886 he became a British subject. He describes in his reminiscences how at the age of thirty-two he felt the call to be a writer and began his first novel, *Almayer's Folly* (1895). It was not published till he was thirty-seven. Conrad's late start in English makes it understandable that his work abounds in uncertainties of idiom. He seems to have thought in French. We are told that his English conversation was unintelligible outside his intimate circle. Yet he is one of the acknowledged masters of English. He is a great stylist, unafraid of eloquence. His style has been called too florid. An admirer might reply that the dominant style of our own day, in comparison with Conrad's, is uncouth and short-winded. The truth is that Conrad's worst fault is over-writing. But we cannot regret that he used so rich a palette. His style is heroic, noble, poignant. He is in literature what Rachmaninov is in music.

Although Conrad wrote so grandly in his adopted language, he lacked self-confidence. He found writing difficult. The reason was partly linguistic. He complained to his collaborator Ford Madox Ford about the inexactness of English. His example was the word 'oaken'. In French the corresponding word means 'made of oak' and nothing more; in English it has emotional associations. Conrad loved the rich suggestive-

ness of English. But he wanted to be precise as well. Another reason for
his difficulties was his perfectionism. Everything in a book must be
significant. There must be no skimping. Finally, Conrad was a profoundly subjective writer. His work drew on latent materials which he
found it disturbing to handle. This may explain the devices he invented
to avoid the effect of straightforward communication with the reader.

Conrad's novels were made out of the life he had lived. He had little
invention. We must remember that he spent his formative years as a
sailor. He had little opportunity for direct study of the people he heard
about. He heard their stories at second hand. Conrad likes to use a
narrator, who is not a mere device for telling the story, but part of it.
The narrator, 'Marlow', is sometimes a clumsy device. He cannot
always have known of the things he reports. But 'matters of conjecture'
are allowed to fall within his range. And in general the device justifies
itself. In any case, Conrad needed it if he was to write at all.

Conrad owed much to his life at sea. He disliked being labelled a
writer of sea stories; but it is a mistake to think that he could have
written just as well about some other mode of transport. In *The Mirror
of the Sea* (1906) he tells us of the fascination seamanship had for him.
He was a sophisticated writer, who closely studied the great European
novelists. But his best characters are sailors: Lord Jim, Captain Whal-
ley in *The End of the Tether* (1902), Captain MacWhirr of *Typhoon*
(1902). Conrad's masters in the novel—Dickens, Flaubert, Turgenev—
had presented their characters against a background of city life, or in
the country. Conrad's heroes have to undergo their ordeals beyond the
bounds of civilization. In his wanderings Conrad had come across many
kinds of men. But he had not, in life, the opportunity to study and
analyse them. His imagination flourished on glimpses. He had to start
from living originals. There really was an Almayer, a Captain Mac-
Whirr, a Mr. Burns of *The Shadow Line* (1917). In real life, such personalities have to be pieced together from guesses and inferences. This
was Conrad's method in fiction.

It has been said that in Conrad's early work, novels like *Almayer's
Folly* (1895) and *An Outcast of the Islands* (1896), we remember the
tropical background rather than the characters. This seems unfair. They
are impressive studies of the moral decay of Europeans in the Far East.
But they move too slowly. The reader becomes impatient. It is in a
shorter tale, *The Nigger of the Narcissus* (1898), that Conrad finds
himself as an artist. His essential theme appears in this simple story of
the quarrels and conflicts of a ship's company, men facing common
difficulties and dangers. *Youth* (1902) strikes a lyrical and elegiac note.
It is a lament for the lost glamour of youthful adventure. *Typhoon* is a
finer story. Its greatness lies not only in its description of the typhoon,

but in the character of Captain MacWhirr ('Can't have ... fighting ... board ship.'). We come close to the essence of what Conrad has to say if we ask ourselves what were the qualities that enabled Captain Mac-Whirr—so comically unimaginative, almost stupid—to bring his ship through the typhoon.

In *Heart of Darkness* (1898) Conrad goes deeper. This is his finest story. Like most of his work, it has an autobiographical basis. Conrad had made a voyage up the Congo in 1890. It made a deep impression on him. Later he was to say, 'I was a child before the Congo.' Out of his memories of this huge remote country he fashioned a story which has had many interpretations. The one certain thing is that it is rooted in the facts of history, the robbery of African peoples by Europeans. The truth is that *Heart of Darkness* is no more to be 'explained' than one of the great plays of Shakespeare. It achieves the resonance Conrad aimed at. Chords are struck in the mind. Some criticisms have been made of this story. Critics have objected to the over-insistence on the sinister, exotic mystery of Africa. They have been unconvinced by the central figure, Kurtz, the man who had become corrupted by the savagery around him. Others have wondered whether Conrad would have done better, like Kafka, to cut loose entirely from the moral-realistic tradition. But the story does not stand or fall by the convincingness of any one character, but by the effect of Conrad's irony in the tale as a whole. *Heart of Darkness* is an ironic version of the story of Stanley and Livingstone.

It is also a story of spiritual breakdown, which is a characteristic theme of Conrad's. We find it in tales like *Falk* (1903) or *The End of the Tether*. It is the basis of Conrad's most famous story, *Lord Jim* (1900). This is a study of what Conrad calls 'romanticism'. So long as it is read, readers will disagree about the idea on which the book turns: honour. Is this preoccupation romantic and noble; or is it morbid and neurotic? Opinions differ. All that is indisputable is its deep personal meaning for Conrad.

Nostromo (1904) has in recent years been commonly regarded as Conrad's masterpiece. Yet it had few warm admirers at the time, and perhaps it has never had many. It is his most ambitious and complex novel. Conrad convincingly creates a fictitious South American state. Jocelyn Baines has shown how he used stories of travel and adventure, and books of geography and history, as well as his imagination and memory. The novel is deeply planned. An expressive symbolism pervades it from first to last. Conrad wonderfully conveys his sense of human life as a precarious poise over abysses. The episode of the night on the Placid Gulf is one of the greatest examples in literature of a writer's power to convey the vast inhumanity of nature. Conrad always felt that modern man takes too much for granted—above all, his safety.

Nostromo is a tale of adventure. In this it is like Conrad's earlier stories, though less exciting. But above all it conveys his power to predict the movement of history in a period that was to come only after his death. We recognize, as if they were contemporary with us, his old-fashioned patriots and Marxist revolutionaries, his defiant reactionaries and men crippled by secret guilt: all the racial and social oppressions of a semi-colonial state. Conrad wrote of these things ten years before the Great War. It may be easier to appreciate *Nostromo* now than it was in his own day.

Yet *Nostromo* is not a deeply moving book. There is something unsympathetic about it. Critics agree that the pivot of the novel is the silver which is stolen by the hero. Silver permeates its imagery and symbolism—a metal, not a human being. This seems significant. There is a great variety of characters in *Nostromo*. But mostly they do not come to life as some of the characters in Conrad's other stories do. The one outstanding exception may prove the rule. Martin Decoud represents the despairing sceptic in Conrad. In the story of his marooning and suicide Conrad evokes 'the deep unbroken solitude of waiting without faith'.

Perhaps Conrad did not wholly succeed in the novel, because it is fundamentally biographical and psychological. At any rate, in the form in which Conrad chose to write, the feigned history, it requires a social world, and perhaps Conrad's standards were too personal and abstract for him to convey this successfully. His specialized, intense approach to human nature may have been more suited to shorter forms. But *Nostromo* is a remarkable achievement. No one could pigeon-hole its author as a mere specialist in 'sea stories'.

The Secret Agent (1907) and *Under Western Eyes* (1911) are still further departures from the kind of work that had made Conrad well known. Of all his novels, these have most in common with the current of European literature since 1945. *The Secret Agent* is a story of anarchists and spies. Conrad emphasizes the seediness and shabbiness of their world. We are far away from the heroism and glamour of the sea. *The Secret Agent* is a masterpiece of sustained irony. The killing of Verloc, the secret agent, by his wife is one of the most effective things Conrad ever wrote. A cruel and painful story is told facetiously, and yet remains imaginatively gripping. This sounds an impossible *tour de force*; but it succeeds. The book is Conrad's most modern novel. Astonishingly, he anticipates the whole trend of the spy thriller from John Buchan to *The Looking-Glass War*. There is no better satire in literature on the whole absurd and frightening 'secret' world of modern international relations.

Conrad's political views are characteristic of him. He is liberal-minded, Western in his outlook. He hates tyranny. On the other hand, he despises the revolutionary riff-raff, the *idéologues*, and the parasites, who out of sheer idleness make trouble and upset civilization. His depiction of revolutionaries is biased and partial. This comes out in *Under Western Eyes*, a story of contemporary Russia. It is more like Conrad's earlier work than *The Secret Agent*. Razumov's story is like Lord Jim's, a study of betrayal of oneself and of others. The earlier part of this story is one of the finest things in Conrad. The writing is taut and compelling. But like *Lord Jim, Under Western Eyes* deteriorates as it goes on: the second part, set in Switzerland, is inferior. *Under Western Eyes* shows the influence of Dostoevsky. Conrad was in some ways hostile to Dostoevsky. He resented the Russian novelist's contempt for Poles. But the political conclusions that Razumov reaches in his despair are like Dostoevsky's. Conrad himself seems to feel this despair. He hates revolution, but he has no alternative to offer. He is pessimistic.

Under Western Eyes is typical of Conrad in another respect. The heroine, Miss Haldin, is colourless, like Antonia Avellanos in *Nostromo*. Conrad's heroines tend to be uninteresting. This may be why he failed to win wide popularity. The majority of novel-readers have always been women, and the great novelists have always appealed to women. Conrad is an exception.

At the time he published *Under Western Eyes* Conrad's fortunes were at their lowest. Neither this book nor *The Secret Agent* had been commercial successes. In 1911 Conrad had to be given a Civil List pension of £100 a year. Then he had a stroke of luck. *Chance* (1913) was a great success. This may have been because of the interest in women which is shown in the book. *Chance* seems to owe something to *Dombey and Son*; but its theme is different from Dickens's. It is a story of modern knight-errantry. It is also very ingenious technically: Conrad won the praise of a severe critic, Henry James, for 'adopting the way to do a thing that will make it undergo most *doing*'. But *Chance* is not one of Conrad's best stories. The hero Captain Anthony is rather incredible, with his exalted romantic egotism. Marlow, the narrator, so effective in *Heart of Darkness*, is tiresome. There is always something absurd about Conrad's English characters. Even Lord Jim is a bit ridiculous. But *Chance* with its romantic theme, the rescue of a woman in distress, caught the public fancy. And encouraged by his success Conrad was able to go on to write a better book, *Victory* (1915). This is the study of a man who feels detached from life, spiritually unrelated to the world around him. We think of the young Conrad's long lonely years with his father. *Victory* is another story of adventure in an exotic setting. But this time its central figure is the detached sceptic, Heyst. He is finally involved in life and brought to pronounce in favour of trust in it, though, ironically, at the moment of his own death. The plot of *Victory* is very melodramatic, and can be made to sound absurd. But it is not absurd in the reading.

Conrad's later books are inferior. *The Rover* (1923) is the best. The story came to Conrad in an inexplicable sudden inspiration. It explores characteristic themes of guilt and anxiety. There are signs of weakness and weariness in it, but the ending is magnificent. Otherwise, Conrad's last phase is one of decline. Success came to him late. He was written out. These inferior books—*The Arrow of Gold* (1919), *The Rescue* (1920), *Suspense* (1925)—harmed his reputation. They reinforced the swing of opinion against him after his death. E. M. Forster's essay on him reflects it.

What sort of writer is Conrad? There is an air of aloofness in his work. His figures are seen at a distance. They are made real to the reader mainly by their environment. Conrad ignored Victorian and Edwardian preoccupations. He was not interested in social abuses or class prejudices. Nor was he particularly interested in psychological subtlety. His best work springs from his admiration for courage and loyalty and the acceptance of a hallowed routine. Conrad's heroes are distinctive. They are not unintelligent, but they are not fashionable or clever or sophisticated. Conrad did not write well of such characters. He wrote better about men who have lost their civilization. If they do not go mad, they become slaves to their vices, or merely to their habits. Some may become heroes, some criminals; none knows why. Conrad likes to start in the middle of a story. For him a man's past lives in his present. How do such people become eccentric recluses? Conrad wondered and doubted. Aldous Huxley complained of Conrad's habit of insisting that he did not understand his characters. But Conrad thought that we can never really know another person. The Court of Inquiry asked Lord Jim for 'the facts', but Conrad thinks this demand for the facts is futile. To know the facts is to know a man's whole life, and this is something we can never do.

Conrad, like James, and unlike Hardy, is a technically sophisticated writer. Like James he shows an obscure sense of guilt and an obsession with betrayal. Conrad was a troubled, neurotic man. Describing a fine day in *Chance*, he speaks casually and in passing of 'the horror of the infinite' hidden behind the brilliant blue of the sky. But he strove for insight. He was a man of warm sympathies; but he thought that sympathy darkens insight. He wanted to be free from illusions. Hence he liked irony. One of his criticisms of revolutionaries, and of women, was that they were incapable of it.

Conrad's weakness as a writer is that he cannot stop. He often spoils his best descriptions by over-elaborating them. His characters have tormented souls, but Conrad laboured on them till the reader is tormented. He is so afraid of *missing* something that he overloads his pages. He does not give the reader enough room. His time-shifts and his mixed-up way of telling the story are perplexing. Rarely is he so clear-cut as in *The Secret Agent*.

But he was a very great writer. His stories at their best are only rivalled by the best of Tolstoy's or D. H. Lawrence's. He had formed an idea of England and the English character. He admired the sense of duty, the practicality, the unsentimental kindness, which he found in Englishmen. His morose and introspective talent worked on this idea and made memorable stories out of it. His work implies his own high moral and spiritual standards, and he assumed that his readers understood them. He could not have paid his adopted country a higher tribute.

No other Edwardian novelist had the genius of James or Conrad. But the novel is a peculiar form of literature, the only one in which ordinariness of mind need not be a bar to success, but may enhance it. Auden speaks in one of his poems of the novelist as one who must 'in his own weak person, if he can,/Dully put up with all the wrongs of man'. We are keeping very good intellectual company when we read Henry James and Conrad; words like 'weak' and 'dully' seem out of place. In comparison, Bennett's or Maugham's minds seem rather commonplace, and Galsworthy's very commonplace indeed. What the Edwardian realists have at their best is an impressive truthfulness. The persons and situations they describe seem utterly credible. The personality of the novelist is so commonplace or insignificant that we can forget about it, as we never can with the greater men. This may explain why some intelligent writers have failed in the novel, while some very ordinary and unoriginal thinkers have succeeded.

ARNOLD BENNETT (1867–1931) was born in the Potteries district of Staffordshire. His background was in the professional middle class, with a great deal of Nonconformist instruction and discipline. He began as a journalist and editor, but in 1900 he gave up full-time journalism for novel-writing. After 1903 he lived largely in France, where he directed British propaganda during the Great War. He emerged after the war as a rich, publicized, extravagant man. His journals, published after his death, give a clear picture of his busy working life.

Bennett preferred to live in France rather than England. But spiritually he was an English provincial who could never forget the part of England where he was born. Nearly all his best work is founded on what he had observed there. The Five Towns have a peculiar character.

In Bennett's time they were horrible. He describes them in *Anna of the Five Towns* (1902). They were mean and forbidding. The poisonous smoke of their ovens and chimneys had soiled and shrivelled the country. For miles around the countryside of England had been destroyed. The people who lived there were sombre, hard-featured, uncouth. The huddled red-brown streets were ugly and prosaic. Bennett, like Lawrence, grew up amid nineteenth-century industrialism at its worst. But the Five Towns also fascinated Bennett. His imagination was stirred by the antiquity of the potter's art. He knew that Burslem, the ancient home of the potter, had a history of a thousand years. And Bennett's comic sense was tickled by the laconic humour of the Five Towns people. His tenderness was stirred by their taciturn stoicism in the face of suffering and death. Bennett was to be their chronicler in English literature.

He was no sentimentalist. Bennett admired commercially-minded, tough people, the successors of the Victorian philistines whom Arnold had ridiculed. But he also sympathized with a quite different kind of men: sensitive people, and especially those who were handicapped in the hard struggle of life. Bennett himself suffered all his life from a stammer, and he was also extremely shy. His novel *Buried Alive* (1908) is an amusing study of shyness. Impediments—physical or spiritual—were one of Bennett's main subjects.

Bennett was influenced, in his picture of human nature and destiny, by what he knew of contemporary science, and by writers like Zola who themselves had been influenced by it. His picture is pessimistic and determinist. Man is not captain of his soul. His fate is fixed by heredity and environment. Only at moments does the illusion of a free spirit emerge. This may happen when we are conscious of beauty. A brief sunshine breaks the clouds over the drab industrial landscape. But it may happen at moments when we are conscious of the futility of existence, as when Sophia Baines, in *The Old Wives' Tale,* looks down at the dead body of the man who had betrayed her. What makes these moments of generosity and detachment in his work so impressive is that Bennett is a plain man. He makes us feel that plain people are capable of them.

But for the most part life for Bennett is just keeping alive. He is preoccupied with what he liked to call 'the human machine' and its breakdown. His novels are a medical encyclopedia. A. E. Housman diagnosed his own Cheyne-Stokes breathing from Bennett's *Clayhanger* (1910). The normal passage of life from youth to old age has for Bennett a mainly pathological interest. The essence of his best novel, *The Old Wives' Tale* (1908), is the scene from real life that prompted it, a pretty young waitress laughing at an ugly, painted, old woman. The theme is that of Virginia Woolf's *The Waves*: the destructiveness of time. But where Mrs. Woolf broods wistfully over time, Bennett confronts it with grim stoicism. 'What Life Is'—so he entitled the last section of *The Old Wives' Tale*. The book ends with the dead woman's rheumatic old dog lumbering up to lick a few scraps of meat from a soup-plate.

Bennett's attitude to life is not tragic. It is resigned. Stories like 'Clarice of the Autumn Concerts', which show people quietly accepting the defeat of their aspirations, abound in his work. D. H. Lawrence said that he hated Bennett's resignation. But Bennett is not a depressing writer. His underlying pessimism often combines with a vein of comedy. In this he is like a poet of our own day, Philip Larkin. Bennett can be a very amusing writer. *The Card* (1911) is a splendid comic creation, and Bennett himself was a 'card'. In his best work humour and ordinariness are tinged with a sadness like Chekhov's. 'The Death of Simon Fuge' is more like Chekhov than any other English writer.

Bennett did not have the traditional classical education of the upper class. This at least spares us the floweriness and conceited affectation which make most of the novelists of his time unreadable. He went to school with the French realists. George Moore had anticipated him in *A Mummer's Wife* (1885). But Bennett pursued his documentary realism more consistently than Moore. And while Moore's master was Zola, Bennett's master was Balzac. He admired, as Henry James did, the 'solidity of specification' of the *Comédie Humaine*. But James thought it had grave limitations. It led to externality, to a diminution of human significance. Bennett in his turn admired James. But he found James's art too hovering and impalpable, lacking the earthiness he thought essential to great writing. On the other hand, Bennett did not care for the minute documentation of Zola and the Goncourts. He did not think a novelist should try to be a sort of literary scientist. Bennett had little in common, temperamentally, with the Aesthetes. But he agreed with them that a novel should be a work of art and have formal beauty. He was interested in the art of the painter. He went to picture galleries to get into the right state of mind for composition. But he has been rightly called our representative realist. He wished to give an impartial, undistorted picture of life.

In a famous essay Virginia Woolf charged Bennett with materialism. He wrote only of the body, not the soul. Certainly Bennett did become very materialistic. In his last novel, *Imperial Palace* (1930), his only positive values seem to be the creature comforts, and the efficient organization, of a modern luxury hotel. How did Bennett come to end his career on so banal a note? Some have thought he was nothing but a corrupt literary businessman. Ezra Pound portrayed such a figure in

'Mr. Nixon' of *Mauberley*. This view of Bennett was partly put about by Bennett himself. He wrote fast and regularly, and took pleasure in his productivity. He made himself into a writing machine. But it is not true that he wrote only for money. Some of his best criticism—broad-minded, curious, tolerant of new developments—was done for the *New Age*, and Bennett was not paid a penny for it. And *The Old Wives' Tale* and *Clayhanger* are not Bennett's only distinguished novels. From his later period we have *Riceyman Steps* (1923) and *Lord Raingo* (1926). Perhaps Bennett was afraid of being laughed at by his commercial contemporaries if he admitted any other motive than money-making.

But Bennett did like the things money could buy. He liked expensive restaurants and fine clothes. He hoped to display the knowingness of a rich connoisseur. And so he exploited his talents to make money. Most of his work will not survive his time. What should last best in it is what came from his heart and his moral feelings. He liked nice, good, simple people—Elsie in *Riceyman Steps*, the two sisters and Mrs. Baines and Mr. Povey in *The Old Wives' Tale*. It is these we should remember when we think of Bennett; not the steam-yachts and the luxury hotels.

W. Somerset Maugham (1874–1965) has remained much more popular than Bennett. His stories have been read all over the world. It seems that they lose little in translation. Indeed, they may gain. Maugham's style, though clear and fluent, is undistinguished. He rarely puts what he has to say in an individual way. In part, this colourlessness is deliberate. Maugham began with the conviction that fine writing should be his ideal. He attempted to model his style on mannered and artificial writers. But he came to realize that such writing did not say the things he wanted to say. So he decided to found his prose on educated speech. There were to be no stylistic flourishes, no evocative phrases, no graceful cadences. Immediate comprehensibility was to be the only criterion. Maugham brought back the plain style of Defoe into English fiction. Writers like Meredith had cultivated all sorts of airs and graces. Old-fashioned writers like Hardy had been heavy, clumsy, and verbose. Maugham restored straightforward writing to the novel at a time when it was needed.

Maugham, like Bennett, reacted against the world in which he grew up. He was born in a higher stratum of the middle class than Bennett, but his rejection of it was more violent and complete. He too left England, but he went farther afield, and seems altogether less rooted. Though Bennett also learned from French writers, Maugham is much more *like* a French writer. He shows a hatred and contempt for middle-class moral standards, tastes, and ways of life which is rare in English literature, but quite common in French.

Maugham, like Bennett, was a shy, stammering man. And like Bennett he had a passion for looking at life from the medical point of view. Maugham had actually been a doctor. The defects of body and mind which his medical experience had shown him made an indelible impression on him. He had to treat children who were born to die of painful diseases. This convinced him that Christianity was nonsense. And it left him with nothing but contempt for the 'religion of nature'—the belief that nature is a beneficent power, preached by writers like Meredith. Maugham's attitude to life was sombre.

Maugham tells us in *The Summing Up* (1938) that as a young man he was deeply unhappy. His desire to succeed in literature was not merely commercial. He was poor, ill, insignificant, nervous, unloved. He must have respect, even if he had to buy it. He bought respect, not by the arduous doubtful struggle of the pure artist, but by applied art. He catered to the tastes of others. The natural goal of his ambition was the theatre. His early plays are imitations of Wilde and of Wilde's master Congreve. He became very successful and his plays had long runs. Maugham was to write other plays later. They succeed in the theatre: Maugham knows his audiences. But his best work is in his novels and short stories.

Maugham began as a novelist only, he tells us, because he thought plays succeeded better if the author was already known as a novelist. His first important novel is *Of Human Bondage* (1915). This was a chronicle novel. There had been many of these, like Thomas Mann's *Buddenbrooks* (1901), or, in England, Wells's *Tono-Bungay* and Bennett's *Clayhanger* and Compton Mackenzie's *Sinister Street* (1913–14). But Maugham adopted a different manner from any of these. He wrote in a detached, objective way. His tone is ironical. Philip Carey, a naïve young man with a club-foot, is led through the futile charade of middle-class civilization. We are shown its cant, its exploitation of the poor, its excitement and perversion of sex. Some criticisms can be made of this novel. Philip Carey is too much of a scapegoat. He has no mind of his own. He just drifts. The author's satire is often shallow. The conventional Christianity at which he mocks is too easy a target. The book is poorly constructed, and it ends weakly. But *Of Human Bondage* is an interesting novel. It asks the question Maugham was always to ask: what is a man's real self? Modern society obscures the answer. It either destroys the individual, or seduces him into conformity. The trend of modern life is towards greater and greater collectivism. Inner freedom disappears. Civilization becomes dull and monotonous. It has no place for the interesting individual: none, therefore, for the creative artist. Such feelings as these led Maugham to travel abroad in search of more inspiring material. *The Moon and Sixpence* (1919) is based on the career of the French painter Gauguin. The hero, Strickland, has been a conventional man who accepts the dull prosaic life of bourgeois society. But he escapes, to begin a new life as a painter and beachcomber in the South Seas. He has achieved his inner freedom.

Maugham's best novel, *Cakes and Ale* (1930), is also based on an actual person. It is famous for its portrait of 'Alroy Kear', suggested by the once popular novelist Hugh Walpole (1884–1941). This vies with 'Harold Skimpole' in *Bleak House* for its vivacity and cruelty to the man satirized. The book contains another portrait, suggested by the old Thomas Hardy. But Maugham's satire is less on Hardy than on the social and academic frauds around him. The theme of *Cakes and Ale* is Maugham's old theme: what is a man's true self? He comes to the conclusion that we cannot know. The relation between the public self and the true self remains an enigma. Human life may be a cosmic farce, a 'jest in an eternal mind'. *Cakes and Ale* is Maugham's best book, because his subject—the smart literary world—deserves his acidity.

Maugham wrote many short stories. Some of them are little more than anecdotes one might hear in the bar of a club or a liner, where Maugham himself may have heard them. After a while we weary of the worldly-wise, urbane pose of the author. We long for Conrad's nobility, his troubled mind, his respect for the mystery of people. Maugham seems in comparison a mere manipulator of formulas. Even in his best work Maugham does not lay his heart bare. He says of Ashenden, the character based on himself, that he admired goodness but was not outraged by wickedness. He is not a moralist; he is an impartial, if sometimes malicious, observer. That, at least, is the impression he desires to leave on the reader. But his best work—*Of Human Bondage, Cakes and Ale, The Summing Up*—suggests that his creative impulse came out of the need to be relieved of suffering.

Maugham is at his worst when he is pretentious. His late novel *The Razor's Edge* (1944), which takes up the current interest in mysticism, is not successful. Although he was interested in philosophy, he is not a profound thinker. His speculations are apt to culminate in abysmal triteness. What is most congenial in Maugham's outlook is his championing of the individual against the collective. Maugham made fun of people's oddities, but it is clear that he liked oddity. He preferred it to pompousness and unction. So long as they exist, Maugham's cynicism is a good antidote.

JOHN GALSWORTHY (1867–1933) was a writer of great fame in his day. He had an international reputation. He was awarded the Nobel Prize for Literature. And for a wide public, in England and in Europe, he has never gone out of favour. His vogue has lately been renewed by television dramatizations of his Forsyte novels. We shall have to wait till 2033 to know if he has 'pleased many and pleased long', by Dr. Johnson's reckoning. But it would seem that to a large number of readers he offers 'just representations of general nature'. Yet the superior critics of today grant him, at most, a similar interest to old bound volumes of *Punch*: a faint 'period' interest, nothing more. This anomaly is troubling.

Galsworthy's best critics have not denied him merit, but they have been very severe. The severest is the best. D. H. Lawrence's essay on him is scathing, but it is terribly to the point. Lawrence's view is that Galsworthy's first good novel, *The Man of Property* (1906), is nearly a great novel. It had the makings of a powerful satire on the 'Forsyte' or bourgeois values. But even in *The Man of Property* there were falsities and contradictions. And Galsworthy's later work shows that he is more and more taking the Forsyte point of view. Lawrence accuses Galsworthy of selling out truly human values to social ones. This criticism might be dismissed as flowing from Lawrence's class prejudice. But a similar line was taken by George Orwell, whose origins were in a stratum of society nearer to Galsworthy's than Lawrence's. Galsworthy, he said, was an Old Harrovian with one skin too few; and later in his life the skin renewed itself.

Galsworthy is in some ways comparable to Charles Morgan (1894–1958), another novelist who achieved European fame, but has been dropped by English critics. Morgan's early novel, *The Gunroom* (1919), about life in the navy, was written out of personal experience and shows deep anger and sincerity. Later, his work became a by-word for spurious art. Perhaps something similar happened to Galsworthy. His personal quarrel with society moved him to write books like *The Island Pharisees* (1904) and *The Man of Property*. Compassion for the poor and the victimized made him write plays like *Strife* (1909) and *The Silver Box* (1909) and *Justice* (1910). But in his later work he seems to be concerned with shoving unpleasantness out of the way, rather than facing social reforms which might threaten his comforts. He wears the blinkers of an English gentleman. He lacks the ruthless honesty which lies at the heart of great writing.

Galsworthy was certainly not another Tolstoy. *The Man of Property* may derive from *Anna Karenina*, but the comparison is damaging to it. Galsworthy is often a very clumsy writer. His dialogue can be quite incredible, his episodes preposterous, his symbolism too obvious. But there are many ways in which his work is enjoyable. Soames Forsyte and the rest may not be profoundly conceived characters, but they are recognizable types of English life which have not completely disappeared even now. The later Forsyte books grew weaker when Galsworthy tried to include people of a younger generation whom he did not understand; but within his range he is clever and amusing. And like all popular novelists he has narrative power and can draw the reader in. He is not so mushy as is often thought. Some of his stories are quite funny, like 'A Stoic', a tale of an old gentleman who, knowing he has not long to live, goes on what would then have been called a 'binge' of eating and drinking, and dies in a blaze of glory. Furthermore, Galsworthy is often astute. He is like a good advocate who not only knows his law, but knows how to talk to the jury. And, within limits, he is tolerant. Galsworthy was not a genius like Lawrence, but he tried harder than Lawrence to understand the point of view of people he disliked. Lastly, like C. P. Snow in our time, Galsworthy gives his readers a pleasant feeling of being in the know. He admits us to the inner workings of the Establishment, the world of parliament and clubs and great country houses. He knows how things are done, how divorces are got, how finance works. At any rate, he seems to know.

But Galsworthy's real power goes deeper than that. One of the most puzzling things in *The Forsyte Saga* is the character of Irene. She stands for beauty—something haunting and unattainable which the 'man of property' strives to possess but cannot. But many others besides Lawrence have found her unadmirable. We dislike Irene and sympathize with Soames. As a wife, a mistress, a mother, she seems utterly selfish. And yet the stories come to life when she is involved, in a way they never do elsewhere. Galsworthy succeeds wonderfully in conveying her spell. To understand why would be to understand why he retains his hold over ordinary readers.

The early twentieth century was a period when critical standards were dominated by realism. Yet it may be that some of the writers whose work will last longest have been far from realistic. A few names may suggest their variety: Max Beerbohm, Arthur Conan Doyle, John Buchan, W. W. Jacobs, P. G. Wodehouse, 'Saki'.

MAX BEERBOHM (1872–1956) was one of those mischievous gadflies who annoy the serious-minded. His *persona* was that of a stranded survivor of the nineties. He said 'I belong to the Beardsley period.' This was a period when a moderate income was enough for security in the vulgar struggle of life. Even luxuries were cheap, and labour was cheaper. It was the period of the Aesthetic movement. Its symbol was the Dandy. The history of dandyism goes back to Baudelaire. It was an artistic protest against the dullness and conformity of bourgeois civilization. Among other things it meant a deliberate cultivation of the trivial.

Wilde's best play, *The Importance of Being Earnest* (1895), is its monument in comedy. The Victorian concept of 'earnestness' is undermined. This is the essence of the dandy spirit.

Beerbohm began as a disciple of Wilde. His short story 'The Happy Hypocrite' (1897) is like one of Wilde's fables. It is the tale of a roué who, to win the love of an innocent girl, covers his face with a mask of beauty and goodness. When the mask is eventually removed, his face has become like the mask. Beerbohm's best story is 'Enoch Soames' (1919). Its background is the decline of the Aesthetic movement. The Wildes, the Beardsleys, the Ernest Dowsons had gone. Their place was taken by imitators, men given over to charlatanism, irresponsibility, or vanity. Genuine artists could keep the tradition going only by satirizing the imitators. But Beerbohm does more than this in 'Enoch Soames'. The hero is absurd but touching. The story is a tiny, elegant, pathetic version of the Faust legend.

Beerbohm, with all his intelligence, did not escape the contradiction in dandyism. The decadent writers hoped to keep their artistic integrity by attacking the philistines. But they depended on the philistines for the civilized life they enjoyed. This was a contradiction which Kipling harshly exposed. That may be why Beerbohm's satires on Kipling are so venomous.

Beerbohm belongs to the history of art as well as literature. Shaw called him the most savage radical cartoonist since Gillray. Some of his caricatures of the Edwardian period have a ferocity which might surprise those who think of 'Max' only as the elegant dandy. A Beerbohm drawing wittily sums up a critical essay. Beerbohm's whole talent lay in criticism. Gratitude is due for his superb parody of Goethe, his attacks on bad writers like Phillips and Jerome, his exposure of Andrew Lang and the 'Oxford manner'. But criticism for him was primarily an exercise of the imagination. He was a superb parodist in *A Christmas Garland* because, unlike most parodists, he could efface himself.

Zuleika Dobson (1911), his most famous satire, is not his most perfect. The later part becomes uncomfortably like a novel. The farcical dénouement is too realistic. But the book should live. *Zuleika* is a witty fantasy about an Oxford which has long ceased to exist, and yet in some ways is still recognizable. It is no doubt a trivial work: Beerbohm was a miniaturist. But when it is forgotten, *The Rape of the Lock* will be forgotten also.

Beerbohm's reputation has fluctuated strangely. To the progressive Edwardians he seemed irrelevant. But the 1920s found him congenial, as he found them. Lytton Strachey was one of the few modern writers Beerbohm admired. In the serious-minded 1930s his stock again sank low. He lived a secluded life in Italy. But in his later years he made several broadcasts from London which made him very popular. His essays and stories were re-read and enjoyed. Today, with the revival of Beardsley and the nineties, and the interest in 'camp' (the modern word for dandyism), Beerbohm should come into favour. His position in literature resembles Charles Lamb's, but his personality is less ingratiating; his comedy rests on something cold and un-genial. Beerbohm's long friendship with Henry James was important to him. He was the only parodist James tolerated. He is best seen as a disciple of Henry James who had his own distinctive talent and his own things to say.

With ARTHUR CONAN DOYLE (1859–1930) we enter the territory of good popular writers. When we think of Edwardian popular fiction, we think of Sherlock Holmes. But Holmes was really a late Victorian. The Edwardian stories show a coarsening and stridency which are absent from the mellow stories of the nineties. Holmes's ancestry is in the Aesthetic movement. He is an eccentric who practises art for art's sake. But his place in folk-lore is that of the great detective, the symbol of intellect, of reason and justice. Today his successor is the double-crossing spy in an equivocal world. JOHN BUCHAN (1875–1940) is more important in the history of modern literature than Conan Doyle. His gentleman-adventurer, Hannay, is the forerunner of Ian Fleming's Bond. Erskine Childers' heroes in *The Riddle of the Sands* (1903) are more attractive than either, free from Hannay's snobbery and self-praise and Bond's cruelty. In his historical novels Buchan is the successor of Scott. He had a particular interest in Scottish character and history. These novels are full of vivid description and story-telling. One of the most unusual and interesting is *Witch Wood* (1927).

Other entertainers whose work is still alive are W. W. JACOBS (1863–1943) and P. G. Wodehouse. Jacobs's attitude towards the English working class is like Wodehouse's towards the English aristocracy. It is humorous, but not essentially satirical. Jacobs wrote in the tradition of Chaucer and Shakespeare, in which low-life characters are treated purely as comic figures. Reacting against this, middle-class novelists of the 1930s romanticized the figure of the exploited Worker. In our own day, working-class life has been used for a sort of sentimental 'objective' sociology. The novelist tries to make himself like an anthropologist who has undergone a patient acculturation. Few authors have achieved 'a central, a truly human point of view' towards the human beings who do the practical work of the world. Jacobs succeeded in his art at the price of remaining stylized and narrow.

P. G. WODEHOUSE (b. 1881) belongs to no particular period. It was in the Edwardian epoch that he began to develop the style which has made him a national institution. But his stories use ancient devices of comedy. Some of his comic routines are as old as Aristophanes. Jeeves, like Sherlock Holmes, now belongs to folk-lore. He derives ultimately from the clever slaves of ancient literature. Wodehouse began as a writer of school stories, and it was out of schoolboy humour that he perfected his unique vein of farce. His style exploits the different levels and registers of the English language. Schoolboy slang, the dialect of young clubmen of a vanished era, the formal manner of old-fashioned editorials, all play their part. Wodehouse seems early to have decided not to let his humour touch anything serious. He could have put a sharper edge on it if he had wished: *Something Fresh* (1915) is a less mellow study of the English aristocracy than those he wrote later. And his stories about Hollywood contain effective satire. But Wodehouse preferred to perfect an art of recreation. It depends so little on fashion and circumstances that it has survived into an entirely different world from his own. It may survive that world too.

Another humorist, H. H. Munro (1870–1916), who wrote under the name of 'Saki', did bring his art into touch with something serious. His *forte* is polite cruelty: he is a peculiarly English writer. He is our only equivalent of the Marquis de Sade. The type of character he most deeply admires is a pathological sadist. His most famous story, 'Sredni Vashtar', is a tale of revenge. More than the other popular writers of his day he signalizes the ominous trends of the twentieth century. Fear and hysteria lurk beneath the light surface. Yet he is witty, epigrammatic, and genteel. His cruelty should appeal to modern taste. But it would find his sickly sentimentality less congenial, and, still less, the positive standards to which he appeals: duty and self-sacrifice.

3

Poetry in the Early Twentieth Century

Hardy—Yeats—Synge—Housman—de la Mare—
the Georgians—Great War poets

THE THREE GREATEST modern English poets are widely agreed to be
Hardy, Yeats, and Eliot. Of these Thomas Hardy (1840–1928) was the
only Englishman. Hardy was the last great Victorian novelist. He gave
up novel-writing before Queen Victoria died. His first volume of
poems was not published till 1898. But Hardy had been writing poetry
since the 1860s, and he often borrowed scenes and situations from it for
his novels. Hardy the poet is continuous with Hardy the novelist. What
is alive in the poems is what is alive in the novels. But he wrote the
poems solely to please himself: while in the novels he was concerned to
entertain his public.

Hardy's novels are old-fashioned in form and style. They depend on
sensational incidents, astonishing coincidences, surprising twists of plot.
Hardy is a story-teller in the tradition of Scott. But he had learned from
George Eliot, and from Shakespeare, how to depict the country people
he loved in a convention of light caricature. And in his early books he
recounts the joys and sorrows, the charm and the humour, of the old
rural life that in his day was vanishing from England. But from *The
Return of the Native* (1878) onwards his books become more sombre
and philosophically preoccupied. Hardy, like George Eliot, was a progressivist, or, to use her word, a meliorist, but he was a half-hearted
one. Again and again he shows human fulfilment and happiness
thwarted by stupidity and selfishness, or by conventionality and ignorance. He did not rule out the possibility of human improvement, but
he was painfully conscious of all the forces, within and without human
beings, that made against it. His tone in his later novels is often peevish
and irritable. But at times it takes on a more tragic dignity, when Hardy
implies that people are up against not only stupidity and ignorance, but
something in the scheme of things. Hardy found it difficult to convey
the sense of fate through conflicts between, or within, individuals. It
was only when he set his characters against the unchanging background

of nature, with its ageless indifference to man's concerns, that he was able to evoke the tragic and unalterable.

In his style, Hardy is often stiff and clumsy. He was an old-fashioned writer, who thought that prose lacked dignity if it was not adorned with long words and classical allusions. His dialogue, especially when the speakers are educated people, is often incredible. Yet he conveys an effect of utter integrity. His greatness lies in his power to unite this truthfulness with a soaring imagination. When we think of Hardy's greatness we think, not of this or that character, but of the tragic plight of humanity itself, seen for a moment against the vast unending background of history, and beyond that, nature and the sky.

Hardy's greatness appears in his poems. Here he was able to disencumber himself from the conventions of Victorian fiction and write as he pleased. Hardy's output was very large, about nine hundred poems. Naturally they are mixed, both in subject-matter and quality. But they have some things in common. Hardy liked to experiment with rhythm and metre. Sometimes a tune came into his head before he had thought of the words to accompany it. He tried to find the right music for different moods. And his moods do vary. We think of Hardy as melancholy, even morbid; but many of the poems are really light verse. Hardy often starts from an anecdote, humorous or pathetic or grotesque, and makes a poem out of it. He had a craftsman's approach to poetry. He liked a poem to be a well-made object. He had been an architect and a draughtsman, and his father had been a musician. He associated poetry with music and singing. He is pre-eminently a lyrical poet.

The strangest feature of Hardy's poetry is his diction. Fundamentally, it is traditional. Hardy never abandoned his first masters, the great poets of the romantic period. But he introduced into this diction a strange mixture of elements. Sometimes he uses provincial or local words, Dorset dialect. Sometimes he is very colloquial, even slangy. Sometimes he is magniloquent, with Latinate polysyllables. Hardy loves to coin new words. Often he uses awkward inversions, or falls into grammatical tangles. Sometimes he sings effortlessly and simply; sometimes he sounds jangling and cacophonous. Sometimes he seems quaint and clumsy; sometimes he seems heavily solemn. This oddity of style makes his page immediately recognizable.

Ford Madox Ford said that Hardy's poetic style seemed to have been borrowed from a country newspaper. Much of his subject-matter might have appeared there too. Unlike most great poets, Hardy wrote about a wide range of ordinary events. He liked to dwell on 'life's little ironies', the sad or strange or funny incidents that we hear about every day. But he also wrote about the routine of day-to-day incidents, the fine mornings and the overcast afternoons, the local gossip and scandals, the births, the marriages, and, above all, the deaths. Hardy was pre-occupied by death. Sometimes he is sad and resigned about it, sometimes indignant, sometimes, in a countryman's way, tickled by some macabre conceit.

Many of the poems reflect Hardy's philosophical ideas. Intellectually, Hardy did not believe that nature revealed any signs of conscious purpose. Organic sentience was a mere accident, and the reflective self-consciousness of man was the cruellest accident of all. But emotionally Hardy was convinced that the amount of suffering and misfortune in the world exceeded what could be reasonably expected from mere chance. He could not help imagining the presence of malign and mocking spirits in the universe, even if their influence upon the blind, unconscious Immanent Will remains unclear. Opposed to them he imagines compassionate spirits, whose influence, if it exists, is small. Both the Spirit Ironic and the Spirit of the Pities are passive spectators.

This half-fanciful mythology provides the framework for the principal work Hardy produced during the Edwardian age, the epic drama of *The Dynasts* (1904–8). It is comparable to *War and Peace* in its vast sweep and its choice of the Napoleonic wars to illustrate a philosophy of history. Some of the most impressive writing is to be found in the stage-directions. We look down from a great height on Europe and the turbulent, urgent, and aimless movement of huge masses of men. More than one critic has aptly compared these stage-directions to a film-script.

The Dynasts and Hardy's last novel *Jude the Obscure* are his most challenging works. *Jude the Obscure* (1895) is Hardy's only modern novel, a story of unhappy, drifting people in a setting of urban life. *The Dynasts* is the only work in which Hardy makes his philosophy explicit. Both are far removed from the Hardy of books like *The Woodlanders* (1887), the quiet annalist of rural life.

Temperamentally, Hardy was an ironist and a satirist. His point of view was like Voltaire's. He had a brisk, shrewd side to his nature, which expressed itself in many caustic observations. But as a boy he had been over-sensitive, even morbid. Like his Tess, he thought the earth 'a blighted star'. And unlike Voltaire he was a tender-hearted, deeply emotional man. Hence his satire and irony directed themselves, not against people, but against circumstances; against the falsities and hypocrisies of social life, but also against the blind cruelty of nature, the fallacy of human hopes, the indignities of time and chance. Satirist and ironist as he was, Hardy is the most moving of all poets. What stirred him to his deepest utterance was memory—the memory of his own past, of the men and women he had loved and quarrelled with and forgotten and remembered. Memory was so vivid to him that it tran-

scended immediate experience. In one of his poems he speaks of some-
one recalling the past, 'not like one who remembers, but one who sees'.
This is true of Hardy himself. A favourite image of his is the ghost, the
revenant, revisiting the scenes where he had lived and been happy and
suffered. In his poems and short stories he likes to draw the picture of a
man who has been away for a long time, so that everyone has forgotten
him, coming back to the house of the woman he loved and looking
wistfully in at the open window. His poems often convey a sense of
poignant desolation. But in his greatest work nothing is exaggerated or
vehement. Faithfulness to the past as it was seems to be his only concern.

Hardy's best poems often turn on the theme of unhappy love. The
image of an unhappy love-affair pervades his poetry. It seems to be a
metaphor for human life. But clearly it had a deep personal meaning
for him also. His greatest poems are intimately personal. Some of them
are to be found among the poems he wrote in 1912-13, inspired by his
feelings after the death of his first wife. Their marriage had been in
many ways unhappy. But after her death Hardy seems to have fallen in
love with her memory. This series of poems is a unique memorial to
her. It is unlike any other poetry. It is elegiac and tragic; at the same
time, it is full of the ardour and passion of love. Hardy's thoughts are
fixed on the dead, but he is not necrophiliac or morbid. What mattered
was that he had lived, and she had lived, and they had once loved.
Reliving their life together, he is filled with grief, but also with joy. As
he realizes the co-presence of these emotions, he is struck with terror
and anguish. That *vanishing* of someone we love, so sadly familiar an
experience, yet so inexplicable and terrible, Hardy conveys as no other
poet has done, in one of his most haunting poems, 'The Going'.

Other great poems are 'At Castle Boterel', 'After the Visit', 'During
Wind and Rain', 'The Self-Unseeing', 'The Wind's Prophecy', 'The
Haunter', 'My Spirit will not Haunt the Mound', 'After a Journey',
'The Glimpse', and 'The Faded Face'. But lovers of Hardy's poetry
will want many others, like 'Afterwards', 'The Shadow on the Stone',
'In Tenebris', 'Wives in the Sere', 'Sweet Cyder', 'Shut Out That
Moon', 'The Darkling Thrush', 'The Family Face', 'The Sundial on a
Wet Day', and 'Family Portraits'. The last mentioned poem is especially
characteristic. Hardy is above all the poet of the traditional family,
with its piety towards the dead, its respect for the old, and its hopes—
in spite of everything—for the children.

In comparison with Hardy, an essentially English writer, the other
great poet of the early twentieth century seems an exotic. W. B. YEATS
(1865-1939) was an Irishman who all his life preserved a sense of his

national heritage. Yeats's poetry belongs to the English romantic tradition as it came down through the nineteenth century. But it differs from English romantic poetry in its Irish subject-matter and its rhythms, based on Anglo-Irish speech.

Yeats's poetry is the record of a personal drama which must be understood as a whole. It is not that he is a confessional poet. He omits much that the curious might like to know about his life and circumstances; and what he leaves in, he often alters. He selects, he arranges, he dramatizes. This was a matter of deliberate literary theory for Yeats. All his life he was concerned with drama and the theatre. He saw a man's life as a series of parts upon a stage. Even his starkest utterances have something histrionic about them. The epitaph he wrote for himself is a rhetorical flourish. In his poetry we never see Yeats without a mask. But even a brief outline of Yeats's biography shows how intertwined his art is with his life.

William Butler Yeats was born in Sandymount, Dublin, of merchant and professional ancestry. His family belonged to the 'Protestant Ascendancy'—the Anglo-Irish governing class. But his father was a poor man of business and mismanaged the family affairs, and they became impoverished. Yeats's father moved to London, where he practised his art as a painter. Thus the young W. B. Yeats grew up in an atmosphere of art and culture, and nostalgia for an aristocratic past. As a young man he seemed to others vague and dreamy. Yeats disliked the London life around him. He longed for the countryside of Sligo, in the west of Ireland, where he had grown up. A moment of nostalgia for it inspired his most famous poem, 'The Lake Isle of Innisfree'.

For Yeats the Irish countryside was not only a memory of peaceful beauty. It was a source for the myths and legends which he craved. He read books of Celtic folk-lore. He sought eagerly among the Irish peasantry for supernatural tales. Like other members of his family, he was 'psychic', and a man of many superstitions. He believed in omens and ghosts. He liked to imagine himself a sage or magician. He tells us that 'deprived by Huxley and Tyndall, whom I detested, of the simple religion of my childhood, I had made a new religion'. This 'new religion' was not mere make-believe. Yeats's mind in some ways was genuinely primitive. He was in touch with the foundation of all real religion, a shared fantasy. His '*Anima Mundi*' was an attempt to find a universal basis for it among mankind. But Yeats's religion seems to lack the ethical connection which all the great religions have had. He was concerned, not with the sanction for a code of ethics, but with ritual, mystery, forms of life. Yeats's first book, with the poetry and folk-tales of the Irish peasantry, already shows his interest in mysticism and the supernatural. He made friends with the Irish mystic 'A.E.' He spoke with the Brahmin sage Mohini Chatterjee. He read books about esoteric Buddhism. We must remember that this was a period when what William James called 'the Will to Believe' was very strong. It was a time when Theosophy and Spiritualism flourished, and more scientifically-minded people looked to Psychical Research for an assurance of human immortality. Yeats himself says that our intellects at twenty contain all the ideas we shall ever really grasp. The Yeats of *The Celtic Twilight* (1893) grew up at a time when strange creeds were in the air.

As a poet, Yeats began in the late romantic tradition. He was influenced by the Pre-Raphaelite school and their successors. William Morris's poetry was one of the main influences on his early work. Morris was a personal friend of Yeats. He was a man of powerful personality and a great practical force in the world; but his conception of poetry was like what Yeats said of his own *Wanderings of Oisin* (1889); 'a region in which one should wander from the cares of life'. Yeats's early poetry has a melancholy, arcane, withdrawn beauty. A poem like 'Who goes with Fergus?' distils in a few lines the poet's love of ancient things. Sorrow and heartbreak do not break the spell, but are blended into the dreamy beauty. There is no moralizing, nothing didactic; no vigour, intellectual or emotional; little sense of the poet himself or his circumstances. All is reverie.

From the first Yeats's subjects had been Irish. But he was not yet clear about the bearings of his cult of ancient Eire on the Ireland of his own time. The traditions of Anglo-Irish poetry had been explicitly patriotic. The greatest poem written by an Irishman before Yeats, J. C. Mangan's 'My Dark Rosaleen', is a patriotic lament, culminating in an invective against the English oppressor. Yeats's attitude to Ireland was more complex. He was a child of the Protestant Ascendancy, who had little in common with the Celtic and Catholic majority. He had no sympathy with those nationalist politicians who worked for a modernized, industrial, bourgeois Ireland. Like the young Joyce, he revered the memory of Parnell as a figure of romance, but he had small understanding of Parnell's methods or aims. Yeats himself was one day to become a senator in the new Irish Free State. But he had no liking for parliamentary politicians. Violent activists were more attractive to him. Yeats was to be growingly fascinated by violence. But for a long time he did not take the activists he knew very seriously. Not until the rebellion of 1916 did he come to realize that there was more in them than attitudinizing.

The political question was crystallized for Yeats by his love for Maud Gonne. She was a political extremist. To the end of his life Yeats half-regretted and half-admired the vehemence with which she flung herself into the bickerings, the journalism, the conspiracies of nationalist politics. None of this was congenial to him. He disliked Maud's ardent feminism. It offended his romantic conception of a beautiful woman's rôle in the world. It displeased his conservative, hierarchical habit of mind. Yet Yeats was to become one of the few memorable modern love-poets. Above all he is the poet of unhappy love: misunderstanding, rejection, bitterness. Some of this poetry may originate as much in literary tradition as in real life. The old Yeats was himself to compare his infatuation with the willed misery that the poets of the nineties made for themselves. But in Yeats life and literature are always inextricable.

Maud's involvement in politics was in the end to divide her finally from Yeats. Yet she too had her romantic, mystical side. She shared in his fantasies about a secret order which was to restore the ancient Ireland of the poets. But here the divergence between Maud and Yeats showed itself. She wished to translate these romantic dreams into immediate, effective action. What she wanted from Yeats was a direct, 'committed', nationalist poetry. Yeats shrank from this. It seemed to him that high poetry must be esoteric. Occultism continued to pervade his poetry and his life. He joined a secret society, he cultivated an acquaintanceship with eccentric mystics.

Many of Yeats's English contemporaries shared his interest in the paranormal. But they were mostly steady men of research, scientifically-minded. Yeats was an anti-rationalist, hostile to the scientific temper. 'Our thoughts and emotions,' he wrote, 'are often but spray flung up from the hidden tide that follows a moon that no eye can see.' In his intuitive way Yeats had grasped the conception of the mind that psychoanalysis was to arrive at later. He was convinced that conscious thought makes up only a small part of the mind's activities. In his essay 'Magic' (1901) he anticipated Jung's theory of the collective unconscious of mankind, which Yeats calls the Great Memory. He explained the sudden leaps in the history of human thought by the intervention of 'unknown instructors'. No better explanation has been found.

Meanwhile a new literary influence had entered Yeats's poetry. Through his friend Arthur Symons he learned of the French symbolist poets, Baudelaire, Verlaine, and Mallarmé. They reinforced his hieratic and cabbalistic view of art. But English influences may have been more important. The Rhymers' Club, the circle of writers to which Yeats belonged, looked to Walter Pater for their philosophy. Yeats's prose in this period, in a book like *Rosa Alchemica* (1896), shows the marked influence of Pater. He came later to react against this mannered, cloistered style. But at the time Pater's influence coalesced naturally with Yeats's cult of aesthetic seclusion and daydreaming. Yeats looked back to the ancient figure of the wizard. He helped to edit the obscure prophetic poems of William Blake, who became another of his cult-figures. Like Blake, he dreamed of the transmutation of life into art.

There can be little doubt that Yeats's esotericism was in part an attempt to escape from painful suffering; or at least to transmute it into something that could be contemplated. And this suffering was due to frustrated love. In *The Wind Among the Reeds* (1899) Yeats writes a new kind of love-poetry. The theme is the spiritualizing of a carnal love that has been renounced. But still the note of longing and regret predominates; the poems are essentially equivocal.

The Wind Among the Reeds has a haunting beauty, but it is very esoteric. And Yeats's Ireland, on which he hoped to base a school of literature, is withdrawn from the joys and sorrows, the struggles and conflicts, of ordinary life. Hence of all forms, drama seemed the least likely for Yeats. *The Shadowy Waters* (1900) is only a drama in outward form: it is really an extended lyric. Yet with the new century Yeats began a close involvement with the Irish dramatic movement which was to continue to the end of his life. The Abbey Theatre, which he helped to found, began as a minority theatre. A new epoch of Yeats's life opened in 1896, when he met its inspirer Augusta Gregory (1852–1932). At Lady Gregory's house at Coole Park he felt that he had revived the relationship of a Renaissance artist to his noble patron. In the same year he met the dramatist John Millington Synge, who was to become another of his cult-figures. Synge's work, said Yeats, 'smacked of . . . all that has salt in the mouth, all that is rough to the hand, all that hardens emotions by contest'. Yeats warmly supported Synge during the outburst of philistine rancour when Synge's *Playboy of the Western World* was produced. In his own plays he followed Synge's example in using peasant idiom and dialect for comic purposes. But Yeats's real medium was verse, not prose; and his best plays of the period are still poems rather than plays.

In the twentieth century Yeats was coming to seem a mere survival from a past age. John Middleton Murry, reviewing his poetry in 1919, concluded that Yeats's inspiration was exhausted: he had nothing more to say. And there are signs that Yeats himself agreed with him. Yeats had always been short of something to say. He always wrote with difficulty. Even in his early work his subject-matter consists mainly of regrets and memories and dreams. The struggle with the drama and 'theatre business, management of men' may have helped to form the more robust style of the later Yeats. His father's wit and irony may have helped too. The elemental simplicity and direct homeliness of Synge played a part. The young American Ezra Pound supplied a personal stimulus. Another minor influence may have been Yeats's discovery of the poems of John Donne. But the most striking difference between Yeats's early work and his later is not so much stylistic as emotional. Yeats writes with an increasing scorn and dismay at the prosaic complacency of Edwardian Ireland. His scorn was above all reserved for the bourgeois elements in Irish nationalism. He wrote bitterly of their deference to lower-middle-class sentiment, their timidity towards the Roman Church, their indifference to art. Ireland under English rule was becoming another nation of shopkeepers. And the more extreme Nationalists seemed to Yeats only talkers and poseurs.

All was 'changed utterly' for Yeats by the Easter Rising of 1916. The gods and heroes had appeared again: beside Patrick Pearse stood the demi-god Cuchulain. But they had reappeared in a way Yeats had not expected, and among men he had despised. Yeats commemorated them in 'Easter 1916'. But the poem disappointed patriots like Maud Gonne. Yeats's mood still remained equivocal. He had little trust in violent revolution. He feared the effects of its fanaticism on the human soul. Long before, in *The Countess Cathleen* (1892), with Maud in mind, he had written the drama of a woman who gives up her soul for her people. Was all this heroic sacrifice worth while? All that Yeats is certain of is that he now sees the past differently. What had been for him mere dreaming, or 'casual comedy', had taken on a tragic dignity. The Easter Rising marked a turning-point in Yeats's poetic career. From now on his antipathy to the age he lived in became more and more emphatic. He now gave full vent to hitherto unuttered emotions— scorn, pride, arrogance, sarcasm. His cult of 'custom and ceremony' continued, in poems like 'A Prayer for my Daughter'; but it was now brandished defiantly, not intoned in an aesthetic cloister.

After 1916 Yeats was no longer satisfied to dwell in the imagined heroic past of Ireland. But his poetry is still nostalgic, backward-looking, full of longing and regret. The difference is that these emotions now take on a tone of mordant bitterness. This is the prevailing mood of *The Wild Swans at Coole* (1917). Some of the poems in that volume show a resentment at growing old. This was not a new theme for Yeats. He had always been preoccupied as a poet with age and time. But here the theme is stated more astringently. Yeats is beginning to speak out. Poems which deal directly with sexual feeling replace the dreamy, languid, shy poetry of his early period. Yeats has become increasingly aware of the confusion and incoherence of modern life. His search for what he called Unity of Being is more desperate.

In the poems he wrote after 1917 we have the first specimens of Yeats's new explanation of life. He had begun to develop what he called his 'system'. This had its origin in Yeats's personal life. Shortly after his marriage (1917) his wife began to produce automatic writing. Yeats based his system on this material, which he was later to expound in his prose book *A Vision* (1925). *A Vision* is the most controversial of

Yeats's writings. Some critics have dismissed it as nonsense. Others have seen deep truths beneath the astrological framework in which Yeats presented his explanation of life. Others, again, have thought that *A Vision* is dealing, under astrological metaphors, with a youthful psychological problem: the 'identity-crisis', the individual's difficult search to discover or create a stable centre of self. Certainly no poet is more preoccupied than Yeats with 'the toil of growing up', 'the ignominy of boyhood', 'the unfinished man and his pain'.

With *The Tower* (1928) Yeats challenges a place among the greatest modern poets. Here he gathers up and renews his themes. In the title-poem he laments and inveighs against old age. In 'Meditations in Time of Civil War' he evokes custom and ceremony in an ever darkening and divided modern world. In 'Sailing to Byzantium' he creates a tension and a balance between the longings of the ageing body and the soul's yearning for liberation. In 'Nineteen Hundred and Nineteen' he evokes the precariousness of civilized life. His poems convey a historical ominousness, a sense of coming disaster. Its finest expression is 'The Second Coming' (1919), a poem which for some readers has come to epitomize modern poetry as Arnold's 'Dover Beach' epitomizes the Victorians or Gray's 'Elegy' the eighteenth century.

Yeats felt the rise of a new force within him. But it made him all the more resentful of the coming of old age. Often he rails against it; sometimes he writes of it elegiacally. Sometimes his attitude is more complex, as in poems like 'Among School Children' and 'All Souls' Night'. These poems are reveries. And Yeats's characteristic mode is the reverie. In poem after poem he broods over his own past, meditates on the phase of Irish history through which he had lived. What did it all mean? What did it come to?

In *The Winding Stair* (1933) the contrasting moods and themes of *The Tower* are more marked. But instead of tension or ambivalence within a single poem, the poems now each tend to explore a single attitude. Some strike a note of stoic acceptance; others, a note of frank sensuality. Some convey the poignant sense of life's passing; others record intuitions of the things that transcend time and mortality. In 'Byzantium' Yeats imagines the purgation that awaits the soul after death. 'A Dialogue of Self and Soul' employs one of Yeats's favourite devices, the debate within himself. The 'Dialogue' asserts Yeats's belief that a man lives through a succession of lives. Oriental religions believed this: but they thought of the succession of lives as a calamity from which men should strive to escape. Yeats rejected Nirvana. In the 'Dialogue' he chooses rebirth, rather than deliverance from birth. Despite all the suffering and ignominy and frustration which human life entails, still he chooses to be born again, to go on with the unending cycle. Yeats's political ideas take on a new symbolic portentousness in this volume. 'Blood and the Moon' was inspired by the violence of the Irish civil war that followed the achievement of independence. Yeats again uses the symbol of the tower, not only as 'an image of mysterious wisdom won by toil', but as 'a bloody, arrogant power'. His thoughts were haunted by eighteenth-century Ireland as he imagined it, the Ireland of Swift and Grattan and Burke. He admired their aristocratic pessimism and contempt for the vulgar. Holding the cyclical theory of history which he expounds in *A Vision*, he is fascinated by the idea that an age of hierarchical, aristocratic power may return. Yeats reaches the summit of his lyrical achievement in this volume with the series of poems called 'A Woman Young and Old' and 'Words for Music Perhaps'. In these he introduces the figure of Crazy Jane, an old mad-woman, as a spokesman for his own anger and defiance in the face of age and death.

Throughout his career Yeats had been a playwright. He constantly experimented with new forms. In his later plays he was influenced by the aristocratic-military drama of old Japan, to which Ezra Pound had introduced him. His two volumes of *Plays for Dancers* (1919, 1921) reflect his preoccupation with an esoteric theatre, an audience of in-itiates, a cryptic, symbolic art. Some of his best poetry is to be found in the lyrics and choruses in those plays, in his translations of Sophocles' Oedipus plays, and in his short prose play *The Resurrection* (1927). Yeats's most striking achievement in drama is *The Words upon the Window Pane* (1934). It is unique among his plays in that it is completely naturalistic, with a modern setting. The last moment is fine. An old ignorant woman, who has been acting as a medium for Swift's voice, is left alone, muttering to herself, when the clients have gone: suddenly she speaks again in Swift's voice: 'Perish the day on which I was born!'

Yeats's last poems and plays are a strange mixture. *Purgatory* (1938) achieves a new rhythm of dramatic speech in verse. T. S. Eliot was to acknowledge his debt to it. The twelve 'Supernatural Songs' show a deep imaginative excitement. Once again Yeats exploits the antitheses and contradictions in himself. The biographer of Yeats must be struck by how different he seemed to different people: memories of him range from the effete fairy-fancier Max Beerbohm caricatured, to the tough old Dublin literary boss Monk Gibbon or Sean O'Casey knew. In his last poems Yeats takes up contrasting rôles, the contemplative saint, the angry old man. He writes ballads inspired by Irish street balladry. He exults in political violence; he exults in the violence of rage and lust ('What else have I to spur me into song?'). In 'The Municipal Gallery Revisited' Yeats's pride is seen at its most sympathetic. It is a tribute to his dead friends and the part they had played in Irish history. A fine late poem, 'The Circus Animals' Desertion', is a review of his whole poetic career. Throughout, he had played parts on a 'painted stage'. Now, in old age, he must make a new beginning from the sordid inner confusion out of which all art is made: he must lie down 'in the foul rag-and-bone shop of the heart'.

Yeats, though a great master of the English language, is an un-English poet. His early poetry has affinities with the vague sad Gaelic poetry of western Ireland or the Hebrides, or with Galician folksong; it is poetry of the Atlantic seaboard. His later poetry also has little in common with English traditions. He hates the middle class, the 'merchants and clerks', the 'hucksters'. His great good place is an imaginary eighteenth-century Ireland: landed gentry, fine horsemen, gracious ladies at the top; peasants, beggars, and priests at the bottom. There is no middle class. Yeats's philosophy is as exotic as his social attitude. He exalts ignorance and folly, even madness, above wisdom. He equates sexual union with mystical experience. He teaches that history goes in cycles: progressive ideas and plans for human betterment are illusions. Some readers find all this so uncongenial that they cannot enjoy Yeats's poetry. For them, he waves his wand in vain: the magic does not work.

Some of Yeats's other readers have been too uncritical. They have gone too far to meet him, forgetting that he himself confessed that much of his work was make-believe, covering the personal uncertainty of a deeply divided man. Yeats attracts cranks. But we cannot be sure whether he himself believed in all his eccentric ideas. Does it matter? The poetry of the past is not judged according to the tenability of the poet's beliefs. What matters is that he should be intensely aware of the world he has chosen to write about. Yeats's capacity for experience continued to the end. Furthermore, his beliefs must be seen in their historical context. Much of Yeats's work was a valid protest against some tendencies of modern civilization, its impersonality, its obsession with money, its mechanical character. However fanciful we may think his fabric of gods and fairies and heroes, it was a genuine attempt to restore a feeling of unity among Irishmen. His work in the theatre also helped to encourage national solidarity. Even the anti-democratic strain in Yeats's work can be excused; at that particular moment of the Irish national struggle, class conflict was less important than the feeling of unity.

But in the end Yeats stands or falls by the power of his writing, and his contribution to the art of poetry. Here his achievement was astonishing. Alone among the poets of his time, he succeeded in renewing himself as an artist and surviving triumphantly into a new literary period.

He created a new kind of lyric verse in the reverie-poems of his later work, more informal and varied in diction, looser in rhythm, than lyric poetry had ever been; yet capable of great dignity, beauty, and majesty. It can still haunt the minds of those who do not agree with Yeats that poetry has only flourished in ages of aristocracy, and who do not share his disillusion with the practical effects of modern civilization, or his doubts whether the concepts of the Scientific Age are ultimate.

Although J. M. SYNGE (1871–1909) wrote in prose, his place is among the poets and beside Yeats. He was a better dramatist than Yeats and less pompous as a writer. Synge's early models were French. But he became dissatisfied with the obscure, cryptic manner of the French symbolist tradition. At the same time, he disliked the opposite school of writing, what he called the 'pallid and joyless' work of realists like Ibsen or Zola. After Synge had spent some time with the people of the Aran Islands, he realized that his true mission as an artist was to use their dialect as the basis for dramatic speech. The outcome was his greatest play, *The Playboy of the Western World* (1907). This play is impossible to classify. The only plausible comparison is with Büchner's *Woyzeck*. In its blend of the humorous and the cruel, the earthy and the imaginative, it strikes deep into Irish temperament and character. The *Playboy* provoked a great storm when it was first produced. It was called an insult to Irish womanhood. But now it has taken its place in the repertory as a dramatic masterpiece, Synge's transmutation of the Oedipus theme. In *Riders to the Sea* (1905), Synge wrote a pathetic drama of the lives and deaths of fishermen. Its sensitive, sensuous art has affinities with some of Lawrence's early tales, like 'Odour of Chrysanthemums'. There is much in Synge's work that suggests an analogy with Lawrence. But Synge's career was short and his range limited. His art was rooted in folk-traditions. In his last, unfinished play, *Deirdre of the Sorrows* (1910), he treated an ancient legend in the style of folk-tale. This makes a contrast to the more sophisticated treatment which Yeats gave it.

Synge's stylization of Irish peasant speech, his earthy humour, his beautiful and curiously un-English rhythms, secure his individual place in literature. But his art achieves its distinction through remaining within strict limits. It is hard to see how any tradition could follow from it. His English disciple John Masefield, in *The Tragedy of Nan* (1909), is less convincing. And the one notable Irish dramatist who succeeded him, Sean O'Casey (1884–1964), was to write not of peasants but of urban, modern Ireland, in plays like *Juno and the Paycock* (1925) and *The Plough and the Stars* (1926). With these plays, the Irish dramatic revival seems to have come to an end. Perhaps it was only possible as a by-product of the Irish national struggle.

ROBERT BRIDGES (1844–1930) will always be linked in literary history with his fellow-poet Gerard Manley Hopkins. He was a close friend of Hopkins, and the first to recognize his genius. But in many ways he disapproved of Hopkins's revolutionary originality, and he has been much criticized for holding back the publication of Hopkins's poems, as a whole, till 1918. Whatever the rights and wrongs of this delay, there is an ironic contrast between the two poets. Bridges lived nearly twice as long as Hopkins, and wrote much more than twice as much. He became Poet Laureate and was awarded the Order of Merit. He died after writing a poetic best-seller. Hopkins died at forty-five, an obscure Jesuit professor of classics, without even a thin volume of verse to his name. But their posthumous histories have been very different. Hopkins has been hailed as one of the fathers of modern poetry. He has been called the greatest poet of the Victorian age. His poems have been endlessly expounded and discussed. Bridges in comparison is little read. His work is neglected by the critics.

Bridges spent his early life as a classical scholar, a traveller, and a hospital physician. He retired from professional life at the age of thirty-seven and spent the last fifty years of his life in what might be called purely cultural activities. He campaigned for phonetic spelling, for a purer English, for an improved hymnal. He made a study of Milton as a verse technician. Above all, he wrote poetry. He tried many kinds of verse—dramas, odes, and lyrics. In his later work he experimented in prosody, writing in various neo-classical and syllabic metres. Bridges was a man of taste, sedate and scholarly, with a chastened pleasure in nature. In his book on Keats he rebukes that poet for his lack of 'dignified passion'. Edward Thompson's *Robert Bridges* (1944) describes the old-world, scholarly atmosphere in which Bridges lived.

It is easy to see why Bridges has been compared unfavourably with the major poets of his time, Yeats and Hopkins. They were turbulent, anguished personalities: Bridges seems too comfortable and sheltered for a great poet. His verse often depends for its effect on our memory of the literary tradition in which it was written. He cultivates classical models; he imitates earlier English poets, like Campion or Blake. But a body of work can be selected from Bridges's output which will bear comparison with any other poet. 'Dejection', 'Eros', 'A Passer-by', 'The Affliction of Richard', the twenty-second sonnet from *The Growth of Love* (1876), 'Elegy among the Tombs', 'The Summer-house on the Mound', and 'The Garden in December' are among the best poems of this century. 'To a Dead Child' is above all the poem which throws doubt on the common view that Bridges's work lacks human interest. I. A. Richards described it as a doctor's poem. It is characteristic of

Bridges's best work; restrained, but compassionate. Perhaps a personal drama is not necessary for the writing of distinguished poetry.

At the end of his life Bridges had a great success with his long poem *The Testament of Beauty* (1929). It was widely proclaimed a masterpiece. But this seems an over-statement. It has interesting passages: but on the whole it gives the impression of senile rambling. We become irritated by Bridges's antiquated words and his fancy spelling. And, to use Johnson's distinction, Bridges thinks in verse rather than poetically. Most of his subject-matter could have been as well treated in prose. Bridges's prose writings, indeed, are among his most valuable. His literary criticism, with all its obvious limitations of sympathy, is full of interest.

Another neglected poet of the time is T. STURGE MOORE (1870–1944), brother of the philosopher G. E. Moore, and a close friend of Yeats. Like Bridges, Moore has been praised by the American critic Yvor Winters, and Winters's discussion of both of them, in *Forms of Discovery* (1968), should be consulted. There is an air of distinction about Moore's work. His thought is austere, though his imagination has a romantic colour. Moore paid no attention to fashion. He worked out his own theory of art and poetry, which he explained in *Armour for Aphrodite* (1929). We cannot but be impressed by the independence of Moore's mind. He seems very sensible and intelligent in his correspondence with Yeats—much more so than Yeats. Yet Yeats's poetry sticks in our minds and Moore's does not. Why is this? The reason may be that Moore, as a poet, turned away from essential experiences of his time. To say this is not to endorse the foolish demand for a poet to be 'contemporary'. There is no reason why every poet must be like Robert Lowell, self-consciously up-to-date. The American poet Wallace Stevens did not reflect the surface of his time in any obvious way. But Stevens's best poetry has a distinguishable sense of the world he lives in. Moore's seems to lack this.

Bridges and Moore may be revived as poets: C. M. DOUGHTY (1843–1926) probably cannot be. Yet he might have been a more powerful writer than either, and the reason for his failure is instructive. Doughty was really a late Victorian writer. His best known prose work, *Travels in Arabia Deserta* (1888), was written after his journeys in the Near East. T. E. Lawrence's *Seven Pillars of Wisdom* (1926) shows its influence. In his prose Doughty, with all his mannerisms, appears as a man of character and integrity. But Doughty thought of himself as primarily a poet. He was convinced that he could reform poetry, and reform England, by reforming the English language. And to do this he went back to the language of Spenser. Hopkins, another experimenter, was critical of this archaism. He agreed with Doughty's criticisms of

Victorian English. But he thought Doughty was making a great mistake in supposing that Elizabethan English was the solution. And this is the essential criticism of Doughty's work. Perhaps a poet will appear who can use it. Then we may see him as an amazing primitive, like Cézanne. As things are, Doughty's long poems, *Adam Cast Forth* (1908) and *The Clouds* (1912), suffer from a fatal defect: they are unreadable. We cannot but admire Doughty's solitary quixotic effort to turn back the current of English life and history. It is not absurd to compare him with Milton. But his great human force spent itself in the linguistic and scholarly. He is remembered, if at all, only as the manipulator of an archaic diction.

With Housman and Walter de la Mare we come to two poets whose work is still alive. A. E. HOUSMAN (1859–1936) began as a poet of the nineties, with *A Shropshire Lad* (1896). And some critics have tried to derive his poetry from characteristic work of that period. But this is a mistake. Housman's note does not belong to any particular epoch. If literary sources are looked for, they are what he said they were: Shakespeare's songs, the Border ballads, the lyrics of Burns and Heine. Farther in the background are Latin epigrams and the Greco-Roman tradition of pastoral poetry, as in Theocritus and Virgil. Housman's pastoralism lays bright colours against the unchanging black background of death.

A Shropshire Lad was originally called 'The Poems of Terence Hearsay'. Terence is a rootless, drifting youth. He feels he is worth little. He expects to die early, never having lived. He has nothing of the countryman's resigned acceptance of a common fate. The thought of death moves him to sarcasm, to despair, to rhetoric. D. H. Lawrence says of him that 'death has filched the pride out of his blood, and there is the conceit of death instead in his veins'. His best friend has taken his sweetheart. He has been in the county jail. His only consolations are football and beer. This character is presented in a series of short lyrics, in a metre recalling ballads and hymns. They are rhetorical, emphatic, eminently memorable. *A Shropshire Lad* made no appeal at first to the public. But when it did, it was taken to their hearts. Edwardian and Georgian readers found Housman easier to assimilate than Hardy. His verse suited a classically trained ear. He had no philosophical framework; his bitterness against God was expressed solely through his moods.

Housman was a distinguished classical scholar as well as a poet. But he achieved his celebrity in a very narrow domain: his *forte* was textual criticism. He said of an editor of Ovid that 'he had no ungovernable passion for knowing the truth about things', and this suggests

Housman's own terrifyingly high standard of accuracy. But Housman had other motives besides the passion for truth in his castigation of erring scholars. We enjoy his own enjoyment of his elegant scorn. And in his own scholarship the desire for fame was a powerful driving-force. He yearned for eminence as a scholar after his failure in his final examinations at Oxford. He determined to build himself a monument. Yet in one of his poems he compares all human ambitions for perpetuity to writing one's name on the sand. The longed-for monument becomes a sandcastle.

Housman called one of his published lectures 'rhetorical and not wholly sincere', and this comment has often been made by readers who dislike his poetry. They find something glib about his pessimism. The epigrammatic crispness of the style seems to run counter to the moping, self-pitying subject-matter. But this contrast of manner and matter reflects something in Housman's temperament. His verse abounds in expressions of the wish never to have been born, cries of protest, denunciations of the 'brute and blackguard' that made the world. But always there is a sense of control and discipline in the versification. Often we have an effect of marching and drilling. Housman, like Kipling and Hopkins, made a cult of the soldier, the 'redcoat'. War is for him a frequent image of human life: 'soldiers marching, all to die'. His soldiers are 'food for powder', 'cheap to the King'. They 'take their wages and are dead'. When they are not at war, they commit crimes, are jailed or hanged. Yet 'the soldier's is the trade'. A poem like 'In valleys green and still' beautifully conveys the deep seductive meaning which it had for Housman.

There are false notes in *A Shropshire Lad*. Housman was not really a dramatic poet. He was a subjective, lyrical poet, like Emily Brontë. His best work did not appear till *Last Poems* (1922) and *More Poems* (1936), published after his death. Throughout Housman's poems his essential subject-matter is proclaimed. Yet he was not a confessional poet, but a shy, reticent man, who shrank from any sort of publicity. His poetry came to him spasmodically, in unpredictable gusts of inspiration. Its sources were latent, unconscious material. But the story behind the poems is not in doubt. Housman's poetry speaks of a passionate love for another man which was not returned. Was this love of a kind which Housman himself felt to be wrong? Housman was a man of stern and austere morality. Not for him could there be the 'transvaluation of values' which a Nietzsche or a Wilde had preached. He held to traditional morality all the more strongly since he had abandoned the creed which enshrined it. Atheist as he was, his verse and prose are saturated in the language of the English Bible. But Housman judged his feeling to be unlucky rather than blameworthy. He regarded it as a given fact of his nature. Hence at the core of his version of the just man's complaint against the universe there lay this private, personal episode.

Housman always insisted on the unconscious origins of his poetry. But it is clear that he worked on the material that came up from below. In 'The Name and Nature of Poetry' he declares that the meaning (that is, the manifest content) of poetry is irrelevant. What matters is the emotional appeal. But on the face of it Housman's own poetry has a great deal of explicit meaning. He is often witty and epigrammatic. It is his liking for finish in phrasing which most reminds us that he was a professor of Latin. His favourite poet was Blake; but his own poems have a much more chiselled, lapidary effect than Blake's. We are always conscious of the scholar's fine judgement controlling his choice of words. It gave us poems like the exquisite 'Parta Quies'.

The pastoral or ballad manners are not Housman's only styles. Sometimes he writes in a vein of noble dignity, as in 'Revolution' or 'Easter Hymn'. At his best he combines lyrical melody with a strong firmness and a command of concise, unadorned statement. Among his best poems are 'Others, I am not the first'; 'Stars, I have seen them fall'; and 'Crossing alone the nighted ferry'. 'It nods and curtseys and recovers' sums up in a few lines Housman's wordplay, his lyrical quality, his liking for the macabre, his hint of mystery.

Housman is the most immediately recognizable of poets. His note is so characteristic that when we find it in earlier poets we do not think of them as influencing Housman, but as anticipating him. His emphatic alliteration, his versification that often suggests a hymn-tune, his caustic or flippant thrusts against his non-existent Maker, are all unmistakable. So are his soldiers, his convicts, his hanged men, his 'lovers of the grave', his wayward, fickle girls, hardly distinguishable from the English landscape that Housman likes to picture as the faithless mistress: 'She and I were long acquainted,/And I knew all her ways.'

The Housman of the verse is the Housman of the prose. He has been caricatured as a crusty, vinous old pedant, furtively penning his tearful poems. But the relationship between the lofty scorn of the prose and the ironic sentiment of the verse may be more complex than that. Perhaps we should see the eighteenth-century wit of the one, like the tough, laconic grimness of the other, as formidable weapons with which Housman defended the secret of his poetic genius: the forbidden longing to look upon 'the west', where the times before birth and after death merge into one. It was that longing which gave us poems like 'Into my heart an air that kills' and 'Far in a western brookland'—summits of romantic lyrical achievement.

WALTER DE LA MARE (1873–1956) began as a writer for and about children. In *Songs of Childhood* (1906) he shows that insight into their thoughts and feelings and imaginings which he was never to lose. He does not sentimentalize them. He conveys the boredom of childhood as well as its joys and fancies. And he did not confine himself to trying to recapture the vision of childhood. Had he done so, he would probably have fallen into false sentiment. Rather, he suggests its survival in the experience of the adult. De la Mare believed that the unreflective responses of childhood could illuminate the world of grown men. He refused to repudiate any stage of the process by which we become aware of the world. He looked inward, as well as backward, for his inspiration. His poems and stories record his explorations of the inner life.

De la Mare wrote a great deal of prose fiction. Some of his short stories are very good. 'Seaton's Aunt' is one of the most frightening ever written, the more so because it refrains from all the common devices for raising a thrill. But we cannot read his fiction for very long without realizing that he was essentially a poet. The traditional subjects of the novel—manners, social criticism, studies of moral conduct—are not at the centre of his interests. His real subject was the imagination. His story 'The Magic Jacket' evokes the ineffable difference between a life with imagination and a life without it.

In some of de la Mare's poems his art is like a game played by children, gravely and solemnly. They are wholly wrapped up in it, they have passed into a timeless world. But in other poems we are aware of the poet as onlooker, responsive to their joy, but conscious, unlike them, of time and mortality. The purity of his lyrical poetry in books like *The Listeners* (1912) and *Peacock Pie* (1913) has been compared with Ariel's songs in *The Tempest*. But de la Mare is never long free from uncertainty and misgiving.

De la Mare's poetry is rooted in literary reminiscence. Critics have spoken of a debt to Blake, to Poe, to Christina Rossetti. All these belong to the romantic tradition. Though he and Eliot admired each other's poetry, de la Mare owes nothing to the modern school. He uses, to excess, conventional poetic diction and ornaments; he repeats the images and symbols, the evocative adjectives, the traditional associations, of late romantic poetry. But the music of his verse is different from anyone else's. And its substance, beneath his art of incantation and spell, is equally characteristic. De la Mare offers nothing optimistic or comforting. Human consciousness and human destiny remain for him inexplicable puzzles. Life is transient and death is final. His fantasy is rooted in no shared convictions or religious traditions, not even in the superstitions of folk-lore. It derives its authority solely from its appeal to the hinterland of the mind.

De la Mare was less successful when he dealt realistically with the painful side of life. But his most powerful poetry is not incantatory. It is like the best nursery rhymes or folksongs. It confronts depressing truths in a direct, simple, amoral way. It is child-like rather than childish. His little poem 'Old Shellover', like Kafka's 'The Knock on the Manor Gate', is one of those very short pieces that convey the essence of an author's vision. Other fine poems are 'The Listeners', 'The Children of Stare', 'The Mad Prince's Song', 'The Ghost', and 'Napoleon'. As late as 1953 he published the most desolating of his poems, 'De Profundis', which makes it clear that his essential materials were tragic.

But on the whole de la Mare's later poetry suggests that, like most minor poets, he had little power of development; he had said his say. The relaxed, ruminative verse of his later years seems to come from the man of letters rather than the poet. As a man of letters—reviewer, critic, and journalist—everyone liked and respected him. And in one particular genre—the anthology of poetry—he did something new and of the greatest value. In anthologies like *Come Hither* he mingled folk-poetry and nursery rhymes with traditionally 'great' poetry. To many young readers he opened up a new kingdom of delight. He showed that the field of poetry is infinite.

Other poets of the late romantic tradition—Flecker, Masefield, Hodgson, Newbolt, Noyes, Gordon Bottomley—were read and discussed at this time. Each had his distinctive voice, and happily each found readers to listen. Flecker's play *Hassan* is still remembered. Masefield was to succeed Bridges as Poet Laureate and achieve a remarkable *succès de scandale* with the 'bad language' of his *Everlasting Mercy*, the story of a scoundrel who is converted to the Salvation Army. Bottomley's 'The End of the World' is a fine poem. More remarkable than any of these poets was W. H. DAVIES (1871–1940). Unlike them, he had had little formal education. He had lived a vagrant life. His *Autobiography of a Super-Tramp* (1908) is a valuable document. Davies's poetry won popularity because much of it is conventionally charming and sweet. Yet Davies could write of the squalid and sordid, as in 'The Inquest', and he had a refreshing vein of quiet sarcasm. Whatever his matter, his verse always retains an attractive simplicity and purity of accent.

It was becoming generally felt at the beginning of the twentieth century that a literary period was coming to an end. There was a demand for a more modern kind of poetry. An attempt was made to supply this, by a group of poets who were known as 'Georgians', after Edward Marsh (1872–1953) had convened them in his anthology *Georgian Poetry* (1912–22). They took their name from the new King,

George V, not because that excellent monarch had any interest in poetry, but to announce the opening of a new epoch. The Georgians have fallen into disrepute, largely because of the later, weaker work in that tradition associated with the *London Mercury* under Sir John Squire (1884–1958). The original Georgian movement attracted some interesting poets, including D. H. Lawrence. But the dominant figure in it was Rupert Brooke. He is still a very popular poet, though he is out of fashion with the sophisticated.

RUPERT BROOKE (1887–1915) was at school at Rugby, where he had a great success, social, intellectual, and athletic. Later he attracted admiring friends at Cambridge, where he became a Fellow of King's College. He travelled widely. In 1911 he settled at Grantchester, near Cambridge, and interested himself in the publication of contemporary verse and the revival of undergraduate drama at Cambridge. There is always a note of undergraduate brilliance and cleverness in Brooke's work. He was a glamorous figure; but under the glamour there were personal immaturities and difficulties, as his letters show. His most famous poem, 'Grantchester', has been described as the prize poem of Georgian poetry. It is a string of wistful home thoughts from abroad. What Brooke wrote best about was personal comfort. On this subject he has many individual touches. 'The Great Lover' is an excellent poem of its kind. In general, Brooke writes best when his touch is lightest. When he expresses his thoughts on grander themes—love and death, beauty and sorrow—he falls into commonplaces. Brooke's work epitomizes the dilemma of Georgian poetry. These poets felt that they must break away from the conventional language of the late romantic tradition. But as soon as they are serious, they lapse into it again. Georgianism was a sunset that was mistaken for a dawn.

Brooke made a determined effort to be modern. He was thought a shocking, immoral poet because he ventured occasionally on unpleasant or unromantic subjects. But all this was to be forgiven when he won posthumous fame as a symbolic figure, the fallen soldier-poet (though in fact he was in the navy and did not die in battle). Henry James and Winston Churchill paid him eloquent tributes. Brooke won his fame because of the sonnets he wrote at the outbreak of war. They put into eloquent language what many people—not only unintelligent patriots—were feeling at the time. In the enemy camp Rilke, like Brooke, hailed the war as an occasion for spiritual revival. But Brooke's 'Now, God be thanked Who has matched us with His hour' was a sentiment soon to become unpopular with sensitive people, and Brooke's reputation suffered accordingly. Had he experienced the full horror of the war he might have gone on to write like Wilfred Owen, though his social background was more like Siegfried Sassoon's or Edmund Blunden's. What

little poetry he wrote after the war sonnets shows an increased sensi-
tivity and thoughtfulness. But there is reason to think that if Brooke
had survived the war, he might well have found his vocation outside
literature.

Brooke, though the most famous of the 'war poets', was not really a
war poet. It is difficult to remain coolly objective about the writers who
were. We are bound to have a warm sympathy with these people, products of a sheltered civilization, who were the first in our history to
encounter modern war. We are bound to give them great credit for the
honesty and sincerity with which they tried to bring home the dreadful
facts to the civilian public, to reveal the reality hidden behind the sooth-
ing language of official communiqués and war correspondents. What
higher task could there be for a poet? But if we are to retain strictly
literary standards, we must admit that the best poetry published during
this period was written by non-combatants: Hardy, Yeats, and Eliot.

SIEGFRIED SASSOON (1886–1967) made it his mission to administer a
healthy shock to the civilian public. His best poem, 'Everyone Sang',
was inspired by the armistice of 1918. Though he continued to write
poetry after the war, his inspiration seems to belong peculiarly to the
war-time period. We must remember that the term 'war poet' has a
special meaning in the Great War period. The 'war poet' did not exist in
the Second World War. The division between soldier and civilian was
less acute and dramatic than it was for poets like Sassoon or Blunden,
Owen or Rosenberg. Sassoon's best work is not in poetry but in his
autobiography. In its war-time sections it describes something that
has now passed away, the paternalism of English officers towards their
men, the spirit of *noblesse oblige*. We see this too in the work of
EDMUND BLUNDEN (b. 1896). Blunden had begun as a poet in a tradition
of English pastoral poetry, and he was later to go back to it. And his
best poems are not those that deal directly with the war. The experience
seems to have been too traumatic for Blunden to assimilate. But his
finest work owes its quality to the sense of unspeakable horror and
chaos in the background. His best poem, 'The Midnight Skaters', conveys the feeling of sinister or tragic things beneath the surface of Izaak
Walton's England. Other good poems are 'The Giant Puffball', 'Journey', 'Report on Experience', and 'The Sunlit Vale'. Blunden's best
known prose book is *Undertones of War* (1928). Its title summarizes the
effect of his best work. He is a quiet poet, literary, academic, nostalgic.
He loves to dwell wistfully on traditional features of English life, like
village cricket. But his undertones linger in the mind when more
strident poetry is forgotten.

By general agreement the best of the war poets is WILFRED OWEN
(1893–1918). Before the war he would have fitted quite happily into the

Georgian school, which he admired. What brought a different kind of poetry out of him was the impact of the war, and his conviction as a young officer that he had a priest-like mission towards the soldiers under his care. He attempted a direct, unrhetorical treatment of the horrors of the Western Front. Owen is very highly valued today. Partly this is because of Benjamin Britten's *War Requiem*, which incorporates some of his poems. He may have been over-praised, because of his subject and his moral attitude. These apart, he might well have been the same kind of poet as Rupert Brooke. On the other hand, a poem like 'The Unreturning', which is not a war poem, is better than anything by Brooke. At any rate, the war, which cost Owen his happiness and his life, brought him out as a poet. He developed a new way of writing verse, with off-rhymes, deliberate understatement, and an avoidance of conventional poetic language. Poems like 'Exposure' and 'Insensibility' were to go deep into the consciousness of the poets of the 1930s. Owen began as a poet under the spell of Keats. And he was the only follower of Keats who was able to develop, not only the aesthetic-sensuous side of Keats, but the more tragic side that comes out in *The Fall of Hyperion*. We see this in his most famous poem, 'Strange Meeting'. Anyone studying Keats will benefit by studying Owen alongside him, just as anyone studying Owen should study Keats. Owen's 'Anthem for Doomed Youth' is a poem Keats might have written had he lived a century later.

Owen deserves his fame. But some have felt that his work has over-shadowed an even more notable poet killed in the war, ISAAC ROSEN-BERG (1890–1918). Rosenberg, unlike the other war poets, served in the ranks. He was little noticed till T. S. Eliot drew attention to him. His work, mostly scribbled in pencil on odd scraps of paper, was not made fully available till the 1930s. Just as Owen is one of the few poets worthy to be compared with Keats, Rosenberg is one of the few worthy to be compared with Shakespeare. He had no opportunity—genius apart —to write anything on the scale of one of Shakespeare's great plays. But his work shows that the spirit in which Shakespeare handled the language can be revived without imitating Shakespeare. Rosenberg was Jewish, and intensely concerned with the place of the Jew in the modern world. He tried to establish an imaginative connection between the unromantic fate of the Jew, in a modern city like London, and the ancient prophetic spirit of the Bible. Rosenberg was a revolutionary innovator in technique. His best critic, D. W. Harding, has shown how, like Blake, he allows his thought to appear in process of formation. The organization of his best poems is pre-conceptual and pre-logical. Like Blake, Rosenberg was a visual artist as well as a poet, and this affected his style. Rosenberg's finest work is to be found in the fragments of his ambitious projects for drama, rather than in complete poems. But those who have read poems like 'Spring 1916', 'Dead Man's Dump', 'Returning we hear the larks', and 'Break of Day in the Trenches', can never forget them.

Poets like Owen and Rosenberg impress us by their promise. EDWARD THOMAS (1878–1917) impresses us by his actual achievement. As the years go by it seems more and more considerable. His name will always be associated with the war period, but he was not a war poet in the sense in which Owen and Rosenberg and Sassoon were. Though he fought on the Western Front, where he was killed in 1917, he wrote little or nothing about his experiences there. Nevertheless, it was the coming of the war, together with Thomas's friendship with the American poet Robert Frost, that brought him out as a poet. He found his poetic voice tragically late; but not too late to produce a remarkable body of work.

Edward Thomas was born in London, the son of a civil servant. He was educated at St. Paul's School, and at Lincoln College, Oxford. He married Helen Noble in 1899, and her memoirs of him, *As it was* (1926) and *World Without End* (1931), are invaluable sources for the student of his life and character. To them should be added Eleanor Farjeon's memoir. Thomas had a wretched life. He tried to live by writing, like Arnold Bennett, but he had none of Bennett's toughness. He wrote many books on country life, books like *The Woodland Life* and *Beautiful Wales* and *The South Country*. They might be called hackwork—they were certainly written for money—if it were not that everything Thomas did was done with care and devotion. He strove to write well. But it was some time before he developed his personal style in prose. For many years he wrote in a style similar to Walter Pater's. But in his interest in the rural life of England he has more affinity with writers like 'George Bourne' and, earlier, Richard Jefferies. Thomas's life of Jefferies seems to have been the one prose book he wrote for pleasure. Thomas was a gifted literary critic. He anticipated many of the positions that were later to be taken by Eliot and Pound. He lived long enough to take a sympathetic interest in the first work of the modern school. He was a sensitive observer of the development of poetry in his own time, and a percipient critic of the poetry of the past, particularly that of the Romantics and the Victorians on whom his own sensibility was nourished.

Thomas's poetry consists largely of his remembered impressions of the English countryside, interwoven with his own personal preoccupations. He was a poet of mood, or, to use Aldous Huxley's phrase about George Herbert, a poet of 'inner weather'. His poetry reflects the country he loved, with its delicate colouring, its cloudy skies, its soft rainy atmosphere, its occasional welcome sunlight. Thomas was of

Welsh blood, and there is a distinctively Celtic strain in his work. But he loved England and the English past and the English countryside. His work belongs to the tradition of Arnold's 'Scholar-Gipsy', but Thomas knew more about the countryside than Arnold, and unlike many romantic poets he could really describe nature. What he shared with Arnold, as a poet, was a tendency to turn away from human life, to find in nature a retreat from the oppressiveness of the world of men. Other poets of his time shared this tendency. But Thomas is distinguished from them by the depth of his melancholy. The circumstances of his life, its poverty and discomfort, might have made anyone sad. To make matters worse, Thomas was melancholy by temperament. Very often he had to struggle against overwhelming black moods. His poetry reflects his depression and sense of aimlessness.

On the other hand, there is a feeling of strength in it too. If we compare Thomas's work with that of his friend and inspirer Robert Frost, it stands up to the comparison very well. Frost is regarded by most American critics as a major poet. He had a long life, he wrote a great deal, he became famous. Thomas is generally accounted a minor poet and is little known. He was killed in the war and left comparatively few poems behind him. But if we ask just how much good poetry was written by each poet, we may conclude that Thomas wrote at least as many fine poems as Frost, and he gives the impression of having been a more substantial poet and a stronger man than Frost. 'I sought yet hated pity, till at length/I earned it,' he wrote in 'There was a time'. That feeling of subdued strength is typical.

Thomas's most striking poem is 'The Other'. It tells the story of a man haunted by an *alter ego*, an anti-self, which finally absorbs him. Thomas came to be obsessed with unrealized possibilities. His discovery that he was a poet meant a new start for him. It is significant that he wrote his poetry under a new name, 'Edward Eastaway'. The Thomas of the prose was discarded. In a new blunt conversational syntax, in new rhythms evolved from prose and everyday speech, he found himself as a poet. Poems like 'Parting', 'Swedes', 'That Girl's Clear Eyes', 'Aspens', 'Tears', 'No one so much as you', 'Celandine', and 'Rain' show that Thomas had done what none of the Georgians had succeeded in doing. He had discarded the Victorian poetic tradition and found a modern style to express a modern way of feeling. At the same time he had retained his sense of continuity with the English past. All that can be said against Thomas is that his range as a poet was limited. His chief subject was his melancholy. But he does not luxuriate or sentimentalize. He was self-preoccupied but not egotistic; he speaks for all intelligent men to whom this world is vain, but who have nowhere else to go.

Thus the Great War produced a few distinguished English poets and a few memorable poems. But the war itself eluded artistic treatment. The most ambitious attempts to render modern war in literature, prose-poems like T. E. Lawrence's *Seven Pillars of Wisdom* (1926) or David Jones's *In Parenthesis* (1937), may be less successful than the books which treat it in an unpretentious, reporting way, like Frederick Manning's *Her Privates We* (1930). What is lacking in English war literature is anything comparable to Remarque's *All Quiet on the Western Front* (1929), which combines the objectivity of good reporting with the creative power of the artist. The writers of the Great War tended to be either reporters or artists, and perhaps it is the reporters whose work has survived best. The ideal union of reporter and artist was not found in any writer on the English side.

4
Joyce and Lawrence

MANY WORLD EVENTS are of little importance to the literary historian. But the Great War marked a definite period in the history of English literature, as well as in human affairs generally. In the 1930s Leonard Woolf called his study of post-war communal psychology *After the Deluge* (1931). That was how literary people felt. The great men of the days before 1914 now seemed antediluvian. Poets like Rupert Brooke and the Georgians, once champions of modern poetry against traditionalists like Newbolt, fell completely out of favour. Many great Victorian reputations also collapsed. Full-bloodedness and confidence were in disrepute. The war had provoked an orgy of rhetoric and emotional propaganda, and writers who were thought, rightly or wrongly, to have anything in common with that were dismissed. The title of C. E. Montague's *Disenchantment* (1922) sums up the general feeling. Blunden conveyed it in his variation of the Psalmist's words: 'I have been young, and now am not too old,/Yet I have seen the righteous forsaken,/His health, his honour, and his quality taken;/This is not what we were formerly told.' Lytton Strachey's *Eminent Victorians* (1918) reflected this change of taste. So did the poetry of the Sitwells and the novels of Norman Douglas and Aldous Huxley.

The most important writers of the new literary period also reflect it. These new writers, 'the men of 1914' as Wyndham Lewis called them, were still an *avant-garde*. Middlebrow literature was well entrenched, and philistinism dominated ordinary reading habits. The optimistic, comfortable tradition of Edwardian literature was not dead. But there were all the signs of a radical change in the literary climate. The 'men of 1914'—Joyce, Eliot, Pound, Wyndham Lewis—were to be eventually canonized as modern classics. Their place may not be so secure as it seemed a decade ago. Wyndham Lewis and Pound (at any rate in England) are less widely accepted than the other two. And the once fashionable aspects of Eliot's and Joyce's work have dated. *The Waste*

Land and *Ulysses* no longer seem the unchallengeable masterpieces they once did. A body of influential opinion holds that neither Eliot nor Joyce, but D. H. Lawrence, was the greatest writer of the time. At any rate, Lawrence, unlike the others, is widely read by ordinary people. It will be said, of course, that they 'read him for the sex', but there is a good deal besides 'sex' in Lawrence's work, and ordinary readers are reading that too. Lawrence has risen in esteem as the personal controversies round him have died down.

Hardy was discovered as a poet in this period. And the poetry of Gerard Hopkins, when it became known, was acclaimed as essentially modern. Hardy and Hopkins, together with Lawrence and James and Conrad, have taken their places beside 'the men of 1914' as the classics of modern literature.

To this period also belong the writers who were called, though not by themselves, the Bloomsbury group, after the district in London in which some of them lived. Bloomsbury existed before the war; but it was the second generation, of Lytton Strachey and Virginia Woolf, that became widely known to the public. Much harsh criticism has been levelled at these writers. Their conviction that they represented the summit of high civilization has been challenged. In their own time, they had many enemies. Besides the taunts of opposing literary factions, they were accused of irreverence by Lawrence, and by the philosopher Wittgenstein. And it certainly looks as if a spirit of reverence would have been as out of place there as a Yorkshire accent. Bloomsbury may have had too good a conceit of itself. The leading families of the intellectual aristocracy in England, while they have produced men and women of distinguished and various talents, have not produced a great writer. Moreover, they have tended to ignore or undervalue the great outsiders—a Wells, a Joyce, or a Lawrence. But of the Bloomsbury writers, E. M. Forster and Virginia Woolf should survive. And Bloomsbury at its best did represent a continuity from the humane rationalism of the eighteenth-century Enlightenment.

We are too near this period to distinguish confidently between changes of taste and changes of fashion. In fashion, the marks of the period are very noticeable. It was the period which Scott Fitzgerald was to commemorate in American literature; the period when jazz was being discovered by the intellectual young. It was the period when Noël Coward (b. 1899) was winning success as a dramatist. Coward's plays do more than any others to catch the surface tone of the period. Plays like *The Vortex* (1924) and *Fallen Angels* (1925) help to fix it in our minds. As a piece of pure theatre, *Private Lives* (1930) is unsurpassed in English drama. Coward exploited to the full the modern technique of underemphasis. He mocked the melodrama and heavy sentiment of the previous generation, substituting his own neater versions. His early plays reflect the self-conscious decadence of the period, typified by exaggerated fashions in clothes, and by cultural eclecticism. We must distinguish what was merely precious and wilful in the period from its genuine individualism. Picasso and Stravinsky, the most admired artists of the period, do not belong only to the history of fashion. But fashion reigned supreme, in this period of private preoccupations, private poetry, and private incomes. Politics were ignored. The 'proletariat', which was to absorb the attention of earnest intellectuals in the next decade, was forgotten. Extravagances and eccentricities continued until the world financial disaster (1929–31) put an abrupt end to them.

JAMES JOYCE (1882–1941) and D. H. Lawrence are among the most widely read of modern writers. Novel after novel, in England and America, reveals their influence. Their work divides opinions. Some readers dislike both. Some admire one and reject the other. Very few seem to care for both equally. This is because of the nature of their work. Each seems to make a claim for his kind of art as the *right* kind. Lawrence had no use for Joyce's work, and Joyce had no use for Lawrence's. We are reminded of Professor Raleigh's story of the idol-maker who found on returning to his shop that the idols had quarrelled and the biggest one had smashed the others to pieces. Joyce and Lawrence are dangerous idols to keep in one's shop.

Joyce was born in Dublin. His family background was shabby-genteel, like Shaw's. Unlike Shaw's it was Catholic, and Joyce was early marked out for the priesthood. But he passed through a religious crisis and left Ireland in 1904 as a self-consciously blasphemous atheist. For the rest of his life he was to be a citizen of the world, like his eighteenth-century compatriot Goldsmith. He studied first medicine and then singing in Paris. Then for ten years he taught languages in Trieste and Switzerland. In 1907 he published his first book of poems, *Chamber Music*, and completed his book of stories, *Dubliners. A Portrait of the Artist as a Young Man* (1916), a novel based on Joyce's early life, and serialized by Ezra Pound in the *Egoist*, was the product of many years' work. What survives of an early version was posthumously published as *Stephen Hero. Ulysses* was begun in Trieste in 1914, serialized in the *Little Review* in New York, and first published as a complete book in Paris in 1922. It became a *casus belli* in the struggle against censorship when it was banned in England. It was eventually admitted into the United States, and for some years it has freely circulated in England. *Ulysses* made Joyce's name the symbol of ultra-modernity. His last work, at first referred to as 'Work in Progress', began to appear in sections in 1924. They were finally incorporated into the complete work, which was then entitled *Finnegans Wake* (1939). Joyce, though outspoken and aggressive on paper, lived most of his later life in quiet retirement in Paris. He had his devoted champions, who supported him financially and published defences and expositions of his work. Everything he wrote cost him years of labour, during which he had to struggle against illness and increasingly bad sight. In the Second World War, after France was invaded by Hitler's armies, he settled in Switzerland, where he died in 1941.

Richard Ellmann has shown the autobiographical basis of most of Joyce's fiction. And even on the surface the relationship between his work and his life is obvious. Joyce was an exile: *Ulysses* is inscribed from 'Trieste, Paris, Zürich'. But Joyce wrote of none of those places. Wherever he went, he remained spiritually in Dublin. The skies did not change the soul. We are reminded of Isaac Bashevis Singer, who has lived thirty-two years in the United States, yet still writes in Yiddish of the ghetto.

But though Joyce's subject-matter was always Irish, he was a European artist. Unlike most English writers of his time, he submitted eagerly to European influences. His greatest master was Gustave Flaubert. Like Flaubert he was a deliberate, conscious artist who drew on the two great currents of nineteenth-century European literature, aestheticism and naturalism. Joyce subscribed to the tenets of the Aesthetic movement. For him, 'perfection of the work' was everything. The phrase is Yeats's, and Yeats's attitude to art and poetry had made a deep impression on Joyce. But he was also keenly interested in Naturalist writers like Ibsen and Zola. Where Joyce differs from his fellow-countryman George Moore, who also submitted to both Aesthetic and Naturalist influences, is that he did not *lean* on his masters. He 'admired and did otherwise'. He was as original a writer as it is possible to be.

This originality makes him difficult to classify. If we define a poet as a man interested in language for its own sake, Joyce should be called a poet. In *Ulysses* and *Finnegans Wake* he was to carry this interest in language beyond what any other writer had ever attempted. But as a poet in verse Joyce is inconsiderable. Apart from two beautiful lyrics, 'I hear an army' and 'Ecce Puer', his main creative effort was to be made outside verse. He also tried his hand at drama, and here too his success was not outstanding. *Exiles* (1918) is interesting to students of Joyce's life and character, but it is so closely modelled on Ibsen as to suggest parody. And there may be a deeper reason for the failure of *Exiles*. Joyce's imagination was not really a dramatic one. Conflict was not part of his essential vision.

It was in prose fiction that Joyce was to show his real originality.

Dubliners, the *Portrait*, and *Ulysses* are his finest works, and they have a unique place in literature. Each is very different from the others, yet they are all unmistakably by the same writer. *Dubliners* consists of a number of short stories and sketches of Dublin life, written in a style of 'scrupulous meanness'. Joyce achieves an effect of sustained externality. He aims at complete fidelity to the observed details of life, to every gesture, tone, and phrase of his characters, to the form and outline and atmosphere of their drab environment. His sentences seem quite ordinary and undistinguished, until, impressed by the general effect of a story, we look more closely and find that not a word, not a rhythm could be altered. Joyce breaks altogether with the traditions of Victorian fiction. There is no moralizing, no explicit authorial point of view, no direct solicitation of the reader.

Dubliners should be read as a whole. But some of the stories are remarkable by themselves. 'A Painful Case' is a desolating story of human loneliness. 'Ivy Day in the Committee Rooms' is a masterpiece of pathos and irony. In every detail it depends on the circumstances of a particular place at a particular moment of history. Yet it can speak to a reader from any small oppressed country which has decided to compromise with the oppressor. The best story in *Dubliners* is the last and longest. 'The Dead' is the finest short story ever to come out of Ireland. Its early part is prosaic and comic. But in the closing pages, as it explores the husband and wife relationship which turns out to be its real theme, it broadens into a moving and poetic art. There is no 'scrupulous meanness' here. To an English taste 'The Dead' may seem morbid, like Henry James's 'The Altar of the Dead'. But Joyce has the advantage over James of drawing upon the peculiar Catholic Irish attitude towards the dead, with its complex mixture of morbidity with piety, of sentimentality with deep tenderness.

The *Portrait of the Artist* belongs to a kind of which there had been many examples; the subjective novel with little external action, having as its theme the spiritual development of a hero whose personality is founded on the author's. Goethe's *Wilhelm Meister* is the prototype. In Joyce's own time there was Lawrence's *Sons and Lovers*. The *Portrait* is a study of adolescence. It is the story of how Stephen Dedalus looks for an order and significance in life amid the muddle and disorder of his father's house; how he resists the temptation to find that order in the Roman priesthood; and how he eventually discovers his vocation to be a priest of art. This story is told from inside. We see Stephen's confusions and immaturities as he tries to assert himself, to mobilize his intellectual resources, so that he can look out on the world with his own eyes. Joyce handles his materials in an original way. A tableau, a snatch of conversation, an ordinary incident, are invested with profound meaning. The book has more in common with a Symbolist poem than with documentary fiction. Joyce has given a creative expression to his doctrine of epiphanies, the 'showings-forth', 'the sudden revelation of the whatness of things', when 'the soul of the commonest object ... seems to us radiant'; the moments of transcendent significance when our life-experiences seem to come together as in a work of art. All his skill is used to convey the inwardness of the experiences which moulded Stephen—his rejection of his mother's religion, his sense of his nationality, his discovery of his vocation to 'forge in the smithy of his soul ... the uncreated conscience of his race'. Where *Dubliners* had been severely objective, the *Portrait* is subjective. But it avoids the sprawling carelessness of most subjective fiction. The consciousness of Stephen, through which we learn his story, is carefully dramatized and controlled.

One marked feature of the *Portrait* is Stephen's passionate interest in words. This was Joyce's own passion, or obsession; and it distinguishes him as a characteristically modern writer. For the romantic subjectivist, a novel was a mirror; for the Naturalist, it was a window; for Joyce it had, above all, to be true to its primary character as a linguistic object. It was through his interest in language that Joyce discovered his sense of the world. The most striking feature of modern thought is its concern with language. Modern philosophers are preoccupied with it. The new science of linguistics has sprung up. Some people have called language 'a useful tool', as if human life would be much the same without it. Joyce knew better. To him language is what defines the human world. Joyce was both professionally and by inclination a linguist. The 'ineluctable modality of the visible' eluded him; but his sense of hearing was as acute as his sight was weak. He was fascinated by the relationship between philosophy and psychology. To him, *how* a thing was said was everything. He refused to accept the usual identification of thought with conscious thought. To him, the human mind was as interesting in its ceaseless, half-articulate inner monologue as in its connected, articulate formulations. Indeed, it was more interesting. The long rumination of Molly Bloom which closes *Ulysses* is an attempt, on an unprecedented scale, to record the movements of a mind on the verge of sleep. *Finnegans Wake* seeks to carry the record into sleep itself.

So it is that Joyce became the greatest technical innovator in the history of fiction. But he was not detached and scientific. There was an emotional drive behind his choice of material which was quite other than the dispassionate curiosity of the investigator. One strong motive in Joyce's work was hatred. He hated his own past in semi-colonial, dirty Dublin, the bickerings of his family, the restrictive religion he had been taught at his Jesuit college, the narrow-minded and provincial patriotism of Ireland. He wanted to avenge himself on the Dublin that had rejected him. And his revenge, an endearing one, was to write a great book about Dublin. He wanted to put *everything* into it. But here his aims conflicted. The formal inventions that make *Ulysses* a handbook of fictional techniques are not compatible with extreme naturalism, which requires the obliteration of the author. In *Ulysses* we are always conscious of the author.

But Joyce's achievement in *Ulysses* was great. He re-created a day in the Dublin of 1904, choosing a date of personal significance to himself. His story, essentially, is of two lonely men who are brought together: the proud, intransigent, guilt-haunted Stephen of the *Portrait*, a self-made 'outsider'; and the Jew Leopold Bloom, whose race stamps him as an alien in the Irish city. *Ulysses* is notorious for the completeness of its portrayal of the modern city-dweller. The element of the indecent and disgusting may not be large, but it is overpowering, like a strong sauce which even in small quantities flavours the whole dish. Some of the incidents in the bizarre surrealist episode of Nighttown must shock any normal reader. The judge who permitted the export of *Ulysses* into the United States remarked that its effect is not aphrodisiac but emetic. Apparently it was all right if Joyce made Americans sick, so long as he did not stir their passions.

But much of *Ulysses* is genial and funny. Bloom is a comedy figure. He is pathetic and likeable: he is also quick-witted and intelligent, though his mind is untrained. His ideas are more interesting than those of Stephen, who, like his fellow-students in *Ulysses*, displays a curious blend of intellectuality and hobbledehoydom. Joyce's contemporary, the Scottish novelist George Douglas Brown, describes similar young men in *The House with the Green Shutters* (1901). But Brown means us to see his students as second-rate minds. It is not clear that Joyce does. At any rate, Bloom in the end overshadows Stephen and every other character in the book. And this certainly was Joyce's intention. After all, Odysseus, not Telemachus, is the hero of the *Odyssey*.

Ulysses, we know, is a parody of the *Odyssey*. But this can hardly be gathered from the book itself. As originally published, its three parts (Telemachia, Odyssey, and Nostos) and eighteen episodes, corresponding to the parts and episodes of Homer's poem, were not titled and numbered. To discover Joyce's intention we have to go to his letters and to the explanatory book by his friend Stuart Gilbert. The Homeric parody is interesting when pointed out, but it is ingenious rather than successful, and it may have led Joyce into some of the ingenuities and pedantries which bore and bewilder many of us.

In the first third or so of *Ulysses* the only important technical innovation is the interior monologue. Joyce was not the first writer to use this method, but he was the first to do so on such a scale. In the interior monologue the thought of the characters are recorded directly, with all the ellipses and wanderings of actual thinking, and without narrative links and explanations. Joyce is not solely concerned with rendering actual thinking. He buries symbolic clues and leitmotifs in his monologues. Nothing in them is accidental or arbitrary. But if the interior monologue had been the only new device in *Ulysses*, it would not have been thought an obscure book. Later on, however, Joyce uses many other technical innovations, which are less functional. Some are mere virtuosity, like the episode which is perplexingly narrated through a sustained parody of all main styles of English prose.

The first third of *Ulysses* is magnificent. But after that it looks as if Joyce had begun to run out of material. His essential material had always been very limited, consisting only of his memories of Dublin and his youth. His fatigue and the state of his health also have to be taken into account. His virtuosity remained. And of this he had more than any other author before or since. He was urged on to ever new heights of it by the well-to-do Anglo-American circle which patronized him. In parts of *Ulysses* we are on the way to the Joyce of *Finnegans Wake*, a Joyce who has lost all capacity for further experience or any thought but the purely linguistic.

Joyce's best work rests not on virtuosity but on something deeply humane: what his Bloom calls, in a touching moment, 'the opposite of hatred'. Beneath his air of arrogance Joyce was a warm-hearted, sentimental, affectionate man, who fought down this side of himself because of some early insult. We are nearer to the secret of his genius in a song like 'The Rose of Tralee' than in music like Schönberg's. A good example of Joyce's warmth of feeling is the episode in *Ulysses* which deals with 'Nausicaa' (Gerty MacDowell). Her monologue has been called a devastating exposure of the effect of cheap fantasy-fiction on a young girl's mind. It is that, but it is much more. It is a most tender and touching thing. We are disappointed when the focus switches back to Bloom and his underwear fetishism.

What is best in *Ulysses* is rooted in everyday situations. Joyce, unlike most modern writers, had a real feeling for family life. Although its appeal has always been mainly to *literati*, the greatness of *Ulysses* does not lie in what it has in common with a virtuoso writer like Vladimir Nabokov. Joyce, like Nabokov, is fond of playing sophisticated games with the reader. But this does not prevent him from giving a convincing picture of a middle-aged husband and wife, bound together by parenthood, and perhaps by something more. Molly may be promiscuous (if only in her imagination) but deep down she is a true Penelope. Joyce's genius in *Ulysses* is in his inimitable eye for the normal. Many readers must have been as astonished as Cyril Connolly or George Orwell at Joyce's seeming omniscience about the little secret oddities and perversities which we all have, but which we all think are quite peculiar to us. He shows us the extraordinariness of the ordinary.

The extraordinariness of *Finnegans Wake* is of a different kind. The 'night language' in which it is written, and which makes it look like gibberish at a casual glance, might be described as Lewis Carroll's 'Jabberwocky' writ large. Joyce invented a language based on Dublin English, but covered with layer upon layer of association, innuendo, and wordplay, drawn from many other languages. At the heart of the book is the family situation of a Dublin publican, a respectable man, like Bloom, who occasionally lapses. On the night of the *Wake* his dreams are troubled by one particular lapse in Dublin's Phoenix Park. 'Whatever it was they threed to make out he thried to two in the Fiendish park', it seems to have involved some mildly improper behaviour on the hero's part, provoked by a young girl, which was witnessed by some soldiers. But this little story can only be dimly discerned through the haze of Joyce's 'night language'. Through the vast linguistic extravaganze there swarm and pullulate symbolic creations of the dreamer's mind, parts or aspects of his personality, which take on sub-personalities of their own. Among these the geography of Dublin, and the River Liffey herself, come to life and further orchestrate the enormous monologue. To complicate matters still more, the dream-personality of 'Earwicker' is also 'Everybody', and the book records a cosmic myth of fall and renewal.

Finnegans Wake offers many pleasures. Some of the puns and *double ententes*, like 'wenchyoumaycuddler', are very funny. The famous 'hitheringandthithering waters of night' have a genuinely poetic quality. But most of the book is not poetry. The suggestiveness of Joyce's coinages is confined to their component elements. They have none of the endless evocativeness of real words like 'rose' or 'blood' or 'star'. And the work as a whole is the product of the will rather than the imagination. It allows no free imaginative response from the reader. He must either reject it altogether, or play Joyce's game by Joyce's rules. It should be added that a surprisingly large number of readers are prepared to do this.

There is some disturbing anecdotal evidence about Joyce's state of mind during the composition of *Finnegans Wake*. His reported demand, that the reader must spend a lifetime studying his work, may have been a joke. But it suggests a weakening hold on reality. What had gone wrong with Joyce may be suggested by a crucial incident in *Ulysses*, when Bloom rescues poor shattered Stephen after the Nighttown horror. Within himself Joyce seems not to have reconciled what

'Bloom' means with what 'Stephen' means. He erected even more barriers to keep out the common reader than Marcel Proust. But Joyce was not really an aristocratic, esoteric writer like Proust. What is saddening about his life and art is that something made him despise and reject people with whom, apart from his genius, he had everything in common.

In his *Study of Thomas Hardy*, D. H. LAWRENCE (1885–1930) speaks of 'the vast uncomprehending and incomprehensible morality of nature, or life itself, surpassing human consciousness'. What he calls the 'morality of life' was to be his subject. How would men and women behave, what would they be like, if they had 'got their lives straight'? He tried to imagine the 'naturalness' of a humanity which recognized its subservience to 'the creative mystery', but remained none the less distinctively human. Lawrence did not deny the part played in life by intellect and will. But he believed that in the modern world they had got out of hand. They had usurped the place of man's 'spontaneous self', for which they should have been mere instruments. Lawrence's desire was not only to write, but to live, as if his doctrine of spontaneity were true.

Lawrence did not win his fame as a philosopher, but as a creative writer, an artist. And like all artists he is better when he reveals than when he expounds. But ethical interest predominates in his work. While a writer like Joyce confines himself to saying 'This is life. Look at it', Lawrence is always saying 'Something is wrong here' or 'Something is right here'. The great temptation for Lawrence was to try to *prove* his points, to 'put his thumb in the balance'. His worst fault as an artist was didacticism. But this did not prevent him from making, as a critic, the finest diagnosis of didacticism that we have. And we must remember that the questions he dealt with were vital and urgent for him. He *needed* answers. It is understandable that sometimes Lawrence made himself believe he had found answers when he had not.

Lawrence was a remarkable and singular man. During his lifetime he made disciples and enemies. He charmed people; he also angered and upset them. Emotional mists surrounded his personality, which are only now beginning to disperse. His letters are among the most interesting in the language. They remind us that in all his work Lawrence has a clear idea of the kind of person he was speaking to. To the flippant or super-ficial, he sounds a grave note, recalling them to 'the symbol of man, alone in the cavern of himself'. But to the easily solemn he speaks like a mischievous urchin. A critic wrote: 'Mr. Lawrence has picked up a thread of life forgotten by mankind.' 'Darn your socks with it, Mr. Muir!' wrote Lawrence.

Lawrence attracts biographers; but his best work can be enjoyed by readers who know nothing of his life, and too much attention has been distracted from what Lawrence actually wrote by a curiosity about his personal problems. However, it must be granted that these underlay his work. His art, like his life, was troubled and restless. Lawrence was the son of a miner and a talented woman with middle-class aspirations. He began work as a shop assistant, then qualified for his teaching certificate at Nottingham, and taught for five years at Croydon. After his mother's death in 1910 Lawrence developed rapidly. His first novel, *The White Peacock*, was published in 1911. After a severe illness he gave up teaching and lived, though precariously, by writing. In 1912 he left England with Mrs. Frieda Weekley, *née* von Richthofen. After her divorce Lawrence was married to her in 1914. They lived for a time in Switzerland and Italy. During this period Lawrence wrote *Love Poems and Others* and his novel *Sons and Lovers* (1913). The Lawrences returned to England and remained there during the Great War. Although Lawrence's health released him from active service, he found the war a painful ordeal. He became the object of public suspicion and official near-persecution from 1916 to 1918, and the patriotic hysteria of the time made an indelible impression on him. During the war his novel *The Rainbow* (1915) was seized by the police and destroyed with the publishers' acquiescence. Its successor, *Women in Love,* was written in 1916, but not published till 1920. After the war, convinced that England was exhausted, Lawrence went to live abroad, mainly in Mediterranean countries. *Aaron's Rod* (1922) is largely set in Italy. He returned to England in 1923, but was soon to resume his wanderings, first in Australia, then in New Mexico, which inspired some of his best prose and poetry. His volume of poems *Birds, Beasts, and Flowers* belongs to that period. Later novels were *Kangaroo* (1923), *The Plumed Serpent* (1926), and *Lady Chatterley's Lover* (unexpurgated edition 1929; expurgated edition 1932), which was forbidden by the Customs to enter Britain. Lawrence was in poor health in his later years, but despite this he managed to produce, besides these novels, many poems, stories, and essays. He died of consumption at Vence, in the south of France, in 1930.

Lawrence, unlike most English writers of this century, was born in the working class. He did not idealize it in retrospect, but all his life he felt uprooted from it. In an autobiographical sketch he speaks of his regret at losing its warmth and directness and human solidarity. His genius gave him an understanding of middle-class culture, but he always felt apart from it. He was to become a famous author without ever acclimatizing himself as a 'man of letters'. He had many literary friends, though he frequently quarrelled with them; but essentially he stood alone, an isolated expatriate.

In his writing Lawrence was impatient with traditional literary standards. The prosaic labours of novelists to 'get things right', the cold-blooded planning and carpentry of successful novels, only bored him. His indifference to literary traditions and conventions was not due to ignorance, for he was a clever, well-informed man, well-read in the literature of several languages. It was due to his conviction of the importance of spontaneity. His artistic ideal had nothing in common with that of Gautier's poem '*L'Art*'. Marble immortality was a vain dream. A work of art was, rather, a flower that is born and gives out its sweetness and dies. He accepted transience as the condition of life.

Lawrence was born in a beautiful part of England that had been made hideous by nineteenth-century industrialism. All his life he hated industrialism and machinery. And, as an inevitable consequence, he hated democracy. He thought it levelling and impersonal, a false egalitarianism inspired by envy. His bitterness was intensified during the war period, when he was assailed by demagogues like Horatio Bottomley. He regretted the passing of an old, ordered, rural England which was, in about equal parts, the product of his imagination and his memory.

Sometimes in his depression with modern civilization Lawrence turned away to the life of wild nature. But this gave him no enduring relief. Like all great writers, Lawrence was essentially concerned with human life. He asked if it was possible for the life of men to share in the wildness and spontaneous beauty of nature, the power and wonder of the cosmos. Sometimes he thought he saw a positive answer in the cultures of primitive peoples. But in his more sober moments he knew that primitivism was an illusion. Sometimes he imagined that ancient peoples, like the Etruscans, had solved the problem of life. But Lawrence knew that, even if his imagination spoke truly, it is not possible for modern men to go *back* to anything. Lawrence has been derided for his primitivism and archaism, as Tolstoy has been mocked for his cult of the mujik. But those for whom Lawrence's and Tolstoy's problems are problems will not want to laugh for very long.

Everyone who has heard of Lawrence knows of his concern with sex. He was to be abused as indecent, or a pornographer, by some, and hailed as a liberator by others. Lawrence's preoccupation with sex had a personal origin. In *Sons and Lovers* he describes a family of boys so dominated by their mother's affection that when they grow up they cannot form satisfactory relationships with women. Lawrence himself had suffered that fate. 'Nobody can have the soul of me,' he wrote. 'My mother has had it, and nobody can have it again.' It is disputed whether Lawrence's analysis of sexual problems owed anything to the ideas of

Freud, which were beginning to be widely known. At any rate, when Lawrence came to study Freud's ideas he disagreed with them radically. Freud held that the price we pay for civilization is the repression of unconscious desires. Lawrence thought that civilization was not worth having at that price. He questioned Freud's pessimistic assumptions about what might happen if men let go of their spontaneous selves. Perhaps it was the repression that was evil, rather than the things repressed. Lawrence opposed all restraints on the sexual life—religious, moral, or merely social—in so far as they were based on fear. In this respect he was on the side of the emancipators. But in other respects he disliked them. He disapproved of promiscuity and casual affairs. He believed that the proper norm of human sexual relationship was the marriage for life. Sexual desire was not just 'normal' but a uniquely precious thing. Lawrence opposed both the romantic idealization of sex and its opposite pole of sniggering lewdness. These poles were connected by an axis: the mistaken dualism of body and soul. For the unitary individuals Lawrence dreamed of, sexual desire would be neither repressed nor sublimated, because it would no longer be a base passion.

Lawrence thought that the satisfaction of sexual desire entailed profound responsibilities. But he was little concerned with the obvious, practical responsibility that it brings: the birth of children. Perhaps this was because he had none. Towards the end of his life he came to see in traditional Christian teaching on the family a wisdom deeper than Bernard Shaw's flippancies. But in his own work the importance of marriage was not primarily to do with bringing up a family. It was the quality of the relationship between husband and wife that concerned him.

This was because of Lawrence's own experience. A crucial moment in his life came when he fell in love with Frieda Weekley. Deep undercurrents brought them together, but on the surface there was much to drive them apart. She was another man's wife, and he took her away from her children. He was the son of an English miner, she was the daughter of a German baron. The wandering life and the childlessness of the Lawrences meant that his experience of marriage was partial and untypical. The married relationship was for him especially difficult. In all Lawrence's writing about love there is tension. Attraction and repulsion go closely together. The relationship between a man and a woman is one long battle. No one can deny the validity of Lawrence's insights; but they are partial. Lawrence seems to have been so disgusted with the cant he heard in his youth about Christian love and self-abnegation, that he concluded they were fraudulent. His picture of marriage, as of life in general, does not allow for genuine altruism.

But no one writer's work contains the sum of human wisdom. Every artist makes his own selection from experience, and Lawrence was no exception. What interested him was the quality of feeling in human life. He rejected the literary tradition which assigns to each person a fixed and definite character. 'The old, stable ego' was an illusion. Much of the rich emotional life which sophisticated people claim to have was, he thought, equally illusory. True feeling cannot be worked up by the mind, in response to some antecedent idea about what one should be feeling. True feeling exists only in the bodily centres. Lawrence tried to render in words the pulsation and relaxation, the ebb and flow, of real emotions. For him, real emotion was intimately bound up with sensation. The sense of touch, physical contact, can bring people together who may be consciously indifferent or even antipathetic to each other. For Lawrence, the mere fact of being alive in the body was a constant source of wonder. He longed to convey that wonder through his art. He sought to break through the deadening habituation of our mental re-actions to the world around us and within us. Above all, Lawrence wanted to destroy the tyranny of the social self that for modern civil-ized people had come to seem the only self there was. It was the 'ulti-mate naked self', discerned by them only at moments of anguish or confusion, that he wanted people to recognize as *themselves*. His main subject as an artist was sincerity.

Lawrence's first novel, *The White Peacock*, is very immature. He writes about cultivated middle-class people with whom he was then not familiar enough. With youthful eagerness he shows off the range of his reading. This book should be supplemented by the memoir of the young Lawrence by 'E.T.', the Miriam of *Sons and Lovers*. We see there how avidly Lawrence read and taught himself. *The White Peacock* already contains themes that recur in Lawrence's later work. One is the charac-ter of Annable, the misogynistic gamekeeper, a curious anticipation of Mellors in *Lady Chatterley's Lover*. Another is the emotional depend-ence of the hero Cyril on George Saxton, the virile, handsome young farmer who fades out in drunkenness and death. Lawrence's next novel, *The Trespasser* (1912), is a study of a passionate love-affair, written with almost unbearable intensity. Much of Lawrence's work is hard to read because of this intensity.

Lawrence found himself as a novelist in *Sons and Lovers*. This novel shows a great improvement in objectivity compared with his earlier work. Yet it is profoundly autobiographical, a book that he had to write. Paul Morel, like Joyce's Stephen Dedalus, is the artist in his family. In his divided home he sides with his mother against his father, and Lawrence seems to side with her too. Yet in many ways Morel, the father, is deeply pathetic. His love for his children, for the son who rejects him, is poignantly conveyed. If we want to understand Lawrence's work we should study the description in *Sons and Lovers* of how it came about that Mrs. Morel first loved Morel. Again and again in Lawrence's stories, men with Morel's quality, vital and sensuous, yet soft and gentle, with something beyond consciousness given out by their whole being, are contrasted with superficial, empty, cerebral people who personify middle-class values. It is as if Lawrence were making amends to his father for the wrong he had done him in life and in *Sons and Lovers*.

Lawrence's early work won him many admirers. But it did not break radically with the traditions of naturalistic fiction. *The Rainbow* was a new departure. Like all real innovations, its originality either went unremarked, or was found incomprehensible or repulsive by critics of the day. It was found morally shocking. The authorities prosecuted it. *The Rainbow*, unlike *Lady Chatterley's Lover* or *Ulysses*, does not affront decency, but it does claim the artist's right to present the reality of human emotions. The incidents that provoked its suppression are those describing the feelings of a pregnant wife, and the infatuation of a young girl with a woman teacher. Today an author's right to deal frankly with such subjects is recognized. But at that time the sensitive delicacy of Lawrence's handling of them passed unnoticed. The subjects were regarded as improper in themselves. *The Rainbow* can never have afforded any satisfaction to seekers for the pornographic thrill. Its prevailing tone is grave, exalted, spiritual. It is a profound study of human emotions, carried out by a genius of exceptional insight.

The Rainbow tells the story of three generations of an English family, concentrating, in each, on the cultural and moral and religious problems of young people. At the same time it conveys a sense of the changes in civilization, as traditional England turned into the England of Lawrence's time. The unifying theme is marriage: *The Rainbow* is the greatest English novel about marriage. Within his broad picture of English life, the farm, the suburban house, the ancient culture of the land, the rhythm of the seasons, Lawrence evokes the rhythm of human passions; the strain of married life which uncovers the naked selfhood of the human being; its humiliations and its triumphs, its ecstasy and its frustration. Critics complained of the burning away of the outlines of the characters, so that one is indistinguishable from another. We certainly have the sense that we are reading of the same persons in different historical metamorphoses. But conventional ideas about character did not interest Lawrence. His aim was to illuminate men and women from within, to show them as creatures of nature like the earth and sky, to depict the conscious mind and the social personality as only the expression, or the frustration, of deeper human needs.

The Rainbow is not completely successful. Some episodes are too obscurely narrated. Fine descriptions are blurred by the writer's emotionalism. And the attempt to bring the whole work to a triumphant symphonic conclusion proved to be beyond Lawrence's powers. But it is none the less one of the great English books. Its style alone puts it in a different category from other novels. It is written in a soaring, yet flexible prose making creative use, at high moments, of the language and imagery of the English Bible. The Lawrence of *The Rainbow* is profoundly traditional as well as profoundly modern.

The Rainbow, though it draws on the author's inner experiences, is not autobiographical. Lawrence told his own story in the verse collected in *Love Poems and Others* (1913) and *Look! We Have Come Through!* (1917). He lays bare—too much so for some readers—the quarrels and intimacies of a difficult marriage. Lawrence's poetry is at its best when it isolates passing moods. 'Life, the ever present,' he said, 'shows no finality, no finished crystallization.' Hence he turned from conventional rhymed verse to free verse. His most original contribution to the art of poetry is the later volume entitled *Birds, Beasts, and Flowers* (1923). He invents a new kind of poem in which he records with matchless vividness his glimpses of animal nature, his sense of momentary *rapport* with the unimaginable unreflective consciousness of non-human life. Lawrence's poetry has been much criticized for its looseness and formlessness. Today it has found new admirers, when interest has revived in the use of poetry for the direct record of experience, rather than for its appraisal and judgement. Lawrence's best poems, such as 'Piano' or 'Ballad of another Ophelia', are more than sketches or improvisations. But much of his poetry, like that in *Pansies* (1929) or *Nettles* (1930), is an occasion for relieving his feelings rather than creating self-sufficient art. For that, we must look more to his novels and stories.

In the shorter forms of prose fiction Lawrence is in some ways more satisfying than in his novels. He is freer from prolixity and repetitiousness. His genius for the glimpse, the intuition of a scene or a situation, was not hampered by the improbabilities that arose when he had to work out his stories at greater length. Lawrence's tales are very varied. In a story like 'The Fox', starting from ordinary, rather inarticulate people, he probes deeply into torturing human desires and needs, the health and sickness of the soul. But he can write equally well of sophisticated people in 'The Captain's Doll'. This comedy of love is at the same time an evocation of the 'darkness' of the human mystery, almost hidden under the surface by-play of social relationships. Lawrence's comedy is always various. The humorous realism of 'Tickets, Please' has little in common with the satire of 'Smile', yet both obviously come from the same writer. In stories like 'The Ladybird' or 'The Woman who Rode Away' or 'The Man who Loved Islands' Lawrence re-creates the fascination of folk-tales and legends, while translating them into stories of modern people. If he is to be represented by one story, it should be 'The Virgin and the Gipsy'.

Lawrence's most ambitious and complex novel is *Women in Love* (1920). This book is pervaded by the malaise that had come over him during the gloomy war years. He believed that a new dark age was coming. Humanity, if it survived the terrible destructiveness that Lawrence foresaw, would have to begin all over again. Lawrence may have been influenced by Edward Carpenter (1844–1929), author of *Civilization: its Cause and Cure* (1889). At any rate, his life-experience and his reading had brought him to convictions which might be described as the opposite of Wells's. Evolution, he thought, was a false idea. There are no new human faculties to develop. The creative mystery of life contains all our powers from the beginning. If these powers are declining now—and Lawrence thought they were—this is because of the blight of civilization. Our urgent need is to exercise our acquired intelligence so as to achieve a full realization of the human spirit in purer and truer relationships. Such were Lawrence's preoccupations when he wrote *Women in Love*. Its central theme is the contrast between a couple who cannot escape their 'mental consciousness' and fail to unite, and a couple who complete each other in 'mystic sensuality' and realize their 'otherness' through physical love. A subsidiary theme is the relationship between the two men of this quartet. The theme of a male relationship, to supplement the deficiencies of the married relationship, is to recur in Lawrence's later work.

Women in Love was planned during one of the most distraught periods of Lawrence's life, when he was living in Cornwall in 1916, harried by local suspicions of the bearded man with the banned book and the German wife, and conducting a seethingly complicated relationship with his neighbours, Middleton Murry and his wife Katherine Mansfield. No doubt as a result of all this, much in the novel is obscure and over-heated. The author seems to mistake a rendering of his personal malaise for a diagnosis of modern civilization. No one who likes Lawrence should ignore *Women in Love*; but only his most fervent admirers can find pleasure in all of it. The novel is carefully written and shows much variety; a whole essay could be written even on minor characters such as the artist Loerke, who appears late in the story. But we vainly seek in *Women in Love* for any release from the inferno of inner violence. Our varying attitudes towards its people, at different moments, are skilfully controlled; but the general nervous tension remains too high. And *Women in Love* ranks with the short novel *St. Mawr* (1925) as among those works of Lawrence which are the most impressive, but most marred by personal bitterness and misanthropy.

Whatever our judgement of *Women in Love*, there is no doubt that Lawrence worked hard to make it a work of art. The same cannot be said of the novels that followed it, *Aaron's Rod* and *Kangaroo*. *Aaron's Rod* begins with a vivid picture of the working-class life Lawrence knew so well, but it turns into a sort of travel-diary, and the treatment of the hero's adventures suggests that Lawrence had lost his hold on reality. Aaron Sisson playing the flute in his back parlour is convincing, but Aaron as the impossible lover of an impossible Marchesa is not. What is much worse, the style of this novel is flat and prosaic. We can hardly believe that some of it came from the author of *The Rainbow*. Another disquieting feature is the introduction of Lawrence and his wife as characters, disguised only by a pseudonym, with the Lawrence-figure preaching the need for all women, and all lesser men, to submit to a hero's 'healthy individual authority'. Lawrence and Frieda re-appear in *Kangaroo*. In this novel there is some vivid reporting of Australia and Australians. But there is a great deal of padding. A whole chapter is made up of newspaper-cuttings. The best thing in *Kangaroo* is the chapter called 'The Nightmare'. We remember it when we have forgotten the contrived and rather absurd tale of Australian fascism which constitutes the main story. 'The Nightmare' has really nothing to do with that story: it is a harrowing account of Lawrence's experiences in war-time England. In its didactic theme, *Kangaroo* continues one theme of *Aaron's Rod*: the leader/disciple relationship. Lawrence is now attracted by masculine comradeship, rather than the family, as the paradigm of the good life.

These novels may be more responsible than any others for the general impression that Lawrence had ceased to be a novelist; that he had become nothing but a little man with a red beard, haranguing his acolytes. Yet it is clear from *The Lost Girl* (1920) that, if Lawrence chose not to become a competent traditional novelist, it was not from want of ability. *The Lost Girl* has some resemblance to *The Good Companions*, with which J. B. Priestley was to win his first popular success in 1929. But in Lawrence's later novels the ideologist is promi-nent. They show, however, some recovery of his creative powers: they contain some invention. In *The Plumed Serpent* (1926) the artist in Lawrence gave us the memorable picture of Mexico as he saw it, the blazing colours of nature in the background, and, against it, the people of Mexico, sullen, bitter, apathetic, sunk in dirt and backwardness. But here, for the ideologist in Lawrence, lay an opportunity. He imagined this beautiful and miserable land as the locale for a religious revival. The religion is not Christianity. In *The Plumed Serpent* the Catholic Church in Mexico is said to have lost its appeal to the masses. In its place Lawrence imagines a religious-political movement, based on the cult of the bird-serpent Quetzalcoatl. It is a cruel and heartless religion. Its leaders put men to death without pity. They paint themselves like savages. There is something masochistic in Lawrence's identification of himself with his central character, a woman, who is made to overcome her revulsion from this barbarism and identify herself with the cause and its leaders. We feel that he shares her every shudder and repugnance. *The Plumed Serpent* is an astonishing feat of imagination. It is also a painful and pathetic book, born out of its author's personal and social despair.

In his last novel, *Lady Chatterley's Lover* (1928), the political preoccupation has gone, and so has the exoticism. Lawrence turns back to the England of his own time, England in process of modernization, which in Lawrence's eyes was rootless, vulgar, and spiritually arid. He seeks desperately to convince his readers and himself that the only panacea is the recovery of naturalness in the sexual relationship between men and women. If his prophecy, his *kerygma*, is that the world can be saved by love, love for him means neither romantic sentiment nor the *agape* of St. Paul. It means the behaviour whereby the gamekeeper Mellors, who figures in the fable as the antithesis of the chilly aristocrat Sir Clifford, converts Connie Chatterley to the acceptance of her own animality. Traditional values are inverted. What the orthodox stigmatize as lust, as shamelessness, as unnatural sexual practices, become cardinal virtues. Essential to this undertaking is the notorious use of the four-letter words. The shocking effect is deliberate. This deliberateness is unattractive: and it suggests a certain falsity. The class in which Lawrence was brought up was unprudish but decent. Lawrence seems to have forgotten that when he drew Mellors. His motives were in part noble. He hoped to cleanse the sexual relationship of guilt and fear. But we suspect other motives. *Lady Chatterley's Lover* is one of those books, like *Jude the Obscure* or *The Way of all Flesh*, which seem to be written out of resentment. They are powerful, but the atmosphere is constricting. The reader feels he is being got at.

About the justification for the book there will be different opinions. Some will see in the belated vindication of *Lady Chatterley* and *Ulysses* nothing but a triumph for the artist's right to represent life as he sees it. Others will regret that, after the battles over Joyce and Lawrence, it has become impossible to appeal to traditional standards of taste and decency without ranging oneself with the 'censor-morons'. Lawrence's own pamphlet, *A Propos of Lady Chatterley's Lover* (1930), suggests that he himself had misgivings. It is hard to believe that he would have approved of the progressivists' use of *Lady Chatterley* as a *casus belli*. There are signs in his last writings that he was going through a new phase in his reconsideration of Christianity. His poem 'The Ship of

Death' suggests that he was reconsidering even the most fundamental of his beliefs, the finality of death. Certainly Lawrence never doubted that modern man had immeasurably lost by the decline of Christian belief.

Lawrence's admirers have seen him very differently. For F. R. Leavis, he is rooted in the traditions of English nonconformity and provincial life. He is the successor of Hardy and George Eliot. This is the Lawrence of *The Rainbow*. For W. H. Auden of *The Orators*, he is a sinister but fascinating prophet of irrationalism, a heroic vitalist and misogynist like Nietzsche. This is the Lawrence of *The Plumed Serpent* and the pamphlet *Fantasia of the Unconscious* (1922). For a writer like Lawrence Durrell, he is a gay, cosmopolitan figure, flouting the stodgy respectability of English ways, light-hearted rather than fanatical in his questioning of social and sexual *mores*. This is the Lawrence who, in Norman Douglas's words, 'opened a little window for the bourgeoisie'. Some support can be found for all these images of Lawrence, and for others. It is difficult to be coolly judicious about him. He will not allow us 'that rather cheap seat in the gods where we sit with fellows like Anatole France and benignly look down on the foibles, follies and frenzies of mankind'. 'Whoever reads me,' says Lawrence, 'will be in the thick of the scrimmage.' But some readers do not want to be. What they dislike most in Lawrence is his scorn for amenity. He himself felt passionately that the educated middle class set too much store by it. His characters are fond of 'jeering' at each other. They can be very unlovely. There is a want of balance and perspective in Lawrence's work, a narrowness of sympathy and an eccentricity. His exaltation of the 'instinctive heart' over the 'abstract intellect' can run to disturbing and sometimes sinister extremes. But when we find him sounding like Hitler, we should remember Lawrence's saying that 'one sheds one's sicknesses in books'. Hitler shed his on the world.

Lawrence's best work comes from the artist in him, and even as an artist his success may have been only partial. He thought that 'vivid individual men' matter more than works of art, and this may apply to Lawrence himself. But he was a great writer. His prophetic-lyrical power is wonderful. His gift for description, when not blurred by emotionalism, is unsurpassed. As a novelist, he is a great figure in the history of the genre. He did not invent technical devices as Joyce did, but he enlarged the essential scope of the novel far more than Joyce. In a famous passage in *Lady Chatterley's Lover* he says: 'It is the way our sympathy flows and recoils that really determines our lives.' If Lawrence's originality in fiction could be summed up in one sentence, this might be the one to choose.

5

Liberal Humanists: the 'Bloomsbury' Group

Forster—Strachey—Virginia Woolf—Keynes, Moore, and Russell—Aldous Huxley—other writers

THE REVOLT AGAINST the Victorian age can be seen as a conflict of generations. One of the books that helps us to understand it was published in 1903, though it had been written some years earlier. This is *The Way of All Flesh*. SAMUEL BUTLER (1835–1902) published many books during his lifetime, but they were little noticed. He was that unluckiest of men, a controversial writer who could not find opponents. But his ideas were to be taken up by later writers like Shaw and Forster and Maugham: and he must be counted an honorary citizen of the twentieth century. *The Way of All Flesh*, published after his death, is his most influential book. It is the story of the mishandling of a son's upbringing by his pious conventional parents. Although Butler does not identify himself with his hero, Ernest Pontifex, preferring to take an onlooker's part in the character of Overton, there can be no doubt that his hatred of his own clergyman father provided the driving-force of his satire. The irony of *The Way of All Flesh* is sometimes cheap. Some of the characters do not come to life. And worst of all, we are not made to care enough about what happens to Ernest, one way or the other. But it is a very enjoyable book. Few things are funnier than the account of giving up smoking for the Lord's sake. The painful comedy of Theobald's parenthood is unforgettable. The coolness of Butler's style is refreshing, after a surfeit of Victorian fervour. And those who resent his attacks on Christianity should remember the form in which he met it. *The Way of All Flesh* has its special place in twentieth-century literature because of its theme of conflict with the father. Other interesting comparisons are Edmund Gosse's *Father and Son* (1907), Lytton Strachey's portrait of Dr. Arnold in *Eminent Victorians*, and Sarah Campion's *Father* (1948), a memoir of the famous Cambridge medievalist G. G. Coulton. The theme was to receive its finest artistic treatment in Virginia Woolf's *To the Lighthouse*. But it is pervasive in writers like Aldous Huxley and Forster.

The reputation of E. M. FORSTER (1879–1970) is very high today. In his lifetime he attracted more personal affection and respect than any English author since Dickens. Many who knew him only through his writings counted him as a friend and a moral influence. If words like 'liberal' and 'civilized' and 'tolerant' can still be used unironically, it is largely because of the work of this quiet, unpretentious, witty writer.

Forster was educated at Tonbridge School and King's College, Cambridge. He was unhappy at his school and gloriously happy at his university. Cambridge dons like Wedd and McTaggart and Lowes Dickinson were formative influences on him. He applied the lessons he had learned at Cambridge in the four novels he published before the Great War, among which *Howards End* (1910) is the most considerable. Of the others, *Where Angels Fear to Tread* (1905) and *A Room with a View* (1908) are comedies of manners, contrasting English conventionality with the colourfulness and vitality of Italian life; while *The Longest Journey* (1907) comes the nearest of all his writings to the autobiographical. Before the Great War Forster travelled extensively. He visited India with Lowes Dickinson. He drafted two novels, but laid them aside. He spent the war on duty in Alexandria. After the war he revisited India and completed and published *A Passage to India* (1924). He published no more novels after 1924, but a great deal of biography and criticism.

The world of Forster's Edwardian novels now seems more remote than Jane Austen's. In them the conflict between individuality and convention, on which they turn, takes a very dated form. Forster himself felt that after the Great War he had lost his subject-matter as a novelist. Yet his early novels still have many readers. This is partly because of his light touch, and the coolness—attractive to modern taste—with which he handles violent and sensational material: emotional disaster, personal catastrophe, sudden death. His casualness looks at first like mere affectation. But it represents something deeply characteristic of Forster's sense of the world: his perception of the element of chance and arbitrariness in life.

Forster's theme as a novelist is the relation between nature and culture. Nature is deeper than culture: it is the spontaneous self, the centre of our profoundest sincerity, which preoccupied D. H. Lawrence. Forster might be described as a Lawrence with less vital force, more wistful, more tentative, more urbane. The similarity of their attitudes towards modern civilization may be seen in Forster's anti-Wellsian fantasy 'The Machine Stops'. But though he recognized the ascendancy of nature over culture, Forster also believed in culture. What he meant by culture was much the same as what Matthew Arnold meant by it. Forster, like Arnold, strove to correct the provinciality and narrowness of the educated class to which he belonged. He was a liberal humanist, but one tempered by a keen critical sense of the shakiness of the humanist position. His novels often describe the chastening of idealistic humanists who come up against not only confusion and stupidity, but deep irrational forces which their humanism cannot cope with. Of such are Philip Herriton of *Where Angels Fear to Tread*, Rickie of *The Longest Journey*, Margaret Schlegel of *Howards End*, Adela Quested of *A Passage to India*.

Forster has retained his popularity because he avoided the pretentious or agitated manner of Victorian fiction. He owed much to Meredith: but unlike Meredith he did not come forward with the air of a master who had solved the problems of life. Yet he is firmly in the English tradition of novelists who teach lessons. He makes no pretence of impersonal aloofness from his characters. His voice is openly heard in his story; but it is a quiet voice. He does not browbeat the reader; he is never pompous. His manner is diffident, his style witty and graceful. He always retains something of the qualities of an essayist.

It is all the more remarkable that the stories Forster tells are so melodramatic. Violent events, sensational confrontations, incredible turns of plot, abound in his work. It has a strain of melodrama. This melodrama reflects a certain rigidity in Forster's moral outlook. For all his tolerance, Forster fundamentally divides his characters into the saved and the damned. He rarely conveys a sense of the *unpredictability* of human nature. Thus he rates low in his scheme of values the kind of human qualities that Kipling admired. But he seems not to allow for the possibility that human beings who have those qualities might have other qualities which would attract him. A Forster novel is a day of judgement: sheep are separated from goats.

In the lay sermons which Forster preached he had in mind a certain type of chilly Englishman, intellectually narrow and emotionally unformed and immature. He thought that this type was produced by upper-class education. Forster, like Jane Austen, who was one of his first models in novel-writing, is preoccupied with education. But he is not so much concerned with education in the family as she is. It was at the public schools to which the English upper class send their children that the future administrators and civil servants acquired their poise and assurance. But this aplomb was the cover for deep insecurities. And when such people went out to govern an empire, their failures in tact and understanding were all the more calamitous.

But Forster was primarily concerned with personal relationships, not as a means to social order, but as ends in themselves. This was the heart of his message. Forster is more concerned with the relationship between one man and another than between a man and a woman. Even a happy marriage, in his novels, is not an example of the 'connection' which for him is the finest human achievement. And when a marriage is unhappy, it is the 'longest journey' Shelley denounced in *Epipsychidion*.

Forster's philosophy, like Lawrence's, was influenced by that of Edward Carpenter. He wrote of Carpenter that 'he will always be known to students of the late nineteenth and early twentieth centuries for his pioneer work; for his courage and candour about sex, particularly about homosexuality; for his hatred of snobbery while snobbery was still fashionable; for his support of Labour before Labour wore dress-clothes; and for his cult of simplicity'. These words tell us much about Forster himself. Like Carpenter he was a democrat, sympathetic to socialism. But he hated collectivism. Lionel Trilling has accused Forster of 'casual anarchism', '*laissez-faire* to the ultimate'. At any rate, he was an individualist who liked people to be themselves. He preferred prigs to snobs, and cranks to conformists.

If Forster is a great novelist, the claim must be based on his last novel, *A Passage to India*. Critics have disputed whether Forster gives a fair picture of India under English rule. But this question is really incidental to Forster's theme. If we compare *A Passage to India* with two later novels, Orwell's *Burmese Days* and Koestler's *Thieves in the Night*, we see how much more they are concerned with topical problems. They are propaganda novels: it is not. Characteristically, Forster states his theme early in the book in a simple way: can an Indian be friends with an Englishman? But his treatment of this theme summons up the whole of Forster's increasingly sombre vision of human nature and destiny. His essential concern, like Lawrence's, is neither political nor social, but religious. But, unlike Lawrence, Forster cannot imagine religious experience from within. Three great religions are passed under review in *A Passage to India*, and none seems to Forster to have the answer to our needs. Christianity is parochial, Islam ethnocentric, Hinduism incomprehensible. Yet strangely enough it is Hinduism, which to the rational humanist seems the most quaint or senseless, that Forster finds the most profound. The naïve reader, attracted by the only sensational incident in this novel, wants to know what happened to Miss Quested in the cave. Was she assaulted by an Indian? If so, which Indian? Or was she hysterical? Did she imagine it? Forster leaves the matter unclear. He imagines a point of view, projected through the traumatic experience of the elderly Mrs. Moore, from which such questions do not make sense, or do not matter. The human voice which asks them comes back in a meaningless boom from the Marabar Caves.

It is as if we could hear the Great War in the hollow reverberation. Although the setting of *A Passage to India* is pre-war, it is radically post-war in feeling. Forster's greatest novel is the one that, more than any of his others, confesses the inadequacy of liberal humanism. Some have thought that the weakness lay not so much in humanism as in Forster's statement of it. During the 1930s he was much criticized for his lack of what is now called 'commitment', his inability to identify himself whole-heartedly with extreme radical or communist positions. Forster himself acknowledged the validity of some of this criticism.

Yet it may be in his very half-heartedness that Forster's value lies. His service has been to remind us of a world outside politics, and of the ends which politics is supposed to serve. In *A Passage to India* one of the characters, looking at the monkeys, is struck by the thought that most of the inhabitants of India do not care how India is governed. At a time of bustle and slogans, Forster's sane perspective brings light and refreshment. His picture of 'Love, the beloved Republic' is admittedly coloured by his temperament, his upbringing, the peculiarities of the declining liberal culture to which he belonged. There will not be another Forster. But this is all the more reason to treasure the one that we have had.

LYTTON STRACHEY (1880–1932) was to personify for the post-war generation the revolt against the Victorian age. He was a product of Cambridge, like Forster; and like Forster he valued aesthetic emotions and personal relationships as the true ends of existence. He was at the very heart of the colony of Cambridge culture known as Bloomsbury. No writer seemed less likely to be popular. But Strachey hit upon the idea of looking with an eye of mockery at some great figures of the nine-teenth century. He showed them shorn of their plumes, but intensely alive. His Florence Nightingale and General Gordon and Cardinal Manning are not the plaster saints of Victorian hagiography: they are real people. Of course, they are to some extent caricatures. Strachey's purpose was entertainment as well as history. And he liked to affect an air of superiority to his Victorian victims. Here time has had its re-venge: in Michael Holroyd's biography of him it is Strachey rather than the Victorians who seems ridiculous. But *Eminent Victorians* (1918) has had a good as well as a bad influence Its good influence is seen, not in the shoal of its imitators, but in those modern biographies which seek for historical truth through imaginative portraiture. In *Queen Victoria* (1921) Strachey attempted to continue his new biographical method with a study of the Queen herself. But something seems to have hap-pened to his purpose while he was writing. He sets out in the spirit of satire, but ends very differently. The famous last paragraph is remote from satire. However unfair or one-sided, Strachey shows historical insight in his writings on the Victorians. This deserted him when he dealt with the Elizabethan age in *Elizabeth and Essex* (1928). Much of it is pure Hollywood.

Some of Strachey's best writing is to be found in his essays in *Books and Characters* (1922) and *Portraits in Miniature* (1931). The last title is suggestive. Strachey was a miniaturist. He was a smaller, more feline Macaulay, who entertained and instructed his readers. His satire was directed at the old order—the public schools, party government, the Church of England, bureaucracy, imperialism. But he is neither a constructive reformer nor a revolutionary. His tone is one of scepticism and mockery. His ideals lay in the aristocratic French eighteenth century, as he imagined it. One of his heroes was Voltaire.

Strachey is not a second Voltaire. But he is a readable and pleasing writer. He aimed at a transparent prose, the equivalent in English of good French prose. Sometimes the effect is commonplace: Strachey is too fond of hackneyed phrases. And there is sometimes a certain poverty in the fine writing with which he evokes a mood, or a period, or the nuances of a character. How trite and sentimental he is on Newman's *Apologia*. But he could be an excellent literary critic. He was one of the few Englishmen to write well on Racine. His essay on Shakespeare's final period is an admirable corrective to over-sentimental interpretations. In all his writing Strachey ministers to the reader's pleasure. Nothing is dull or wooden. He can tell a story well, describe a scene vividly, sketch a character as firmly as an eighteenth-century master. His worst fault is that he encourages his readers to feel superior to some famous man because they live later. Strachey's finest quality is his hatred of cruelty and intolerance. When he is possessed by it, he forgets pose and pastiche and recovers the true spirit of the Enlightenment.

The biographer and critic Hugh Kingsmill Lunn (1889–1949), who wrote under the name of HUGH KINGSMILL, owed something to Strachey. But at his best he was a better writer. Kingsmill was not backed by Bloomsbury, won no great fame in his lifetime, and has been undeservedly neglected since his death. His lives of Dickens, Matthew Arnold, and D. H. Lawrence share Strachey's debunking tendency, but Kingsmill's diagnosis of what was wrong with these writers goes very deep. His life of Dr. Johnson, whom he loved, provides a positive counterpart to these deflating studies. Kingsmill has explained his own aims in *The Progress of a Biographer* (1949). He is an interesting writer who will repay critical attention.

It is not yet clear whether VIRGINIA WOOLF (1882–1941) will be classed among that select company of writers who outlive their time. At present there is a note of uncertainty in most critiques of her work. Yet she seems to have been a genius in some sense in which Lytton Strachey was not, and in which even E. M. Forster was not. She belongs to the company of Henry James and Conrad, of Joyce and Lawrence. But the range and scale of her work is so much smaller that comparison is difficult.

Mrs. Woolf was the daughter of Sir Leslie Stephen, the distinguished critic. She was brought up partly in London and partly in Cornwall. She married Leonard Woolf in 1912 and collaborated with him in the Hogarth Press, which pioneered the publication of experimental and controversial writers. Her early novels, *The Voyage Out* (1915) and *Night and Day* (1919), were followed by *Jacob's Room* (1922). Later novels included *Mrs. Dalloway* (1925), *To the Lighthouse* (1927), *The Waves* (1931), *The Years* (1937), and *Between the Acts*, which was published posthumously in 1941. Mrs. Woolf wrote a great deal of criticism. The critical essays which represent her best may be found in the two volumes entitled *The Common Reader* (1925, 1932).

Virginia Woolf was a born writer. E. M. Forster said of her that 'she liked writing with an intensity that few writers have attained, or even desired'. She derived many of her ideas from her circle. And in this circle personal relationships, it seems, tended to lack depth and stability. This may partly account for the bloodless grace and cool detachment of her work. Yet in her best novels, *To the Lighthouse* and *The Waves*, we feel that her relationship with a few people mattered deeply to her. Her essential subject-matter may not differ as much as it seems to do from that of the traditional novelist. But her way of presenting it is very different. She tried to capture in her style the actual experience of life as it is lived, the flow of perceptions from moment to moment, a thought as it is actually thought, a feeling as it is actually felt. In her conception of consciousness and the self, she has affinities with thinkers of her time, the French philosopher Bergson, and the French novelist Marcel Proust, whose last book was published in 1927. She may also have owed something to the novelist Dorothy Richardson (1872–1957), a pioneer of the method known as the 'stream of consciousness'. But essentially her approach and style are original.

Mrs. Woolf's first novel of promise was *Night and Day*. This novel is rather neglected, because its main themes are developed more convincingly in *To the Lighthouse*. And it remains on the whole faithful to the traditional form of the old-fashioned novel, which she was later to ridicule. Her new technique first appears in *Jacob's Room*, in which she draws an impressionistic sketch of a volatile young man. *Mrs. Dalloway*, which followed, raises the question of Mrs. Woolf's debt to Joyce. Six lives, in essence, are shown in a cross-section of time—one day in the neighbourhood of Bond Street. This suggests the influence of

Ulysses; but while Mrs. Woolf had certainly read *Ulysses*, her published references to Joyce are patronizing. What is odd in *Mrs. Dalloway* is the relation of the heroine Clarissa to the shell-shocked soldier Septimus. These characters never meet, but their lives are mysteriously linked. Later Mrs. Woolf indicated that in some way Clarissa 'was' Septimus. We must remember that there was a strain of insanity in Mrs. Woolf's family. More than once in her life the stress of composition provoked mental breakdowns, and in fear of their recurrence she was to drown herself.

In *Mrs. Dalloway* the central consciousness is a woman who seems very limited intellectually. Mrs. Woolf was an ardent feminist, and campaigned for the emancipation of women. Yet her women characters, like Mrs. Dalloway, seem to exhibit the traits of women to which men have felt superior—lack of intellectual interest, a habit of inconsequence. This may have been merely character-drawing. But Mrs. Woolf herself shows inconsequence in her feminist pamphlets; and in her literary criticism the voices of Dr. Johnson and Walter Pater are disconcertingly joined, at times, by the voice of Mrs. Nickleby. In her novels Mrs. Woolf tends to regard reasoning as a typically male faculty. In a curious way she both exalts and disparages masculine intellect.

Mrs. Woolf's attitude to men may have been largely conditioned by her own experience. She admired her distinguished father, and seems to have identified with him in many ways: she was mannish, she smoked pipes and cheroots. Yet she also felt hostility towards him, and this hostility was bound up in her mind with the effect of her mother's death, and the premature death of her brother Thoby. In *To the Lighthouse* Mrs. Woolf, perhaps for the only time, was able to transmute her psychological problems into a work of art. Here, more than in any other of her novels, she reconciled intellect with intuition. The main character of *To the Lighthouse*, Mr. Ramsay, is based on her father Leslie Stephen. In the presentation of him there is an element of satire in Lytton Strachey's manner. Mr. Ramsay is an 'eminent Victorian'. He is 'seen through', with his masculine confidence, his lack of self-knowledge, his self-pity, his egotism. But there is more in him than that. Although he is too conscious of his own pathos, he is really pathetic. We sense in his presentation, not only the anti-Victorianism of Mrs. Woolf and Strachey, but the personal problem of a daughter with a beloved and difficult father.

To the Lighthouse has another theme, Mrs. Woolf's growing preoccupation with Time. The middle section of the novel, 'Time Passes', anticipates her later prose-poem *The Waves*. But, contradicting the sense of endless flux, the central symbol of the novel is the Lighthouse. It is a true symbol; its total meaning is unanalysable. But its recurring beam, compared in the last part of the book to the movement of the painter's brush, is related to the sense of finality which the completion of a work of art can bring. And this is related in turn to the figure of Mrs. Ramsay, who has died in the course of the novel. She is the figure whose sensitiveness is contrasted, in the organization of the work, with the intellect of her husband. In the end it is the intuitive feminine mind of Mrs. Ramsay which brings serenity and peace.

By the late twenties Mrs. Woolf had become the centre of a cult. But she was little read by the general public. Her idiosyncrasies deterred readers accustomed to ordinary novels. As her journals show, Mrs. Woolf was very concerned with the barometer of her own reputation, and it is possible that in the fantasy *Orlando* (1928), and the novel *The Years* (1937), she attempted to reach a wider public. But neither shows her strength as an artist. *The Years* looks like a compromise between the method of the ordinary novel and Mrs. Woolf's own poetic method of creation. As such, it is disappointing, and often strangely lifeless, as if Mrs. Woolf had exhausted her subject-matter.

It was in *The Waves* (1931) that Mrs. Woolf wrote her last successful novel. This is the most experimental of her novels, the farthest from conventional notions of character, story, and plot. It shows, in semi-dramatic structure, a group of characters at certain stages in their lives, different times and seasons. It is a prose poem, held together by the symbolic use of the sea, recurrently punctuating the sextet of voices with its sound and movement. *The Waves* is a strange book. It is as if some-one were to write down their dreams, very poetically, but without comment or interpretation. The only clue to its meaning lies in Mrs. Woolf's obsession with death. At the end the sea, which stands for death, has the last word: 'the waves broke on the shore'. In *To the Light-house* and *The Waves* the preoccupation with death is overpowering. But we also have the sense that Mrs. Woolf was groping for insights of a glory that transcends the flux of change and time. She seems to have sensed that this glory did not belong to works of art or human beings in themselves, but was merely a reflection of another glory that is not in this world. Virginia Woolf, daughter of the Leslie Stephen of *An Agnostic's Apology*, never came near any sort of reconciliation with formal religion. But her two best novels convey her sense that the mutability which obsessed her was not ultimate and absolute. Had she survived her last illness, her art might have taken a new direction. But her last, unrevised novel, *Between the Acts* (1941), is aimless and drifting.

Virginia Woolf will never be a great favourite, like Jane Austen. We come to know her characters only from the inside, if at all. They are wraiths. In her pamphlet, 'Mr. Bennett and Mrs. Brown', she attacked the Edwardian novelists for their desertion of Mrs. Brown, the old lady in the railway carriage, the symbol of reality. But she seems unwillingly to have accepted the premises of Wells, Bennett, and Galsworthy. They had materialized; she would spiritualize. The result is that, if *The Waves* is her best work, *The Waves* represents more than any other of her novels the desertion of Mrs. Brown.

To write of the culture which produced Forster and Virginia Woolf would be to write a whole chapter in the intellectual and social history of England. They belong to the last phase of liberal humanism. Some documents of that phase are the autobiography of Leonard Woolf, Mrs. Woolf's life of the art-critic Roger Fry, a cult-figure of Bloomsbury, and Clive Bell's *Civilization* (1928), a *jeu d'esprit* which is none the less a provocative statement of Bloomsbury's doctrines of art and the good life.

With two other names associated with this circle we pass from talent to genius. JOHN MAYNARD KEYNES (1883–1946), through the practical force of his ideas in economics, is one of the few men in history who have decisively affected the life of the whole world. But as a writer he belongs to a particular moment of English culture. His attitude towards the Victorian solemnities of the 'dismal science' of political economy closely resembles Strachey's attitude to Florence Nightingale or General Gordon. Keynes is brilliant, ironic, mischievous, the supercilious intellectual alternately amazed or amused by the follies of businessmen and the confusions of doctrinaires.

What is most astonishing about Keynes is his range and versatility. What is astonishing about G. E. MOORE (1873–1958) is his power to restrict, to narrow down, to focus closely. Moore brought to philosophy the outlook, and the limitations, of a research scientist. But he had also the rare virtues of candour, simplicity, and disconcerting directness. In his time philosophy was dominated by the obscure metaphysics of Idealism. Moore, like the child in Hans Andersen's story, cried out that the emperor was naked. He asked the obvious questions which the ordinary man was too over-awed to ask. Moore arrived at the remarkable view that the strange things philosophers say (such as 'Time is unreal', etc.) were the result of *mistakes*. This view is implausible. But there is no doubt that philosophers, like other thinkers, do make mistakes, and Moore's insistence on clarity and bent for analysis will always be needed. What attracted philosophers to Moore was the inhuman patience with which he examined statements and arguments and asked just what they meant. What attracted Bloomsbury to Moore was something different. In *Principia Ethica* (1903) Moore had arrived at the conclusion that the only ultimate sources of value in the universe are the appreciation of art and beauty and the enjoyment of sensitive personal relationships. This doctrine was congenial to Bloomsbury. And Moore's attack on philosophical pontiffs had something in common with their attack on Victorian father-figures. If they committed the sin of Ham, so did he. *Principia Ethica* might be compared to Pater's *Renaissance* in its rôle as a sacred book for the younger generation. But Moore, like Pater, was to see his work used for purposes that he might not have approved. In many ways, as Keynes pointed out, he remained a great Victorian. The armchair antinomianism of Bloomsbury was not the intended sequel of his 'intuitions'.

Moore's distinction lay in the comparatively narrow field of professional philosophy. His older Cambridge contemporary BERTRAND RUSSELL (1872–1970), while his distinction in that field cannot be questioned, had a much wider scope. His work, in John Wisdom's words, extends from 'the icy regions of logical space' to 'the equatorial jungles that lie between us and the conquest of happiness'. His genius in logic and the philosophy of mathematics must be judged by his peers. It is where Russell's work approaches ordinary human concerns that doubts arise about his achievement. How far will posterity judge him to have been a great philosopher in the traditional sense, a man of wisdom? What was the gain and loss to English civilization when the Cambridge of Russell and Keynes succeeded the Cambridge of Maitland and Sidgwick?

For many decades Russell, the Whig aristocrat with his democratic views, was a vivid feature of the English scene. The grandson of a Victorian Prime Minister, he knew and corresponded with almost every famous man in the world. He did more than any other thinker to bring philosophy out of the ivory tower. In this respect his rôle was like that of Sartre in France. He had always shown an urgent and practical concern with the terrible problems of our civilization. In his work on education and politics, in his popular books on marriage and morals, he was always passionately involved in contemporary questions. During the Great War he suffered imprisonment for his opposition to militarism, and in recent years he was again sent to prison as a result of his active struggle against nuclear armaments. He campaigned for what he thought true and right. He was popular and unpopular, but his course was always unswerving. We might contrast his extreme old age with that of Shaw, cosseted by the admiring public. Russell remained crisp and emphatic amid the false genialities of our time. He may be called the last of the great Victorians; or, perhaps more appropriately, the last voice of the eighteenth-century Enlightenment. Yet he shaped the course of English philosophy in our time.

In Russell's philosophy the moral and spiritual aspects of experience are merely subjective, matters of feeling only. Yet it was these that engaged Russell's whole being. Among the great rational humanists, he has been famous for his passionateness. But in his writing he cannot convey it. His poetic eloquence is not moving. He cannot command a warm humanity when he is speaking of himself, or of others, or of God. His best writing is distinguished by dry wit, by gaiety, by intellectual brilliance. But a whole dimension seems to be missing from it. What this is may be suggested by a glance at D. H. Lawrence's best work. Russell had a famous encounter with Lawrence during the war years. At first they were attracted to each other, but soon became enemies. Lawrence was to diagnose Russell as 'immature' and caricature him in *Women in Love* as 'a bottle of compressed tabloids'. Russell, years later, was to portray Lawrence as a half-lunatic fascist. It is one of the calamities of history that these two great Englishmen could not teach one another anything.

Joyce and Lawrence, Forster and Virginia Woolf, are the dominant voices in English fiction in the 1920s. But some other writers whose work first appeared in this period may be mentioned. These are Aldous Huxley, Ford Madox Ford, Katherine Mansfield, Ronald Firbank, and T. F. Powys.

ALDOUS HUXLEY (1894–1963) belonged to the intellectual aristocracy of England. He was the grandson of T. H. Huxley and the son of a niece of Matthew Arnold. By temperament he was an observer, a collector of human curiosities. Some of his best writing is to be found in his collected essays. Although Huxley often changed his conscious philosophy, his outlook on life always remained that of an aesthete. He valued 'experience' above everything else. In his early work he advocated the 'Whole Man'; in his later work he became a journalist-polymath of the scientific age. Throughout his career he retained his breadth of intellectual interests and his omnivorous curiosity.

Huxley's early novels won fame for their febrile brittleness, their reflection of the deflationary, mocking spirit of the post-war generation. They satirize the perversity of sophisticated culture in our time, living on the inherited capital of a religious and moral tradition which is losing its vitality. These early novels have less in common with conventional fiction than with the satirical extravaganzas of Peacock, or Anatole France, or Norman Douglas in *South Wind* (1917). But Huxley, unlike Douglas, is a moralist. There is a note of protest in his work. Like the hero of *Antic Hay* (1923), 'he picked up his pen and denounced'. A didactic impulse in Huxley inhibits his gaiety.

This didactic strain was to become stronger in the novels of Huxley's middle period. And so did an element peculiar to him, a curious cold disgust, a fascinated repugnance at 'the Human Vomedy' (as Huxley's typewriter once called it). Huxley in his early and late books was to extol the pleasures of the senses; but a certain dualism, the dualism he condemned both in the sensualist and the ascetic, is never absent from his own work. Horrible incidents abound in it. An early chapter of *Eyeless in Gaza* (1936) describes boys at a boarding-school tormenting a boy they have caught masturbating. Later, a dog falls out of a plane and spatters two embracing lovers with its blood.

From the thirties onwards Huxley, under D. H. Lawrence's influence, became more and more gloomy about the future of the age of science. In *Brave New World* (1932) he gave us a memorable example of a gloomy modern genre. Comparing it later with Orwell's *Nineteen Eighty-Four*, Huxley claimed that his own prophecy was more likely to resemble the actual future than Orwell's. Orwell gives us a nightmare of crude sadism; Huxley, inspired by books like Pavlov's *Conditioned Reflexes* (translated 1927), and Russell's *The Scientific Outlook* (1931), shows us a humanity cushioned, buffered, and denatured by a scientific bureaucracy. *Brave New World* is more forceful than Huxley's early satires because Huxley has arrived at a more satisfactory resolution of his own point of view. He no longer protects himself by satirizing everything. In *Brave New World* he puts himself behind his Savage who comes from outside and claims for man the privilege of individuality and freedom, even at the price of suffering and misery.

But Huxley's Savage does not really have the best of the debate with his Controller. And Huxley's later work might be described as an attempt to find a more convincing affirmation of human dignity than he could offer in *Brave New World*. Despairing more and more of modern society, he turned in his retirement in California to Oriental mysticism. He attempted to revive the ancient elevation of the contemplative life over the active. In *Grey Eminence* (1941) he explored the personality of the seventeenth-century mystic Père Joseph. But the moral of this book is ambiguous. Père Joseph shows the detachment which Huxley claims to be the only means of salvation for modern man; and yet Père Joseph was the accomplice of Richelieu in the destruction of Europe during the Thirty Years War.

Huxley's later novels, such as *Time Must Have a Stop* (1944), though they contain amusing satire in his old manner, are predominantly gloomy. But late in his life he began to strike a more positive note. He experimented with the drug mescalin; he speculated optimistically on the benefits of a technique of sexual intercourse known as *carezza*. An unsympathetic critic might see in this Huxley's surrender to the American intellectual environment of modish nostrums. At any rate, Huxley is more convincing as a satirist and an aesthete than as a prophet. His gifts were essentially those of an anthologist, not of a mystic. Mystics do not make anthologies of mysticism, like *The Perennial Philosophy* (1946); but in the end this and the literary anthology *Texts and Pretexts* (1932) may turn out to be the most purely enjoyable of Huxley's books.

FORD MADOX FORD (1873–1939) was the best literary editor England has ever had. As such, he has a footing in two literary periods. Before the Great War, he published Conrad and Hardy in the *English Review*; after the war, he published Pound and Hemingway in the *Transatlantic Review*. As an author in his own right, Ford made it his aim to introduce into English fiction the objectivity and realism of the great French novelists. In his concern with the medium of literature he had much in common with his friend Ezra Pound, and his place in literary history is beside the 'men of 1914'—Pound, Joyce, Eliot, Wyndham Lewis. Ford sought to express the essence of his experience as a man who had lived through the Edwardian age and the Great War. He wrote a series of novels, centring on the life of a character called Tietjens. Ford has most of the traditional qualifications of a novelist: the power of description and scene-setting, the evocation of character in dialogue, the blending of reflection and generalization into narrative. Formally, too, he was a fine craftsman. His construction is subtle. His handling of the time problem is complicated, but dexterous. Yet for some mysterious reason Ford's novels are not memorable and, in some essential respect, not convincing. *The Good Soldier* (1915) does everything a novel should do, except the one thing necessary: it does not compel belief. There was some kind of artistic truth that Ford, man of honour and intelligence as he was, could not command.

It is probable that the talent of KATHERINE MANSFIELD (1888–1923) was less than Ford's. Yet her best stories—stories like 'The Fly' or 'The Doll's House'—stick in our minds like poems. They have the indispensable ingredient of reality. Katherine Mansfield had something in common with her friend and rival Virginia Woolf. They were both consciously emancipated women, who protested against male dominance. But the best of Katherine Mansfield's work, the art of the short story as she perfected it, does not rely on any special 'message'. She was essentially an observer of life, ironic and realistic. Unfortunately her talent was pulled in a different direction, perhaps under the influence of her husband John Middleton Murry (1889–1957). Murry was a distinguished literary critic, but he had a tendency, very marked in his middle-period work, to lapse into a sickly pseudo-religious sentimentality. We see Katherine Mansfield, under this influence, striving for a sort of pathetic purity that does not ring true. Her real talent is not engaging, sweet, or gentle. She casts an ironic cold eye at human baseness. Lawrence perhaps took something of 'Gudrun' in *Women in Love* from

Katherine Mansfield: mocking and aloof, cultivating perfection in *small* forms of art. Katherine Mansfield was influenced by Chekhov, but she is very different. Chekhov, like the Shakespeare of the Sonnets, was essentially a parental writer. And there was nothing motherly about Katherine Mansfield's gifts.

RONALD FIRBANK (1886–1926) is one of those writers who belong peculiarly to a period, yet who seem more important now than they did at the time. He is a writer of a kind some people detest. Words like 'perverse', 'precious', 'decadent', obviously apply to him. He seeks nothing but what he finds 'amusing'. His novels are very short, very mannered, very affected. The author of *Prancing Nigger* (1925) is clearly a spiritual descendant of Wilde. But where Wilde was large and generous, Firbank is small and feline. A book like *Concerning the Eccentricities of Cardinal Pirelli* (1926) is an easy target for literary moralists. And yet the heavy adjectives of moral criticism seem to miss the mark with Firbank: or rather, they hit it too completely. Firbank deliberately taunts and challenges the assumptions of the serious critic; yet after a while we begin to recognize a certain integrity in his point of view. Harold Nicolson (1886–1968) portrayed a character based on Firbank in his *Some People* (1927). But Nicolson's conventionality prevents him from seeing just how subversive Firbank was. He makes the character based on Firbank 'redeem himself' by going to fight in the Great War. The real Firbank made no such accommodation with convention. He remained an outsider, perverse and mocking. E. M. Forster took Firbank seriously; Evelyn Waugh admitted his influence. But both Forster and Waugh (from *Vile Bodies* onwards) are moralists: Firbank is not. There is no protest in his work, unless just keeping a certain point of view alive is a protest.

To go from Firbank to the work of the Powys brothers is to be reminded that it is hard to generalize validly about modern literature. No writers could be more different: yet none could be imagined in any other period than the twentieth century. J. C. Powys, T. F. Powys, and Llewelyn Powys have an unmistakable flavour in common. It is either liked or disliked, like nutmeg. J. C. and Llewelyn Powys have their admirers: but the most substantial talent among the brothers may turn out to be that of T. F. POWYS (1875–1953). Theodore Francis Powys developed a specialized art of fiction. The main tradition of the English novel has been biographical and psychological: the feigned history has been its dominant type. Some novelists have tried to alter this tradition. But they have paid a price. They have been ignored by ordinary readers: and they have been accused of 'escapism', of evading their responsibilities as novelists, by sophisticated ones. This happened to Powys. Like J. M. Synge, he chose a particular region, with its special customs and folkways and its own dialect of English, as the basis of his art. He drew upon the speech and manner of life of people in Dorset, a region far from London, where traditional ways still survived. But Powys's novels are neither realistic accounts of country life, nor romances like those of Mary Webb (1881–1927). Powys's novels are essentially the expression of his own peculiar vision, rooted in the Bible and Christian tradition, but reflecting his own pessimistic, sceptical temperament. His best-known story, *Mr. Weston's Good Wine* (1927), turns on the fancy that God comes to a little Dorset town in the guise of Mr. Weston, who has two wines to sell, one that makes people happy and fulfilled, the other that brings oblivion and peace: the wine of love and the wine of death. Love and death are Powys's preoccupations. And he comes to be more and more preoccupied with death. We are reminded of Freud and his belief in the death instinct. Freud was not supported by all his disciples in this belief; and Powys lost some admirers when he began to persist in the pessimistic, death-centred tendency of his inspiration.

But in Powys's best work, what would be unpleasant or horrible in real life is curiously transformed. His art has a Biblical foundation; his style has a limpidity that recalls the Cowper of the letters and the Wesley of the journals. A story like 'When Thou Wast Naked' has a wonderful transparency and beauty. But Powys's art, even at its best, is precariously poised between cruelty and sentimentality, and often sentimentality overpowers it. A writer who entitles an anthology of his stories *God's Eyes A-Twinkle* cannot complain if critics dismiss him as a whimsy. Charges of 'escapism' are too easy to make: but there do seem to be serious inherent limitations in Powys's desire to turn away from the language of his own time, to seek out old words and phrases, to model himself on earlier writers. To reassure ourselves of the comparative richness of his work, we need to turn to a writer like David Garnett (b. 1892). Garnett has charmed many readers with his fables and fantasies; but Powys's art has deeper roots in the England of the past.

6

The New Poetry

Eliot—Pound—Hopkins

FOR MANY READERS of our time the name of T. S. ELIOT (1888–1965) is virtually synonymous with modern poetry. During the 1920s Eliot was an *avant-garde* figure, a centre of controversy, a party leader. By the 1940s he had conquered the literary establishment and was generally accepted as the leading writer of the age. Many of his critical dicta achieved a world-wide fame. His taste for Dante, for the metaphysical poets, for French symbolist poetry, his comparative distaste for Milton and for much nineteenth-century poetry, shaped the opinions of a whole generation, and left a lasting mark on school curricula and university syllabuses. In his later years Eliot became somewhat remote from the world of literary movements and fashions. And since his death his reputation has been in a sort of critical limbo. This often happens when a writer has commanded the literary scene for a long time. But there is plenty of evidence that Eliot's poetry is still cherished and his influence active.

Thomas Stearns Eliot came of an old-established American family with ancestral English connections. He was born at St. Louis, Missouri. From 1906 to 1915 he studied literature and philosophy at Harvard, the Sorbonne, and Oxford. He made personal contact with French poets of the symbolist school, and with the Anglo-American movement known as Imagism, which included such writers as Ezra Pound, T. E. Hulme, and 'H.D.'. Eliot was employed in Lloyds Bank in 1916. He was assistant editor of the *Egoist* from 1917 to 1919 and founded the *Criterion* in 1922. Shortly afterwards he was made a director of Faber, the publishers. A book of poems, *Prufrock and Other Observations* (1917), was followed by a volume of criticism, *The Sacred Wood* (1920). Eliot's most famous poem, *The Waste Land*, was published in 1922. During the 1930s Eliot first reached a wide public with his play *Murder in the Cathedral* (1935), which was followed by another play, *The Family Reunion* (1939). Eliot published much criticism and miscellaneous prose, mainly lectures and addresses. His standing in the literary world reached its greatest height with the series of poems called *Four Quartets* (first published together in 1943, though the poems had previously appeared separately, starting in 1936 with 'Burnt Norton' in *Collected Poems 1909–35*. After *Four Quartets* he returned to the drama. His later plays are *The Cocktail Party* (1950), *The Confidential Clerk* (1954), and *The Elder Statesman* (1959).

Eliot's early background was scholarly and conservative. Harvard, the Sorbonne, and Oxford before 1914 were strongly traditionalist in outlook. Eliot studied under men like Irving Babbitt and George Santayana. He interested himself in the history of religion, especially Buddhism. He wrote a philosophical treatise. But Eliot was also a practical man, who was to become a successful publisher, editor, and man of affairs. And Eliot's best work is always between two worlds, the world of the mystic and the world of everyday life. The success of his poetry lies in bringing them together. Eliot's worldly side has been seen by some critics in the seeming astuteness with which he made a career and conquered the literary world by transposing the iconoclastic ideas of Ezra Pound into a 'sly, polite, insinuating style'. It may appear also in his keen awareness of social values in the England which he had made his home. But the worldliness in Eliot was an advantage to him as a poet, not only as a man of letters. It gave a reality and a rootedness to his perceptions. He was not an ivory tower poet.

Eliot as a young man abandoned America and sought to become a European writer. For a while he even seems to have thought of becoming a French poet, like his fellow-countryman Stuart Merrill. Some of his early poems were written in French. But it was soon clear to Eliot that his future as a poet lay in the English language. In London and Paris Eliot was drawn to the Imagist poets because, like them, he wanted to correct the loose expression and woolly sentiment of contemporary poetry. He disliked the vague poeticism into which the romantic tradition had degenerated. A new start had to be made. Eliot planned to create a different music, to give poetry a greater informality, to bring it closer to the spoken language. But Eliot was also impatient with the carelessness and formlessness of contemporary free verse. He wanted to tighten it up, to return to rhyme and strict forms where these were appropriate for special effects. Above all, he sought expression in poetry for the secret, subconscious currents of the mind. He invented a method of using literary quotations and reminiscences with seeming casualness, but in obedience to these deeper impulses. Eliot, like his friend Pound, was preoccupied with craftsmanship. He thought twentieth-century verse lacked standards. He looked, for a new start in poetry, to neglected traditions. So he turned to Elizabethan drama, to Jacobean and

Caroline poetry, to the poetry of Donne and the Metaphysicals. What interested Eliot above all in these writers was their use of the spoken word, the colloquial language and rhythm that had long been absent from serious poetry. But French influence on the early Eliot was more immediate than these. And deeper and more lasting than any other influence was Dante, the medieval poet who still grips us across the centuries because he is so graphic and unconventional. Dante was to remain Eliot's master from the beginning to end.

Besides Eliot's consciousness of his special needs as a poet, he had a general interest in literature. He was keenly aware of its precarious status in the modern world. In this he resembles Matthew Arnold. Eliot often quarrelled with Arnold's ideas. He may have associated them with the stuffy-genteel New England tradition that had bored him as a young man. But we feel that this was something of a family quarrel. In his literary and social criticism Eliot is essentially in the tradition of Arnold. But the sort of poetry Eliot wanted to write was very different from Arnold's. And as a thinker he looked for more precise philosophical and religious standards than he found in Arnold's prose writings. Moreover, Eliot was more eclectic than Arnold. He shared to the full the twentieth-century interest in what André Malraux has called *le musée imaginaire*. His imagination throve on fragments of remote and alien cultures. He explored the myths and legends of the past. Eliot's philosophical preoccupation is also characteristic of our century. He was preoccupied with Time, the enigmatic dimension, which seems to obstruct our contact with spiritual realities. In his later poetry Eliot strives to give meaning to the idea of non-temporal existence. At the beginning of 'Little Gidding' he evokes, through a description of a winter landscape, his sense of a 'timeless moment'. And this idea underlies his insistence, in his early criticism, that what he calls 'tradition' means seeing past and future with the same eyes. Eliot's 'tradition' is not conservatism: it involves a recognition that every period changes. He sought for what Goethe called permanence in change; whether in art, or ethics, or literary form.

The *Prufrock* volume (1917) has a peculiar and unforgettable place in English poetry. These poems introduced readers to a new manner in verse, with its apparent freakishness and inconsequence, its urban setting, its abrupt transitions from clipped satire to lyrical beauty, its sordid episodes. The poems show the influence of the French poet Jules Laforgue, a minor symbolist who invented a technique of discontinuity to express his own blend of romantic wistfulness and self-deprecating irony. But Eliot's transposition of this French voice into English poetry was an original creative feat. In a poem like 'Portrait of a Lady' a new music emerges in English poetry: a versification based on the speaking voice, but employing for variety and contrast effects which draw on a whole body of literary tradition. To the bewildered, this new poetry seemed maddeningly impressionistic. Yet it had a unity of tone. Looked at from the perspective of Eliot's later work, his poetry down to 'The Hollow Men' seems to be a pilgrimage through the inferno of modern city life. The inspiration of Dante is clear. But besides Dante there was another poet, associated with him in Eliot's mind, Charles Baudelaire, the first great poet of the big city.

In the poems of 1920 Eliot abandoned the special free verse effects of the *Prufrock* volume. Most of the poems are in stanzas, with tight, regular rhythms. They express a sophisticated sense of the meanness of the unheroic present. In them Eliot now adopts the manner of another French poet, the Gautier of *Émaux et Camées*. But the best poem in the volume is written in a kind of modernized Jacobean blank verse. This is 'Gerontion', the most obscure of Eliot's poems. Through cunning technical means 'Gerontion' conveys the rootlessness and disintegration of a modern mind. Like all Eliot's early poems, it abounds in cryptic, suggestive, inexplicit effects: 'The word within a word, unable to speak a word.'

This mysteriousness attracted some readers and repelled others. In its day *The Waste Land* (1922) became a by-word for obscurity. It is the consummation of Eliot's earlier manner. It evokes an urban civilization which has lost its roots and is dying of spiritual thirst. Eliot employed, as the framework of this poem, mythical symbolic material he found in *The Golden Bough* (1890–1915) of Sir James Frazer (1854–1941) and Jessie L. Weston's *From Ritual to Romance* (1920). *The Waste Land* abounds in vivid episodes, startling transitions, erudite allusions. A few months later Eliot added notes sometimes as cryptic as the lines they purport to elucidate, which increased the effect of eccentricity and mystery. Yet many lines and passages clung to readers' memories. The last section, 'What the Thunder said', is the most mysterious and haunting of all. There were not wanting interpreters who claimed for *The Waste Land* a peculiar relevance to the spiritual sickness of the post-war generation. In particular, the poem's presentation of modern sexuality, as joyless and sterile, compelled attention. It was acclaimed, too glibly, by many who suffered from what the poet himself was acidly to describe as 'the illusion of being disillusioned'. *The Waste Land*, like Pound's *Mauberley,* reflects a sour, negative attitude to everything characteristic of modern life. So powerful was its influence that a whole pseudo-sociology was developed in keeping with that attitude. Today *The Waste Land* sounds less like the authoritative epic of modern disintegration. We see it rather as the expression of the plight of a poet who always finds it hard to speak out, and has to put on a series of masks before he can do so.

For Eliot's insistence on impersonality, classicism, and tradition should not mislead us. The poets and artists and polemicists with whom he consorted were not conservatives but aggressive radicals of the Right. T. E. Hulme (1883–1917) proclaimed that all poetry more than twenty years old should be burned. French political thinkers like Sorel or Maurras favoured violence and extremism, not the cautious gradualism of a real traditionalist. Pound supported Mussolini. Wyndham Lewis wrote a book in favour of Hitler. Eliot himself in the *Criterion* expressed sympathy with the reactionary movement of the *Action Française*. His ideals were far removed from the traditional humanism of a poet like Bridges. The decorum of his prose style does not conceal his irrationality and impressionism. Words like 'impersonality' and 'classicism' need re-definition when we are discussing Eliot. It is true that he is not a personal poet in the sense that Yeats is. With Yeats we always think first of the poet, and discussion of his career inevitably brings in personalities and public affairs. With Eliot we think first of the poem, the thing made, rather than of the poet. In this sense Eliot may be called impersonal. But he has little in common with the balanced, generalizing poets who take their origin from Greek humanism. His work reflects the aesthetic ideas of an age as far removed as possible from the Greek ideals of serenity and harmony. Private need and personal impulse play a large part both in Eliot's style and his matter. Though his personality and literary ideals are so different from Wordsworth's, the whole body of his work deserves, as much as *The Prelude*, to be called 'the growth of a poet's mind'.

But with 'The Hollow Men' (1925) the growth of Eliot's mind seemed to have stopped. This poem is an unforgettable expression of dryness, sterility, emotional bankruptcy: the landscape of Ezekiel, described in ultra-modern verse techniques. Its prophetic imagery, the desert and the dry bones, were to recur in 'Ash-Wednesday' (1930). But they recur with a difference. A new and positive preoccupation had entered Eliot's poetry: the Christian religion. Yet there is nothing dogmatic about 'Ash-Wednesday'. For the Eliot of this poetry, Christianity was still something aspired to, a matter for exploration and self-questioning, not for preaching. Its style, its versification, its symbolism, all suggest that the poet had reached a spiritual crisis. He was groping towards a religious affirmation that, with the whole of his being, he had not yet reached. 'Ash-Wednesday' is one of the poems of Eliot that most resists paraphrase. Its manner is distinguished by hesitance, suggestiveness, obliquity. But we cannot miss the confessional note in the poetry, the note of repentance, the sense of advancing years. From now on the religious preoccupation was rarely to be absent from Eliot's verse or prose. After 'Ash-Wednesday' Eliot abandoned the mordant phraseology and allusive sarcasm that first made him admired. This change of manner was regretted by many of his admirers. And so were the Anglo-Catholicism and political conservatism to which Eliot committed himself.

Eliot had never been universally accepted. Many traditionalists still resented the innovations of his poetic style, and disliked many of his critical ideas and attitudes. They were repelled by the cold lucidity of his prose quite as much as by the cold want of lucidity of his verse. They were exasperated by the difficulty of reconciling the Eliot of the prose, severe and prim, with the Eliot of the verse, impressionistic, syncopated, dream-like. In the 1930s the various currents of opposition to Eliot were at their strongest. The older generation of readers were sceptical about 'modern poetry'; the younger generation, if not distracted by the temptations and menaces of Russian or German collectivism, were preoccupied by social and political problems to which the later Eliot seemed irrelevant. There was also a pause in Eliot's poetic progress in the thirties. In a lecture given years later he was to speak of the three voices of poetry: the first voice, that of the poet talking to himself, or to no one; the second voice, that of the poet talking to an audience; and the third voice, that of the poet speaking through a dramatic character. Eliot's early poetry had been mainly poetry of the first voice. But in the thirties the second and third voices predominated in his work. Much of Eliot's contact with his public was now made outside poetry. His prose writings became less concerned with qualities of style in authors who appealed to him, and more concerned with questions of culture and public affairs—the place of Christianity in a secular society, the problems of social change, the scope and function of education. He wrote in the guarded, endlessly self-qualifying manner of a half-hearted reactionary.

Eliot's 'third voice' is also very evident in his poetry of the thirties. It was then that he began his major effort as a playwright. He had no wish to emulate the example of Yeats in writing a specialized, esoteric drama. Eliot wanted to conquer the West End theatre, to reach the ordinary play-going public. This desire was prompted not so much by an ambition for commercial success as by Eliot's view of his chosen genre. Eliot believed that drama, to be truly drama, must work at several levels. Drama is not an esoteric cult, but a public art. The great dramatists of the past had been able to work at many levels of response, ranging from the level at which we respond to the straightforward story and the characters, to the level at which we appreciate the poetry and the latent meaning of the play. Eliot wanted to emulate them. So it was at this time that he assisted in the composition of the religious propaganda play *The Rock*, and wrote two more important plays: *Murder in the Cathedral*, a drama on the martyrdom of Thomas Becket in 1170, which was performed in Canterbury Cathedral; and *The Family Reunion*, in which Eliot adapted the thematic material of Aeschylus's *Oresteia* to the conditions of modern life and the modern theatre. Of these two plays, *Murder in the Cathedral* is more successful as a play, though the student of Eliot may find it less deeply significant. Traces of the poet's private obsessions appear in the shrinking disgust with physical life expressed by the Chorus; but otherwise Eliot's poetry is subdued to its historical theme. Eliot starts his story at the end, with the death and martyrdom of Becket. His theme is the question: what is true martyrdom? For Eliot, it is not only the sacrifice of one's *life* to God, but the sacrifice of one's *will*. *The Family Reunion* does not succeed so well in adapting the ancient to the modern. Its obsession with guilt and sin seems too inward and personal, not fully dramatized or given its 'objective correlative'—to use a phrase Eliot himself made famous in discussing *Hamlet*. His own play seems an unsatisfactory compromise between his private poetry and his public, explicit manner.

Eliot himself was dissatisfied with these plays. But he continued to be fascinated by the theatre. It was only when the outbreak of the Second World War forced him to discontinue playwriting that he turned back to poetry and wrote his masterpiece, *Four Quartets*. This consists of four poems, 'Burnt Norton' (which had been written earlier), 'East Coker', 'The Dry Salvages', and 'Little Gidding'. The *Quartets* rank in modern European poetry with Rilke's *Duino Elegies*. Eliot created a new form, inspired by instrumental music, in which to unite complex strands of thought and feeling about the past—his own past, and the historic past—in its relation to the present; to explore the significance of time, and the possibility of eternity. Queen Mary Stuart's motto, 'In my end is my beginning', a phrase used in 'East Coker', states the total theme of the work. We cannot recapture the semblance of the past, because it is into our own time-bound consciousness and our memories that we look for it. But if we can unlearn our preoccupation with self, we may purge our minds of vanity, and hear 'music heard/So deeply that it is not heard at all'. Among the images Eliot uses are, in 'East Coker', the agricultural rituals and dances of ancient England; in 'The Dry Salvages', where he returns to his native America, the ancient river Mississippi which serves modern needs; and in 'Little Gidding' the ruined chapel to which Charles I returned in the hour of his distress, a place where the memory of Civil War conflicts has vanished, but 'prayer has been valid'. The lesson of *Four Quartets* is the need to abandon fear about the future, but also, as a necessary consequence, to abandon hope. It is here that Eliot makes his sharpest challenge to American activism. We must learn to live for the present, for those moments in which, for Freud, we experience 'the return of the repressed', and, for Eliot, we touch a timeless dimension in which the real meaning of life is found. In the philosophical framework of these poems Eliot is indebted to one of his early masters, F. H. Bradley (1846–1924). But agreement with Bradley's metaphysics is not necessary in order to appreciate them. The *Quartets*, even in their most philosophical-looking passages, are poetry, not philosophy.

But they are difficult poetry. In 'East Coker' the poet speaks of his 'intolerable wrestle/With words and meanings'. And there is no doubt that what he wished to convey is hard to approximate in language. *Four Quartets* has not been universally admired. Eliot was accused of psychic impressionism, of gloomy mumbling. Part of the explanation may be that in Eliot's early work his 'impersonality' required him not to impose his own views or ideas on the readers. His figures, his images, his transitions, were left to speak for themselves. When he began to make his attitudes more explicit, as in *Four Quartets*, he was found less congenial by some of his early admirers. The technical skill, and variety of verse-forms, with which Eliot developed his new style were agreed to be remarkable. And no one could deny the austere seriousness of these poems, their meditative tone, their emotional restraint, their penitential quality. But some of those most in sympathy with Eliot's religious position found him too coldly remote from ordinary life, and too disdainful of its possibilities. He was for ever castigating the conscience of his readers, asking them to see life in this world as self-deceiving and essentially unreal. Such poetry could never be widely popular. It is otherworldly, yet its other-worldliness lacks fervour. It does not so much affirm religious faith as undermine the alternatives. To appreciate such poetry requires the reader to participate, as far as he can, in the ascetic self-discipline of the poet. Such an effort is beyond the capacity, or the desire, of most readers.

Yet, with all its exacting demands, *Four Quartets* was to raise Eliot to the summit of literary fame. After the war he returned to the drama. And here, paradoxically, while he attracted a wider public than before, with *The Cocktail Party* and its successors, he began once more to lose some of the allegiance of the intellectual community. Eliot's later plays have a style and a wit far beyond the cruder art of an Osborne or a Wesker. They are at the moment dated, because Eliot used the conventions of West End comedy, which is now unpopular; but their brilliant writing will surely bring them back into favour. Yet Eliot was not a born dramatist. What he says of Browning is true of him: we remember the poet by the dramatic monologues, the *personae* through which he speaks in his poems, rather than by the characters in his plays. Gomez or Julia or Eggerson are less vivid than the characters in Eliot's poems. Eliot's genius seems to be for the presentation of humours, or grotesques, rather than for the drama of human relationships. So it may be that his most interesting work in dramatic form is the fragmentary 'Aristophanic melodrama', *Sweeney Agonistes* (1932). And of all Eliot's works this is the one that may have most to say to us at present. In it he is farthest away from the sedate and Olympian figure of *Four Quartets*, or the sly, cryptic, urbane personality implied in the later plays. And it is here that he exposes most nakedly the boredom, nausea, and horror that fostered his creative impulse. 'Birth, and copulation and death./ That's all, that's all, that's all, that's all,/Birth, and copulation, and death.'

Although he lived for some years in England and was deeply involved in English literary life, EZRA POUND (b. 1885), unlike Eliot, did not become a British subject. And, outside a small circle of admirers, his reputation in England has never been high. What reputation he had was largely due to his connection with Eliot, and it disappeared altogether during the Second World War, when Pound broadcast from Rome in favour of Mussolini. Many English readers have been content to leave judgement on his work to American critics. But Pound has an important place in the history of English poetry. He had an extraordinary gift as a talent-spotter. He was one of the first to recognize Eliot's genius, and worked with generous disinterestedness to promote the cause of Eliot's poetry. He was a pioneer in the recognition of Joyce. He encouraged Yeats's emergence from the Celtic twilight. Pound urged on poets the importance of technique and craftsmanship. He spared no pains to rewrite, to correct, to advise. This technical concern has always attracted young writers, from the far-off days of Imagism to the present-day school of American 'projectivist' poets. Pound's most famous performance as a craftsman was his work of revision on Eliot's *The Waste Land*, which in its original form seems to have been sprawling and shapeless. Pound was also keenly interested in the work of modern musicians and painters. But above all he was devoted to the art of writing. It is this devotion which makes his handbooks, like *The A.B.C. of Reading* (1934), so attractive. We must not be too solemn about Pound's 'chucking out' of established reputations. What matters is what he leaves in. He finds poems we had missed. His worst fault as a critic is his underrating of the importance of content. This may explain his cult of the medieval Provençal poets, who are tedious because they care little about their meaning, so long as they can fit it into a complex rhyme scheme. But Pound's activities on behalf of poetry can do nothing but good. In everything he has written he appears as one of those rare people—especially rare in the literary or academic worlds—who have a genuine love of literature.

Pound would not have been effective as a propagandist for poetry if he had not had creative gifts himself. He began as a poet in the late romantic tradition: Quiller-Couch included two of his poems in the *Oxford Book of Victorian Verse*. His masters were Browning and Swinburne. In dreamier moods he took up the style of the early Yeats. But early in this century Pound began to write a more modern kind of poetry. He introduced witty, satirical observations of contemporary life. He tried to eliminate abstraction and verboseness from his verse. Throughout his career Pound was fascinated by papyrus fragments, which seem to leave us with the pure essence of poems, without continuous syntax, framework, or verbal padding. In his short poems, and later in his long series of *Cantos*, he attempted to emulate this effect. Conventional metre was rejected along with conventional diction. The technical innovations were accompanied by a change in emotional tone. Pound, like Eliot, was in sympathy with the anti-humanist doctrines of T. E. Hulme and Wyndham Lewis. Satire and irony replaced pathos. Warmth, tenderness, and gentleness were banished as sloppy sentimentality. High decorum and the grand manner were rejected as spurious. Everything was to be hard, external, linear.

In so far as Pound was not a satirist, his positive inspiration came from his idea of Europe. He saw in the relics of European civilization valuable things that were lacking in the past of his own country. The emotional core of a poem like 'Provincia Deserta' is the sense of wonder that someone from a completely different civilization, modern and American, should be alive in this ancient land, with its ruined castles where the troubadours had sung. In all Pound's dealings with the past we feel an underlying sense of wonder. Beneath the mask of the ironical modernist he is essentially a Late Romantic and an Aesthete.

The drawback of Pound's early verse is that he had very little to say. None of it seems to be poetry that he *had* to write. But the opposite is true of the sequence of poems, *Hugh Selwyn Mauberley*, which Pound put together after the Great War. Through Pound's favourite device of the *persona*—here, a disappointed Aesthete—Pound sums up the literary epoch through which he had lived. The poems illustrate Pound's stylistic ideals. They are not discourses but *objects*. One of them is called 'Medallion': and we feel that Pound thinks of a poem as something tangible. In its subject-matter, *Mauberley* records a moment of history. But the impulse behind it is not merely historical. The war is dealt with directly in only two poems of the sequence, but it is always in the background, giving depth and poignancy to what otherwise might have been only a 'period' satire.

Pound was less successful in the *Cantos* in finding something of his own to say. This lengthy and still incomplete work, which has been coming out in instalments since 1925, is his most comprehensive attempt at a critique of modern civilization. It uses the method Eliot used in *The Waste Land* and 'Coriolan': sudden unexplained shifts of perspective from one historical period to another. But the use of that technique in a very long poem is self-defeating. Moreover, the *Cantos* are too esoteric. They are an album of Pound's interests and obsessions, rather than an organic whole. And Pound's worst side appears in them, his truculent didacticism, and something worse, his attraction towards fascism and anti-Semitism. In the *Cantos* the poet's mind appears horribly disordered and diseased. Yet there are passages of great beauty. The late 'Pisan Cantos' (1949), though obscure and esoteric, draw effectively on Pound's experience as a prisoner of the Americans in Italy, and on his nostalgia for England. But the *Cantos* as a whole, like *Finnegans Wake*, reflect a sort of artistic megalomania: they try for a cultural comprehensiveness that cannot be achieved by one mind—certainly not by Pound's.

Pound's best work has been done when his subject-matter was provided for him, and all he had to do was to 'make it new'. His genius is that of a translator. Pound revived a conception of translation which had been dormant since the eighteenth century, when it was called 'imitation': the transposition of ancient works into a modern setting. Creative translation is essentially a form of literary criticism: the comparison through craftsmanship. Pound's work as a translator has been very influential. It has seriously discredited the taxidermist notion of translation. He has not always been successful. Some of his 'mistranslations' seem merely pointless, or howlers. But classical scholars were wrong to deride *Homage to Sextus Propertius* (1919). It is as much about England during the Great War as about Augustan Rome. J. P. Sullivan has authoritatively explained (in *Ezra Pound and Sextus Propertius*) Pound's aims, and his successes and failures, in the *Homage*. In his *Cathay* Pound has been called the creator of 'Chinese poetry' for our time. And in his early translations of Japanese *Noh* drama, which he worked up from Ernest Fenollosa's prose versions, he is clearly the inventor of the modern idiom in verse.

Pound's last major translation is his greatest work. *The Women of Trachis* (1954) vies with *Samson Agonistes* as the most remarkable play in English to be inspired by Greek tragedy. Where Gilbert Murray (1866–1957) had acclimatized Euripides to a taste which favoured Swinburne and Morris, Pound, by his strange pseudo-colloquial style, neither quite English nor quite American, brings out in his translation of Sophocles just how *alien* Greek tragedy is—as remote as a *Noh* play.

Pound's Heracles is the most effective of all his *personae*. Few things in poetry are more impressive than the sudden change in Heracles when he realizes that what has happened to him is not a mere accident, a stupid atrocity, but predestined from the beginning. 'What splendour, it all coheres.' We have become used to the commonplace that tragedy is dead in the modern world. Perhaps *The Women of Trachis* will one day be recognized as the exception.

Can it be said of Pound's own poetic achievement that 'it all coheres'? He is a comparable figure in English literature to Ben Jonson. Most of Jonson's work is a mosaic of translation from ancient authors, but his own great character comes through. The same may be said of Pound. In England he has been generally judged inferior to Eliot. Yet the *Homage*, *Mauberley*, and *The Women of Trachis* do not suffer in comparison with any poems of Eliot. And for some younger readers— not only in America—Pound has come to seem the original stimulating genius, and Eliot a mere consolidator. There may be non-critical reasons for this view. Pound gained dignity from his long imprisonment in an American mental hospital. He could no longer be easily derided as a bore and a crank, or denounced as a fascist. As a symbolic figure Pound the 'caged panther', the irate half-crazy old outcast, was more attractive than Eliot with his O.M. and his Anglicanism and his playful verses about cats. For a widely agreed comparative judgement on the work of both poets we may have to wait till personal accidentals no longer seem important, and recent political controversies cease to burn.

GERARD MANLEY HOPKINS (1844–89) has long been reckoned one of the major English poets, though the body of his poetry is so small that some of his admirers know it by heart. He was born and died in the nineteenth century, but, except to a few close friends, his work was unknown in his own time. The handful of poems placed in anthologies by his friend Robert Bridges, from 1893 onwards, aroused interest in Hopkins's work, but the demand for a full collection was not met until 1918. Soon many of those who enjoyed the work of Eliot and Pound were eager to welcome Hopkins as a pioneer of modern poetry. The novelty of his diction and versification, the timbre of his verse, with its charged intensity, singled him out as unique among Victorian poets, the only one who was spiritually akin to the new movement of twentieth-century verse. Attentive readers were later to discover that Hopkins was in many respects a man of his own time. He is very different from Eliot, or Pound, or the later Yeats. But those early enthusiasts were not wrong. The qualities which attracted the moderns to Hopkins's verse are really there. He is much more a part of the twentieth century than his contemporary Doughty, though Hopkins died in 1889 and Doughty lived till 1926. The truth of the matter is that Hopkins's unique individuality transcends all such classifications as 'Victorian' or 'modern'.

Hopkins was not only a poet but a painter and a musician, a scholar and a Jesuit priest. At Oxford he experienced the influence of Matthew Arnold and Walter Pater, but after his conversion to the Roman Catholic faith in 1868 he abjured his earlier enthusiasms. He joined the Society of Jesus and adopted the rule of its founder St. Ignatius that in all his thoughts and actions he should strive for identification with Jesus. He learned not to deny himself sensuous experiences, but to enjoy them sacramentally. A flower, a landscape, a view of Oxford, still stirred his poetic sense, but now he saw the indwelling presence of God in each thing's distinctive form and pattern. We see here an affinity with the Ruskin of *Modern Painters*. And Hopkins's notebooks, which are filled with delicate renderings of nature in drawings or word-pictures, have a likeness to Ruskin's. Hopkins also has affinities with Pater, whose critical writings lay stress on the importance of particularity. But the philosophy which informed Hopkins's thought about nature was different from Ruskin's or Pater's. It was closely linked with a confessional Christianity. Hopkins was interested in the medieval philosopher Duns Scotus, who emphasized the metaphysical significance of the individuality of each created thing; but his interest in the particular, as the index of reality, was formed independently of Scotus. In so far as any philosopher influenced him in this matter, it seems to have been his older contemporary John Henry Newman. Hopkins admired Newman's *Grammar of Assent* (1870), and towards the end of his life he planned to write a commentary on it. This philosophical preoccupation has a direct interest for the student of Hopkins's poetry. Hopkins coined the word 'inscape' to describe the essential individuality of created things. Not only nature, but the human spirit, has its distinctive inscapes. Hopkins made it his purpose as a poet to render them.

Hopkins defined poetry as 'speech framed to be heard for its own sake and interest over and above its interest of meanings'. 'Some matter and meaning,' he said, 'is essential to it, but only as an element necessary to support and enjoy the shape which is contemplated for its own sake.' 'Poetry is in fact speech for the inscape's sake—and therefore the inscape must be dwelt on.' Victorian poetic diction would not do for this new vision. So Hopkins recreated Anglo-Saxon words and phrases. He drew upon dialect words. Hopkins had a scholarly, antiquarian side to his mind: he sympathized with scholars like Furnivall or Barnes, who campaigned for a 'pure', 'Teutonic', English. But he was no archaizer. When Barnes recommended 'pitches of suchness' as a better way of saying 'degrees of comparison', Hopkins remarked: 'We *ought* to call them so, but alas!' He could not approve of Doughty's attempt to revive Elizabethan English. To him it was, however beautiful, a dead language. Similarly, there was for him no question of reviving the classical quantitative metres in which his friend Bridges was interested. For Hopkins, prosody must be based on living speech. What he called 'sprung rhythm' consists, he said, 'in scanning by accents and stresses alone'. He uses slack syllables, which do not count metrically. He eliminates, so far as that is possible in an uninflected language, the particles and merely grammatical parts of speech. Sometimes, as Bridges complained, this leads to oddity and obscurity. But Hopkins was prepared to run that risk if he could get into verse 'the naked thew and sinew' of English. In the same way he did not scruple to offend a traditional ear with his emphatic alliteration, his internal rhymes, his clashing dentals and sibilants, his sequences of stressed monosyllables. The dissonant, chromatic effect of his verse, which dismayed his first readers, was to attract the taste of the twentieth century, weary of the unfailing sweetness and liquidity associated—fairly or unfairly—with the name of Tennyson.

Nearly all Hopkins's poetry is devotional. He writes with the enthusiastic intensity of the Catholic convert. But he differs from earlier convert poets, such as Crashaw, in that his devotional life and rhetoric are English, not Italian. His favoured shrine is Walsingham, not Loretto. Furthermore, Hopkins's temperament as a poet was different from that of most devotional poets. His poetic gifts were aesthetic and sensuous. However, he put 'beauty of body' below 'beauty of mind', and 'beauty of mind' below 'beauty of character'. For Hopkins, a poet does not only perceive beauty around him and try to reproduce his impressions of it in the best words; with God's inspiration he can be raised above himself and convey what is beyond the range of human observation, a sense of the indwelling presence of God in the world. It was in this way that Hopkins answered the old question, 'Does the poet imitate or create?' According to Hopkins he does both.

The emotional quality of Hopkins's verse is intense and ecstatic. His verse, he said, was 'poised but on the quiver'. Phrases like 'the horror of height' and 'the swoon of a heart' are typical of him. His most ambitious poem, 'The Wreck of the Deutschland', is charged with emotional intensity. Hopkins lavished the resources of his new style on this poem, written to commemorate the disaster in which five German nuns were drowned off the English coast. It celebrates and vindicates the ways of God to man. Tragic accidents are merely the most spectacular examples of His chastening of the human soul and recalling it to his true destiny. By a daring use of imagery Hopkins connects the shipwreck with his own spiritual crisis. It is here that the poem falters. There is a tissue-rejection between the nuns' tragedy and triumph, and the commemoration of the poet's own sufferings and ecstasies. But 'The Wreck of the Deutschland' has some marvellous stanzas. It is an astonishing metrical and stylistic achievement. Hopkins's best poems are usually shorter than the 'Wreck'. Many are sonnets. But Hopkins's sonnets are not like anyone else's. They show a fresh and unconventional handling of language and rhythm. 'Felix Randal', a lament for a dead blacksmith, reaches one of the highest points that English poetry has ever reached.

Hopkins's total output was small. He felt a conflict between the demand of poetry and the demands of his vocation as a priest. In this battle, poetry lost. And in such poetry as Hopkins did write there is often conflict and self-torment. His later poetry shows signs of his bad health, and his feeling that his creativity had declined. His inner struggles, his mortifications and frustrations, culminate in the so-called 'terrible' sonnets, such as 'Carrion Comfort', 'No worst, there is none', 'To seem the stranger', 'I wake and feel the fell of dark', 'Patience, hard thing!', 'My own heart let me more have pity on'. These poems reveal the dark side of 'inscape', that vivid sense of selfhood, 'that taste of myself which is more distinctive than the taste of ale or alum, the smell of walnutleaf or camphor'. This is now no longer, as in a poem like 'The Windhover', an occasion for rejoicing in God's creation, but a burden and a punishment. Through these states of aridity (as a disciple of Ignatius would call them) Hopkins still bears his 'burning witness'. But he is obsessed, as in 'Spelt from Sibyl's Leaves', with a sense that 'the skeined stained veined variety' of life is now separating into 'two flocks, two folds—black, white; right, wrong...' Hopkins's later poems are focused on the appalling and sublime alternatives of salvation or damnation.

These poems have attracted readers whose interest is psychological rather than theological. Of the masochistic and homosexual element in Hopkins's sensibility there can be no doubt. And we can see the appeal of Hopkins's later work to a taste in poetry which had rediscovered the devotional poems of Donne, recognized a major poet in the Yeats of *The Tower*, and rejected the ideal of classic serenity. We feel in Hopkins's 'terrible' sonnets the identity of the poet and the man. But if general human interest is a criterion, Hopkins's range is narrow. Some of his poems are cluttered and obscure. There is a want of balance and perspective in his mind. It is true that his letters, particularly those to Bridges, contain fine human insights. They often discuss—and they demonstrate—Hopkins's conception of a *gentleman*, which for him, as for Newman, was important. But they make it clear that Hopkins's literary interests were primarily aesthetic and technical. He would not have agreed with F. R. Leavis that 'questions of technique...cannot be isolated from considerations of fundamental purpose, essential ethos, and quality of life'. Hopkins will praise a poem of Bridges for its style and then add: 'The meaning is bad.' Poetry for him was a secondary activity. Other things were so much more important to him that he wrote little.

All the same, Hopkins was a great poet. What Arnold said of Gray can be said of him: he is the scantiest and frailest of our classics, but he is a classic. His work shows the true mark of the great poet: the capacity for constant development. In his early poetry he followed Keats and the Pre-Raphaelites. Later, he began the complex experiments which were to intrigue twentieth-century readers. But even as he experimented he felt the dangers of over-elaboration, eccentricity, and obscurity. So in 1887 we find him saying that 'my style tends always more towards Dryden'. We find him studying Donne's *Holy Sonnets* and cultivating 'a more Miltonic plainness and severity'. Milton had always been a model of style for Hopkins; though he thought Milton 'a very bad man', he drew his usual distinction between the man and the poet. It is Milton's sonnets that inspired such poems of Hopkins as 'Andromeda' or 'St. Alphonsus Rodriguez'. We must remember that Hopkins died prematurely. If he had lived longer, and continued his development towards a more austere and 'smoother' style, the technical elaborations of his middle years would have fallen into perspective. It would then have been beyond doubt that Hopkins was not an English eccentric but an English classic.

7

From Auden to Orwell

Auden—Empson—Graves—Novelists of the thirties—Criticism in the thirties—Churchill—Literature in the forties—Dylan Thomas—Joyce Cary and Angus Wilson—Orwell

THE NEW WRITERS of the 1930s shared a definite sense of reaction against the temper of the previous decade. Novelists like Lawrence, Huxley, or the Powys brothers were stigmatized as morbid, socially irresponsible, navel-staring. The brittle gaiety of the twenties now seemed as alien as its despair and hysteria. The new writers had in common a sense of urgency, a crispness, a shedding of affectations and frills. Where the twenties had been indifferent to political or religious commitments, the thirties were obsessed with them. The day of the cultured *rentier* was over. The harsh, bracing facts of modern society had to be understood, the growing menace of the international scene confronted. Many tried to persuade themselves that the marriage of Civilization to the hideous Industrial System, which 'Max' grimly cartooned, had regained its honeymoon spirit. The Mexican painter Diego Rivera caught the mood of the time in his mural *The Belt Conveyor* (1931). It shows part of the assembly line at an automobile plant, a team at work, while white-collar workers watch and marvel. This was how the intellectuals of the thirties wanted to feel.

There was a similar change of mood in the Edwardian age after the eccentricities of the nineties. But the thirties were more preoccupied with politics than the Edwardians had been. For the intellectuals of the time the crucial event, emotionally, was the Spanish Civil War (1936–9). It was seen in simple symbolic terms, as Rupert Brooke had seen the Great War. This was a time, said the poet Day Lewis, to 'declare one's allegiance'. Ralph Fox, who was to die fighting for the Spanish Republic, expressed this sense of occasion in *The Novel and the People* (1937). Auden's 'Spain' rendered it in poetry. The process of enlightenment about the Spanish War was to come later, in books like Gerald Brenan's *The Spanish Labyrinth* (1943) and George Orwell's *Homage to Catalonia* (1938). At the time, it provided what the writers of the twenties had felt they lacked: a Cause. Strong feelings were not confined to the intellectuals of the Left. General Franco had passionate supporters among literary men, such as Belloc, who described the war in Spain as a battle between Christ and Anti-Christ, or Roy Campbell (1901–57), a violent rhetorical poet of South African birth who had found his spiritual home in traditionalist Spain.

The Spanish War was for many a signal instance of 'the menace of Fascism'. A sense of menace dominates much writing in the period before the Second World War. Wells's *Shape of Things to Come* (1933) predicted the total destructiveness of air bombing. F. L. Lucas, who spent the year 1938 mainly in Cambridge, entitled his diary of that year *Journal under the Terror*. Winston Churchill was to call the first volume of his war memoirs *The Gathering Storm*. William Empson had already used this title for a book of poems, and both Empson and Churchill meant the same thing. England was waiting for the war. Auden's early poems and plays capture, best of all, this moment of ominous expectation. Hitler and Mussolini dominated the European stage. Roosevelt's America stayed aloof. The Stalin régime in Russia continued on its enigmatic and ruthless course.

But in the world of literature and ideas there was none the less a feeling of hope and confidence. Modern problems were vast and frightening, but they were formulable. They could be tackled by deter-mination and will. There was a rush among the intelligentsia to commit themselves to ideologies, to creeds, to scientific theories, which claimed to have the answers. Some found the answers in psychoanalysis. Others turned to the Roman Catholic Church; others, again, to the 'Oxford Group' of Frank Buchman. But the most widely attractive of all the creeds, the one that most manifestly seemed to have the answers, was Marxism. To the spell of Karl Marx (1818–83), perhaps the most effective teacher since Christ, the English intellectual community were belated in succumbing. But Marx and Lenin soon became for them what Luther and Calvin had been for their Elizabethan ancestors. Documents of the time describe the religious experience of conversion to Marxism: *The Mind in Chains* (1937), edited by Day Lewis, and retrospective studies like *The God that Failed* (1949), edited by R. H. S. Crossman, or Arthur Koestler's *The Yogi and the Commissar* (1945) and his autobio-graphy (1952). To be fair to Marx, whose actual thought is difficult to interpret, the Marxism of the thirties was an emotional attitude rather than a philosophy. In so far as the English Left writers had an ideology, it sprang from certain of Marx's later writings as simplified by Engels, vulgarized by the *epigoni*, and grafted on to English moralizing and the guiltiness of English public schoolboys. The atmosphere of schoolboy rebellion is very marked in the early work of writers like Auden and Isherwood, Edward Upward and Rex Warner. The Russian 'comrade',

faintly comic to an English ear, was assimilated to schoolboy cama-
raderie. The red flag was intertwined with the old school tie. This poli-
ticizing of literary culture was a curious and untypical phenomenon in
English life. In the work of the most publicized writers it was to be
short-lived and superficial: but at the time it had a remarkable
intensity.

It was not only that Marxism gave emotional satisfaction to such
people, or to the young poet Stephen Spender, or to brilliant youths like
Julian Bell or John Cornford. It seemed to be scientifically sound and
obviously *right*. The rich were getting richer, the poor were getting
poorer. This was a time of economic depression and mass unemploy-
ment. The Marxist apocalypse seemed to be in sight. The word 'proletariat' was much used. The American realists of the period were popular. Books like John Steinbeck's *The Grapes of Wrath* (1939) were read
eagerly. The editors of magazines and journals were quick to display
their contributors' working-class credentials. The devil-figure was the
capitalist: Nazism and Fascism were regarded as merely his by-
products. Mammon was the enemy. Not until the Russo-German pact
(1939) did many intellectuals realize that Moloch had taken his place.

For many years W. H. AUDEN (b. 1907) has been an American citizen.
And his career falls into two phases, before and after 1939, which may
be called the English Auden and the American Auden. The English
Auden belongs to the 1930s, from *Poems* (1930) to *Another Time*
(1940). To English critics he seems quite different from the American
Auden; but American critics find no difficulty in seeing Auden's work
as a coherent whole. The American Auden has helped them by discard-
ing much of his early verse and rewriting much of what remains. But
here we shall discuss only the English Auden: the Auden who excited
his readers.

The background of Auden's early work is significant. Eliot had become the master of modern poetry. *The Waste Land* had joined *Ulysses*
as a contemporary classic. A book like I. A. Richards's *Principles of
Literary Criticism* (1924) taught that poetry must be complex and
ironic. The young Auden, responsive to all this, discarded early models
such as Hardy, Frost, and Edward Thomas, and became difficult,
esoteric, allusive. Yet it was at once felt that he was not merely imitating Eliot, but going in a different direction. Other young Oxford poets,
Stephen Spender (b. 1909), Cecil Day Lewis (b. 1904), and Louis Mac-
Neice (1907–63) show his influence. Young Cambridge poets like William Empson (b. 1906) and Charles Madge (b. 1912) have testified to
their excitement on first reading him. It was felt that he had a special
kerygma for his generation. Madge wrote in 1933: 'But there waited
for me in the summer morning/Auden, fiercely. I read, shuddered, and

knew.' It is hard to recognize this fierce figure in the urbane and humorous man of letters we know, the successor to Eliot's mantle as a genial Christian–humanist sage. But there can be no doubt that many outside Auden's circle were convinced that history had written a prophetic part for him, even if he was playing it in a school blazer.

Auden's work created the imaginative landscape of the 1930s. We see it in novelists like Graham Greene and Christopher Isherwood, as well as in the poets. Its characteristics are unmistakable. There are the depressed areas and the rusty machinery. There is the peculiar schoolboy atmosphere. And there is the Germanism of the sensibility: partly archaic, deriving from the Icelandic sagas, hard-bitten and laconic, and from the Anglo-Saxon poetry Auden studied at Oxford; partly modern, deriving from an interest in contemporary Germany which Isherwood and Spender shared. All three had lived in Germany during the waning years of the Weimar republic. And on all three the Germany in which Hitler was coming to power made a deep impression. This is the background of the charade 'Paid on Both Sides', which first made Auden well known. Through a cryptic story of hereditary feuds it conveys the poet's sense that English bourgeois civilization had struck an 'air pocket' of history. Auden's early poems convey a vague sense of impending disaster, which Empson was to satirize ('Waiting for the end, boys, waiting for the end'). But they also suggest a positive remedy for the modern malaise. They speak in the tones of the healer, the therapist. The son of a doctor, Auden was keenly interested in modern psychology, especially of the more unorthodox brands. He had become convinced of the underlying identity of physiological and psychological ills. And this psycho-somatic diagnosis he extended, ambitiously, into the political and social *mal du siècle*.

Some readers were impressed. But others were irritated. They disliked the play made with fashionable names like Marx and Freud, the self-conscious up-to-dateness of Auden's verse. Great poets have not usually reflected the contemporary scene in this obvious way. Dissatisfaction was increased by Auden's most equivocal bequest to English poetry, his unvarying lacquer of smartness. His smart manner forbade any appeal to the deeper imagination and emotions. It seemed heartless. Something must be conceded to that view. But we must remember that by temperament Auden has always been a counter-romantic. He was hostile to the egotism of the romantic poets. He cultivated a more business-like, technical approach to poetry. He did not wear his heart on his sleeve. And curiously enough, with all his smartness and glibness, Auden can be more touching than any other poet of his school. His lyrics exceed in range and number those of any other modern poet, and they include such moving lines as those beginning 'Lay your sleeping head, my love'.

The impersonal, clinical surface of Auden's verse covers deep disturbances and stresses. His early poetry is composed upon two themes, one private, the other public. And so much is one theme treated in terms of the other that it is often difficult to say of a poem of Auden's just what it is about. The private theme is the theme of growing up, of overcoming the immaturities and confusions of adolescence. The public theme is the theme of England waiting for the war. Both themes are treated with an air of ominousness, as in the play Auden wrote with Isherwood, *The Ascent of F6* (1936). The storm is gathering.

The most interesting work by the English Auden is *The Orators* (1932). The American Auden has professed himself unable to account for it. Yet this weird, demented extravaganza may have more to say to us than the 'minor atlantic Goethe' of Auden's later work. It evokes, in its surrealist way, the England of his youth, under a series of timid governments, waiting for an inevitable war and the catastrophic social changes which (it was supposed) war would bring. The underlying private theme is the psychological problems of the chief *persona*, the Airman. What brings these themes together is the resentment of the social group to which Auden belonged, a professional class which felt itself growingly impoverished. This emerged in a political radicalism not of the Left but of the Right, and an art corresponding to it, sporadically vivid, patchily satiric, surrealistically incoherent. The later Auden chose not to go that way. But in *The Orators* he came nearest to making a virtue out of his chief defect, the uncertainty he arouses—and may himself feel—whether his jugglings with incompatible tones are deliberate, or miscalculated. And it is *The Orators* that ends with the best poem Auden has ever written ('O where are you going?').

It is in 'Spain' (1937) that the liberal humanist in Auden finds his best expression. He had been listened to as a *vox clamantis*. Now he speaks more positively. He recaptures the idealism which led young men to go to Spain and give their lives there. In the lines that speak of 'Time, the refreshing river' Auden has given his answer to the defeatism of T. S. Eliot. He gives a voice to the inarticulate longings of ordinary people for a better future. Yet in the same poem he can end, quite congruously, on a tragic note: 'History to the defeated / May say alas but cannot help or pardon.' Auden has now repudiated these lines and discarded the poem. He seems to agree with his critics that the hopes expressed in 'Spain' for a better future are naïve. At the same time, he has abandoned the tragedy, as well as the hopefulness, of 'Spain'.

When the thirties came to an end Auden was in the United States. He remained there during the Second World War. This made him unpopular in England. The whole Auden style fell into disrepute. And when

Auden's popularity revived, it was with a different public; no longer the young intransigent *avant-garde,* but older, more academic readers. His most attractive work was now to be found, not in his long moralizing poems, but in light verse. Those who could not take him seriously either as a Marxist–Freudian prophet, or as an Existentialist–Christian sage, could now enjoy him as a promoter of wit and gaiety. Auden has a collector's eye for good aphorisms. His own prose, as in *The Dyer's Hand* (1963), is highly aphoristic. We feel that the later Auden is not quite the sort of writer he wants to be. He admires the poetry of John Betjeman; he would like to have written the early part of *Pickwick,* or the works of Wilde or Firbank or Wodehouse. But his conscience compels him to preach and to moralize. Auden as a man of letters is sane, humane, and witty. He has been hostile to that *esprit de sérieux* which inflates writers' egotism and impels them to quasi-Messianic claims. He has revived the old conception of a writer as a professional craftsman, who teaches and entertains rather than 'expresses his personality'. He has an active, lively mind, open to new ideas. As a critic he is tolerant, wide-ranging, and generous. He can appreciate both Kierkegaard and Sydney Smith. But his best poetry seems to have drawn upon dark uncertainties which the older Auden has resolved or outlived.

The poets associated with Auden in the thirties were soon to find their own voices and go their own ways. Day Lewis emerged as a traditional poet of accomplished craftsmanship, finding his roots in earlier poets like Hardy or Meredith, and eventually following Masefield as Poet Laureate. Spender, with more original poetic force and imaginative impulse, succeeded less well in finding a secure technique in verse. We remember his work in striking passages and images rather than in complete poems. MacNeice at first seemed likely to prove the most ephemeral of these writers, a clever vogue-poet with an attractive style in light verse (as in 'Bagpipe Music'). But in the end, more than any other of these poets, including Auden, he seems to have found within himself a capacity for further development. His later work suggests that he had become a meditative poet, perhaps better grouped with Edwin Muir or Robert Graves than with the school in which he made his début.

A glance at anthologies of the period will show Auden's dominating influence. But some poets managed to remain aloof from it. Eliot was still a formidable figure in the background; and Herbert Read (1893–1968) remained attached to the school of Eliot and Pound. His best poem, '1945', was to be written later. Read is not at his best in poetry when he thinks or argues, only when he illustrates and describes. His most enduring work is likely to be neither his verse, nor the prose he wrote in the course of promoting *avant-garde* movements in art and literature, but his autobiography, *The Innocent Eye*, and *Annals of Innocence and Experience* (1940), in which he appears as a likeable and sensible Yorkshireman, with a rare capacity for linking his evocation of childhood with the experience of the grown man.

An Autobiography (1954) by EDWIN MUIR (1887–1959) has also a good chance of becoming a minor classic. It is a story of a poor boy from the Orkneys who became one of the most respected Englishmen of letters of the thirties; poet, translator, and critic. At first glance we might be tempted to assign it to a too familiar genre. But Muir's autobiography has little in common with self-satisfied narratives of 'making it'. It is distinguished from all such by its genuinely visionary quality, which invests Muir's accounts of quite ordinary events, such as dreams or illnesses, or the commonplaces of literary life, with an extraordinary light and significance. Muir was primarily a poet; but for long his quiet voice and his comparative indifference to technical novelty prevented him from making much impression. It was only late in his life that he proved able to convey the power of his vision in poems which won the awed admiration of T. S. Eliot.

The Sitwell family, Edith, Osbert, and Sacheverell, were praised and abused in their day as the last word in ultra-modernity. EDITH SITWELL (1887–1964) was one of those eccentric aristocrats, like Lady Ottoline Morrell, who enliven the drab English scene from time to time. She wore flamboyant clothes. She intoned rather than spoke her poems. More than any poet since Yeats she adopted the public posture of the Poet, inspired and exotic, a macaw among the chaffinches. Her early work, as in *Façade*, has a conscious picturesqueness, an ear-catching originality of rhythm, a keen sense of belonging to a particular moment of history. Edith Sitwell has a place in English poetry similar to that of Rex Whistler in English painting. She was an incantatory poet, comparable to de la Mare, or the early Yeats, or the Stevens of 'Peter Quince at the Clavier'. When in her later work she became distraught with the agony of the modern world, the atrocity of war, the peril of the H-bomb, her poetic voice coarsened and her talent failed.

Before Auden was launched, the Cambridge poets William Empson and Ronald Bottrall (b. 1906) had staked their claims as potential leaders among the post-Eliot poets. Bottrall was a talented poet, but most of his work looks like variations on themes of Eliot, Pound, and Hopkins. Only in a few poems, such as 'On a Grave of the Drowned', does he seem fully personal; but where he does, he has added to the memorable verse of our time. WILLIAM EMPSON (b. 1906) drew his inspiration from the revival of seventeenth-century poetry, particularly that of Donne, to which Eliot had given impetus. He had formed his extraordinary poetic style while still an undergraduate. His manner stands out as one of the most immediately recognizable in English poetry, with its punning, riddling quality, its taut rhythm, its intricacy and sophistication, and its multi-faceted vision. Critics have said that Empson's later poems are inferior to his earlier. But this seems false. 'Aubade' is quite as memorable as 'Arachne'. Nor did Empson's intellectuality always result in mere ingenious headwork. His best poem, 'To an Old Lady', with all its wit and cleverness, has a tender gravity of feeling. Empson's work was small in quantity. It was overshadowed in the thirties by Auden's, and in the forties by the baroque-decorative poetry that was then in fashion. It was in the fifties that he became a major influence. And it was then, by contrast with his imitators, that his true originality emerged. Empson's imitators tended to replace his taut rhythm with a mechanical, inflexible beat. His air of limitless sophistication deteriorated, in their work, into a facile mannerism. The poise of Empson's best work is essentially inimitable. It is the expression of a complex mind trying, with some difficulty, to establish harmony among its moods and impulses. Confusion and hysteria lie just beyond the limits of that poise, and something more disturbing still, the 'deep blankness' which is 'the real thing strange'. In his literary criticism Empson's ingenuity and subtlety also left a distinctive mark. A pupil of I. A. Richards, he enthusiastically adopted an analytical approach to criticism. In *Seven Types of Ambiguity* (1930) he developed the method of analysis pioneered by Robert Graves and Laura Riding in their *Survey of Modernist Poetry* (1927). He studied the plurality of meanings in poetry. Sometimes his analyses were unconvincing or irresponsible; but no one who has read this book attentively can have been unaffected by it. In his later criticism, as in *Milton's God* (1961), Empson became more concerned with wider questions about an author's meaning and the interpretation of works of literature as a whole. But he did not neglect his interest in verbal detail. In *The Structure of Complex Words* (1951) he offered an original, and still largely unassessed, contribution to lexicography albeit of a uniquely Empsonian kind.

The poetry of ROBERT GRAVES (b. 1895) is very different from Empson's, but in his own way he also has been preoccupied with the supreme problem of an intelligent man in our time: how to preserve sanity in a world of madness. This is the theme of Graves's war autobiography *Good-bye to All That* (1929), which first made him well known. It seemed to many a cool, even callous book. But it brought out, all the more because of that, the real horror of the Western Front. We notice Graves's emphasis, amid all that horror, on the soldierly virtues of discipline and regimental pride, the things that keep men sane.

Graves began as a poet, and it may be by his poetry that he will be remembered. But his most popular writings have been in prose. In *I, Claudius* (1934) he invented a new genre, which has had many imita-tors, the imaginary historical memoir. This book, with its successor *Claudius the God*, makes the Roman Emperor Claudius a real charac-ter, struggling for sanity and decency in a crazy world. The historical material is genuine, but it is handled in a modern, cool way. Much of the comedy arises from ancient Romans talking like Noël Coward characters. Graves's prolific prose writings include his explorations of the world of early Christianity, which he treated fictionally in *King Jesus* (1946). But there may be more true insight into Christianity in his early poem 'The Scapegoat' than in *The Nazarene Gospel Restored*. Graves's most important prose work is *The White Goddess* (1948). It can be described as a study in the pre-history of ancient myths and legends. But essentially this strange book is as *sui generis* as Yeats's *A Vision* or Burton's *Anatomy of Melancholy*. Graves stood apart from most of the writers of his time. He had little use for the Auden school, nor, after the 1920s, for the American–French modernism of Pound and Eliot. His rugged independence appears in *The Crowning Privilege* (1955), in which he attacked all the contemporary poets then in fashion. Graves's standards for good poetry are true inspiration and honest craftsmanship. His fiercest sarcasm is reserved for those who either dishonestly pretend to the one, or lazily fall short of the other.

In his own poetry, Graves began rather whimsically, as in his early volume *Fairies and Fusiliers* (1917). But in the 1920s he became a con-scious modernist in poetry. He aimed at the difficult, the metaphysical, the complex. During the thirties he was living at Majorca, away from the English scene. His work seemed obscure and eccentric. But his popularity revived with the volume of poems he published in 1945. Since then, he has usually been thought one of our most considerable poets. Graves's poetry has two aspects. One of them is represented in *The White Goddess*: the mythical element. Although he attacks Yeats, his appeal here is to the poets who have gone the way of Yeats. He seeks to recover the original, magical power of poetry. And in his poem 'To Juan at the Winter Solstice' he creates an effect of mystery and wonder almost without parallel in English verse. But for some readers Graves's incantations do not enchant. They seem too self-possessed, too intellectual. And this brings us to the other side of Graves's poetry—its astringency, its wit, its coolness. This aspect of Graves's work has been more influential. Since the fifties it has attracted poets who have no interest in *The White Goddess*, who think of themselves as counter-romantics. But Graves's own counter-romanticism is that of a romantic. His own poetry is more complex than either of the schools of poetry it has influenced. Its roots lie in psychological problems. He was severely wounded in the Great War, and he has told us how he recovered from his traumatic experiences through a sort of self-analysis. But in his best work the inner fires are still smouldering. In his love poetry—and Graves is one of the few memorable modern English love poets—we have a constant sense of delight surrounded by disaster. Even the attainment of the end of love seems to bring not happiness but a brooding, torpid feeling. His poetry can be full of fierce gaiety. And it is not always fierce: his 'satires and grotesques' are enjoyably cheerful. But the prevailing note of his poetry is sadness. Graves is an isolated figure in English literature. Although he has become well known in the modern world as a charming (if sometimes irascible) personality, the roots of his poetry are in the past, in the world of an English gentleman before 1914. In so far as he can be compared to writers of our time, his place may be with men like George Orwell or Wyndham Lewis, who have stood by themselves at the risk of being written off as cranks.

The central tradition of the English novel, the feigned history, has declined in this century. Some have even thought that only writers of low literary pretensions, like Warwick Deeping in his sincere and moving *Sorrell and Son* (1925), have written it with any conviction. The reason may be that the classical novel is the product of the liberal civilization which emerged at about the time of Swift, and ended about the time of Lawrence. And it is significant that critics have doubted if either Swift or Lawrence were really novelists. The best English novels since 1930 have tended to draw upon the resources of other genres, the fable, the satire, the thriller, the journalistic report, the political tract. The popularity of non-naturalistic experiment is significant. But prose fiction is so commodious a form that we have no hesitation in describing as novelists such varied writers as Isherwood, Ivy Compton-Burnett, L. H. Myers, Arthur Koestler, Wyndham Lewis, Evelyn Waugh, and Graham Greene.

CHRISTOPHER ISHERWOOD (b. 1904) was closely associated with Auden and collaborated with him in three plays. He gave a striking picture of the young Auden in his autobiography *Lions and Shadows* (1935). Isherwood's fiction began in the tradition of E. M. Forster. He has told us how impressed he was by Forster's casual, unrhetorical handling of sensational events. And it was in a Forster-like mood of rebellion and protest against the middle-class world of his upbringing that he wrote novels like *All the Conspirators* (1928) and *The Memorial* (1932). But these novels fail to live in comparison with the books that he wrote later, such as *Mr. Norris Changes Trains* (1935), *Sally Bowles* (1937), and *Good-bye to Berlin* (1939). These books are a kind of reportage. The author is a 'camera', a neutral observer of piquant or mysterious or horrifying events. In Isherwood's later work, such as *Down There on a Visit* (1957), the drawback of this method is obvious. His detached manner of presenting the homosexual underworld makes it look as if the author is not so much sophisticated as morally too imbecile to realize that the behaviour he describes is shocking to normal people. Isherwood's best work is neat, spare, limited. He never coins a startling phrase, but he never wastes a word. Mr. Norris and Sally Bowles are vividly drawn sketches. But the lack of a point of view soon means a lack of substance of interest. Isherwood's work, like Auden's, declined after he settled in America, but more sharply. It is to be noted that he went to California, like Huxley, not to New York, like Auden. His later work is coloured by Californian eccentricity and religiosity.

IVY COMPTON-BURNETT (1892–1969) is the opposite of Isherwood, in her total lack of surface contemporaneity. Her novels consist almost entirely of stylized conversations in mysterious country houses about sixty years ago. Yet her novels reflect an awareness of barbarism that would hardly have been possible in such a writer before 1914. Her subject is the oppression of human beings by one another, especially in a family. Moral monstrosities—cruelty, vice, crime—lurk beneath the polished surface of Ivy Compton-Burnett's dialogue. But nothing happens on stage. Everything is reported or implied: Ivy Compton-Burnett had studied Greek tragedy. Her novels have intense admirers. Her most attractive qualities are her dry, ironic wit, her hatred of tyranny and cruelty, and the essential realism of her vision: she depicts a world in which wickedness usually triumphs. But Ivy Compton-Burnett has thrown away the realistic novelist's strongest instrument, the differentiation of characters by speech. The question is whether this can be done without an effect of frivolity. Few readers can fail to derive pleasure from pages or passages in books like *Men and Wives* (1931) or *A House and its Head* (1935). But for many of us, prolonged reading is difficult, because our pleasure is too purely intellectual. There is no objection to melodrama and improbability in fiction, but they must be made to happen. The question is whether Ivy Compton-Burnett can make them happen.

L. H. MYERS (1881–1944) is one of those English writers whose reputation might stand higher if he had been a German. His masterpiece, the series of novels brought together as *The Near and the Far* (1943), can be compared with the work of Thomas Mann. But the philosophical novel has never really flourished in England, and Myers, who was above all a philosophical novelist, does not have many readers. This is a pity, because no serious writer of our time surpasses him in depth of interest. In his inferior work he is not much better than the Charles

Morgan of *Sparkenbroke* (1936), applying a lofty tone to banal adulteries. But even in his inferior work Myers, the child of a great Cambridge academic family, has much more intellectual distinction. In his best work this is his chief asset as a novelist. The setting of *The Near and the Far* is the India of the Emperor Akbar, in the sixteenth century A.D., and the plot is concerned with the intrigues over the succession to Akbar. But Myers's purpose is not that of a historical novelist. He uses, on a larger scale, the strategy Johnson used in *Rasselas*; he brings out the permanent character of the problems he deals with by placing them in a remote and sparsely described setting. Much of the interest lies in dialogues and discussions. There is, all the same, incident, plot, and suspense in Myers's book. His best critic, D. W. Harding, has aptly compared it to a detective story. But Myers had little interest in manners, or in presenting a lively realistic surface. In this respect he deserted the main stream of English fiction. Yet he was no antiquarian. He was exclusively preoccupied with twentieth-century problems. Above all, he was preoccupied with morality. Moral significance, he thought, must be the paramount criterion of value. For Myers, art, religion, spirituality were all manifestations of the moral consciousness. They can never be separated from general human values. Such a separation led, in his view, to triviality and vulgarity. He found this vulgarity even in the Bloomsbury group, who prided themselves on superiority to the common herd. Myers satirized them in his account of the nasty colony of aesthetes set up by Akbar's vicious son Daniyal. But Myers's questioning of liberal humanism went far beyond one local modern set. He extended his criticism to its ancient Greek sources. Myers's essential concern is with the relation of man to God. The choice of India for his setting is not merely a technical device: it is in the thought of ancient India that modern man finds the greatest challenge to the progressivist, activist, and pragmatic assumptions which govern his world. Myers's temperament, then, was essentially religious. This is what drew him, in the thirties, towards Marxism and Soviet Russia. 'Regeneration is there,' says one of his characters in *Strange Glory* (1936). But *Strange Glory* is also a condemnation of the materialism of Soviet Russia. And Myers, like many others, was to give up the communist faith. *The Near and the Far* closes with the psychological teaching of a guru. But we are not really convinced by the guru. Nor, it seems, was Myers himself. He was an unhappy, neurotic man, and the coming of the Second World War heightened his unhappiness. He committed suicide in 1944. Myers's strength lies in the questions he asks rather than the answers he finds. Not a born novelist, he found a way of using the novel to ask them. His work belongs, with *Women in Love* and Santayana's *The Last Puritan*, among the few philosophical novels in English that can stand comparison with Mann's *The Magic Mountain* or Goethe's *Wilhelm Meister*.

With ARTHUR KOESTLER (b. 1905) we are brought back directly to the contemporary world and the politics of the thirties. Koestler was one of those who helped to dispel the comfortable illusions of the English Left in the Popular Front period. He had the advantage, like Orwell, of having been directly involved in European communist politics. Koestler is a Hungarian by birth: he wrote his early work in German. His most famous, and best, novel is *Darkness at Noon* (1940), a fictional account of the great Russian purge trials of the thirties. Koestler conjectures that the explanation of the 'old Bolsheviks'' confessions, which mystified the world, was their spiritual bankruptcy. They knew that Stalin's régime was corrupt and wicked, but they were trapped in the logic of the ideology which had produced it. *Darkness at Noon* is in some ways a documentary work. Its only essentially fictitious element is the use of a single typical figure to stand for the whole group of the accused. Koestler even introduces facts and figures, and uses statistical arguments. His interest is in a particular ideological problem, rather than in the general human consequences of Stalinism. For these, we have to go to a work of our own time like Solzhenitsyn's *One Day in the Life of Ivan Denisovich*. Koestler's novel is at its weakest when his hero, Rubashov, is presented at the end as a martyr. What makes *Darkness at Noon* a work of art is Koestler's inward handling of the ideological problem. This has to do with the question of ends and means. In *The Yogi and the Commissar* Koestler distinguishes between the Yogi, or saint, who thinks that as the end is unpredictable, only the means count, and the Commissar who believes that human nature can be 'changed from without'. What is interesting in *Darkness at Noon* is that Koestler's fundamental sympathies are with the Commissar. He can present the *impasse* of the 'old Bolshevik' from within. *Darkness at Noon* shows up most English Left writing of the thirties as puerile. Koestler ranks among the most distinguished of Conrad's successors. In his other novels the artistic element is less and the topical, propagandist element is greater. It is significant that in his later work he has abandoned fiction. He now writes as a *philosophe*, like Wells, making it his mission to explain the discoveries of modern science and deduce the social consequences of the new knowledge.

In PERCY WYNDHAM LEWIS (1882–1957) we have a voice from the Right. Lewis became an ostracized figure in the 1930s because he admired Hitler in the days before Hitler came to power. Later he changed his mind. He was in fact always an English patriot and a democrat. But the stigma remained. Lewis was one of the 'men of 1914', whom Pound supported: he shared many artistic and political prejudices with

Pound. He was a painter as well as a writer: he launched the movement called Vorticism. He became well known as an extravagantly irascible and quarrelsome figure on the literary scene.

Lewis made himself a satirist of the twenties and thirties. His work will need many footnotes: he calls himself 'the Enemy', but it is sometimes unclear what he is the Enemy of. He derided the self-pity of the intelligentsia of the twenties, their tendency to blame the war for everything, their use of the state of the world as an excuse for boorish egotism. He attacked the modern cult of youth as a value in itself, which excused every form of misbehaviour. He satirized the eclecticism and rootlessness of modern artists. In *Paleface* (1929) he mocked the primitivism of D. H. Lawrence. In *Time and Western Man* (1927) and *Men without Art* (1934) he scored some shrewd hits on contemporaries like Joyce and Virginia Woolf.

Lewis's essential outlook already appears in *Tarr*, written in 1914. The painter Tarr, he says, 'had no social machinery but the cumbrous use of the intellect. He danced about with this, it is true. But it was full of sinister piston-rods, organ-like shapes, heavy drills.' This suggests Lewis's own writing: jagged, harsh, brutal. Lewis exemplified the anti-humanist trend of the school of Pound and Eliot and T. E. Hulme. He liked straight lines, sharp edges, violent effects. He disliked softness and vagueness, the tentative and the oblique. He is a peculiarly un-English writer. He shows that hostility to nostalgia which is so characteristic of modern painting and music. Some fellow-artists admired him enormously. The novelist F. M. Ford said that he was 'so great a realist he makes you shiver'. The painter Sickert called him 'the greatest portrait-ist who ever lived'.

As a writer, Lewis has serious defects. His satires are too long. All the great satires have been short. Cartoon-caricature protracted to the length of *The Apes of God* (1930) is intolerable. And as a satirist, Lewis's peculiarity is that he can only satirize himself. His victims are merely hallucinatory extensions of his own strange, wilful personality. At present he is not a needed writer. As an anti-humanist, Samuel Beckett has superseded him. But if he was the least in genius of 'the men of 1914', he was at any rate one of those independent, individual writers who prevent literature from falling completely into the hands of cliques and gangs. He stood outside all of them: he attacked them and they attacked him. This made for a liveliness in the literary world which is sadly lacking nowadays.

GRAHAM GREENE (b. 1904) is the leading exponent in English of the existentialist-psychological fiction which has dominated European literature since the forties. One characteristic of this new literary period is that the old snobbery of literary genres has been given up. It is now recognized that thrillers, or romances, or spy stories, or space fiction, can be as well written, and as deserving of intelligent interest, as any other literary form. Furthermore, it is widely agreed that these traditionally inferior genres are especially suited to the age we live in. 'Escape' literature used to be contrasted with 'reality', which meant the prosaic, secure, everyday world of most English readers. But today even the English reader must recognize, if only because of newspapers and television, that the late twentieth-century world is becoming more and more like the world of thrillers and spy stories and space fiction. The commonplace world is losing its ontological prerogative.

Greene's distinction in English literature is that he made the thriller a serious form. The thriller must be distinguished from the detective-story. In the thirties the English detective story was at its best. Writers like Dorothy Sayers, John Dickson Carr, and Agatha Christie brought this peculiar game with the reader to perfection. Agatha Christie (b. 1891), the world's most popular modern English author, England's answer to Simenon, bears the same relation to Jane Austen as Simenon does to Balzac. Her stories, like Jane Austen's *Emma*, offer a puzzle to be solved, and affirm reason and morality in the solution. The detective story cannot do without poetic justice. But in the thriller the problem is insoluble, and reason and justice, if they exist, have to be created by the decisions of the protagonist. The philosopher Guido de Ruggiero thought it was in the thriller that such existentialist concepts as *incarnation, the wager, the leap, anguish, bad faith*, and *the void* found their fitting artistic expression. Kierkegaard, the inventor of existentialism, was intensely interested in crime. He even thought of becoming a policeman. Dickens and Dostoevsky, who of all nineteenth-century novelists have most to say to us, were preoccupied with the psychology of the criminal. And the finest work of the greatest modern European writer, Franz Kafka's *The Trial*, opens in the very tones of the thriller, when Joseph K., 'without doing anything wrong', is suddenly arrested one morning.

If Edgar Allan Poe invented the detective story, John Buchan, in *The Thirty-Nine Steps* (1915), invented the modern thriller. But no psychological or moral problems are posed for his hero, Hannay (in so far as Buchan dealt with these, it was through the more introspective character of Leithen). In this respect Buchan's Hannay, with all his difference in *mores*, leads straight to Ian Fleming's patriotic epic of James Bond. The more serious tradition, which leads to Greene's 'entertainments' and the work of John Le Carré, includes *The Secret Agent* of Conrad, and the *Ashenden* of Maugham. In the thirties its leading masters included Eric Ambler and the English-educated American writer Raymond Chandler, whose stories of a Californian 'private eye' link the

English thriller with an American tradition, the hard cool style of Dashiell Hammett. The thriller can be of various kinds. At the moment, types of spy story have reached a high point of development; but books like Charles Williams's *The Greater Trumps* (1932), and John Fowles's *The Magus* (1966) in our own time, show that quite different varieties are possible.

Greene is the successor of Conrad. He has turned the thriller into a genre which uses the modern international world as material for art. His best work lies in what he calls entertainments: *The Ministry of Fear* (1943), *The Third Man* (1950), *Our Man in Havana* (1953). Greene is at his best when, like the film director Alfred Hitchcock, he uses an idiom of suspense. It is suspense in art that enables us to enjoy a sense of heightened awareness. His humour co-exists happily with his seriousness, because both are founded on the same perception: the element of absurdity in life. The perception of the absurd is part of the essential philosophy of the thriller: the intervention of the contingent and arbitrary, which deny tragedy to man. In the thriller these provide not only the comic relief but the shocks and surprises which are essential to its nature.

In some of his novels Greene was especially preoccupied with Catholicism. He presents it, in *Brighton Rock* (1938), *The Heart of the Matter* (1948), and *The End of the Affair* (1951), as an obsessional neurosis. But his presentation is not clinically objective. He has acknowledged that his conversion to the Church was deeply influenced by the accidentals of his own troubled childhood and youth. He was led to form clearly the concept of damnation: salvation he seems to have accepted only as a logically entailed possibility. Greene's Catholic characters seem neither to have good reasons for their beliefs, nor to find any joy in them. Their religion appears as something that has been arbitrarily inflicted on them. They take a morose pleasure in the intellectual and moral contortions it demands. Here Greene may have been influenced by the French novelist François Mauriac. But more probably it is from Eliot, and from Baudelaire through Eliot, that he derived the idea that the sexual act is more interesting if it is regarded as evil. Yet in his earlier novels it is shown as compelled and repulsive, rather than excitingly wicked. The grounds for his attitude seem merely emotional, or superstitious. Greene's general religious position seems to be that 'faith' is not so much the expression of the matured convictions of a whole person, as something which you either have or you haven't, which you can find or lose, like a talisman. This conception appears at its most absurd in his plays.

Greene's novels are not at their best when he is closest to the moral-realistic tradition, the art-form proper to agnosticism, according to which we are all different shades of grey. Melodrama is a better form for Christianity, which divides men into saved and damned, the sheep and the goats. It is true that no sane Christian claims to know *now* who are the saved and the damned. In *this* world everything appears in varying shades of grey. But art is not life. There is no objection, in art, to a proleptic eschatology. The name for it is melodrama. In *The Power and the Glory* (1940) Greene makes a fine use of melodrama. The sinful priest and the virtuous atheist confront each other. The persecution of the Church, the distinction between priest as priest and priest as man, the continuity of the priesthood ('the power and the glory, for ever and ever')—these were things that had forced themselves on the writer. *The Power and the Glory* was a book he had to write. The exotic background of Mexico is essential to the theme. Greene's Mexico is 'a state of mind'. As such, it is unclouded by everyday accidentals and ambiguities. The choices have to be made, the chase pursued. The contrast with Greene's later novel, *A Burnt-Out Case* (1960), is striking. Here we feel that Greene is deliberately re-charging his imagination, soliciting his material.

EVELYN WAUGH (1903–66) has often been bracketed with Greene as a 'Catholic novelist'. But they are very different. Greene has always remained a man of the Left. A novel of his like *England Made Me* (1935) has the typical anti-capitalist bias of the thirties. Waugh was a man of the Right, and not the radical Right of Wyndham Lewis, but the reactionary, traditionalist Right. Greene's book about Mexico is the record of a spiritual experience: Waugh's is propaganda for British oil interests. Greene opposed colonialist war and tyranny in Vietnam, Cuba, Haiti: Waugh defended the Italian invasion of Abyssinia. Greene's manner, until his later work, is stiff, inflexible, suspenseful; Waugh's is consciously elegant, relaxed, and vivacious. Yet both belong peculiarly to the recent epoch of literature. They both have a high technical skill and a lively, entertaining surface. Some readers may not care for either Waugh or Greene, but few readers can have been bored by them. Since Forster gave up writing fiction, no English novelist has excelled them in vividness of description and immediacy of presentation.

Waugh began as a satirist, displacing Aldous Huxley as the latest smart name in fashionable fiction. He was a better writer than Huxley, more economical, less pompous, far defter at catching the tone and manner of the 'bright' society he was writing about. His early books are farces in the tradition of Voltaire's *Candide*, showing the adventures of an innocent (in *Vile Bodies* he is less innocent) in a crazy smart world. Waugh concentrated on an upper-class set. It seems to have been a set to which he came from outside. And a *parvenu* quality, which made him tiresome as a man, has left its mark on his writings. The social climber who is irascible and self-conscious about his position is not an attractive figure. But niceness is not an asset to a satirist. Waugh's early satires are centred on daring people. They attracted him; but he keeps direct comment out of his books. Outrageous or horrifying events are presented in a poker-faced way. A prison chaplain's head is sawn off by a lunatic. A lover is made to eat his mistress's body at a cannibal feast. Such things horrified older readers. They could find nothing funny in *Decline and Fall* (1928) or *Vile Bodies* (1930) or *Black Mischief* (1932). Younger readers enjoyed Waugh as a purely frivolous writer, like Firbank.

But there was a serious side to Waugh's satire. And it was when he came to reveal what he was in favour of that he began to dismay the frivolous. Before *A Handful of Dust* (1934) Waugh's interest had been mainly in the daring, or in clowns and buffoons. Now he became interested in a different kind of character: the upright. Tony Last in *A Handful of Dust* belongs to this category. Dull and limited as he is, with his upper-class English inhibitions, he represents in Waugh's mind an aristocratic and romantic ideal. The book is about his betrayal by his wife, a typical 'modern' woman. We are left in the dark about her motives and her personality, as about those of her seedy lover. By a technique of omission and exclusion Waugh conveys an acute sense of the brittleness and pointlessness of modern high society. *A Handful of Dust* is full of things that make us laugh. Even the fate of Tony Last is funny, stranded in South America reading Dickens to a half-caste. But it is also very painful; and so is the whole book. Some scenes in *A Handful of Dust* vie with scenes in Huxley's *Point Counter Point* as the most painful in modern fiction.

In *Brideshead Revisited* (1945) Waugh revealed, too egregiously for some, the extent to which his Catholicism was bound up with romantic snobbery. But he defended with dignity class-attitudes that are usually held only by unintelligent people. Compared with two novels more or less contemporary with it, Huxley's *Time Must Have a Stop* and Maugham's *The Razor's Edge*, Waugh's novel has an essential seriousness which partly redeems its absurdities. Waugh's lighter stories show the advantage to a humorist of a serious point of view. *Scoop* (1938) is a satire on high-powered journalism that has lost none of its point. *Put Out More Flags* (1942), more than any other novel, captures the atmosphere of that strange period of the phoney war (1939–40). *The Loved One* (1949) is not only black humour about the 'American way of death', but a serious criticism of the false attitude to life which underlies it.

Waugh's later work shows an almost unique development in a satirist. He became broader and more humane without going soft. *The Ordeal of Gilbert Pinfold* (1957) showed his own understanding of the cruelty and obsessions and snobbery which had motivated his early work. *Sword of Honour* (1965) is Waugh's finest work, and the best English novel inspired by the Second World War. The hero, the wartime officer Crouchback, is a study of the upright man. He is dull, conventional, and ultimately wrong in his romanticizing of the war, as he is made to realize. He is not likeable. But his utter integrity and honour come through. Waugh sees clearly, as in his earlier work he seemed not to, a distinction between the merely cultural and the spiritual. Crouchback's Catholicism is not just sentimental piety about his family. It is a real force to him and to the reader. The climax of *Sword of Honour*, a series of three novels, is Guy's vain attempt at an act of compassion: 'in a world of hate and waste ... a single small act to redeem the time'. What is most remarkable in *Sword of Honour* is the treatment of Guy's erring ex-wife, Virginia Troy. She is a figure of the modern world that Waugh and his hero detest. Unlike them, she accepted change as the evidence of life. It is evidence of Waugh's humane development as a writer that we come, as we do, to like and respect her.

In the literary and social criticism of the thirties the outstanding figure is Eliot. Many of his views were violently disagreed with by other critics, but it was he more than anyone else who formulated the issues. J. M. MURRY (1889–1957), a distinguished editor and critic, was influenced by Eliot's ideas, but worked out his own position. He and Eliot were often led to more precise formulations of their own thought by their controversies with each other. Murry's best criticism was written when he was not too closely identified with his author, as he was in his books on Shakespeare, Keats, and D. H. Lawrence. His essay on the eighteenth-century poet Collins suggests that he wrote better on authors towards whom he could feel the right blend of sympathy and detachment. His books *Aspects of Literature* (1920) and *The Problem of Style* (1922) show him at his best. In the thirties Murry became more and more preoccupied with attempting to work out a religious philosophy for modern man. He is less successful here than in his purely literary criticism. G. Wilson Knight (b. 1897) shared Murry's religious preoccupation, and went farther than Murry in the affirmation of a personal faith. Knight's religious intensity and the visionary quality of his imagination made him, in *The Wheel of Fire* (1930) and its successors, the most original interpreter of Shakespeare's plays since the great work of A. C. Bradley.

Even more influential in our time has been the criticism of F. R.
LEAVIS (b. 1895). It has been said that he dominated English criticism
as Keynes did economics. Leavis won his fame as a teacher at Cambridge University. He believed in the paramount importance of English
literature, not merely as an academic subject, but as something which
could transform the minds and lives of intelligent people in our society.
Leavis was very conscious of living in a period of cultural decline, and
this gave an urgency and sharpness to his pronouncements. As a literary
critic, he proposed a bold transformation of the historical perspective of
literature. He took up the cause of Eliot in *New Bearings in English
Poetry* (1932). He followed this with *Revaluation* (1936), in which he
extended his revision of the history of English poetry to earlier periods.
The Great Tradition (1948) revealed a shift of Leavis's interests to the
novel. He had now come to feel that, since the nineteenth century, prose
fiction had largely superseded poetry as a means of expression for the
greatest literary artists. This shift coincided with his growing belief that
Lawrence, rather than Eliot, was the supreme genius of the age. Leavis's
influence derived part of its strength from his activity as a literary
editor, the dominating figure of the group centred on the periodical
Scrutiny, which firmly maintained the Cambridge tradition of independent liberal humanism amid the ideological battles of the thirties. Leavis
is rare among writers in that his creative force has expressed itself entirely through discussion of the work of other men. As a critic of
academic background, he is almost unique in having actually influenced
literary taste and judgement in his time.

In one respect Leavis departed from the critical tradition of Cole-
ridge: he disclaimed the necessity of formulating the theoretical basis
of his views. The only first-rate English book on aesthetics was written
by the Oxford philosopher R. G. COLLINGWOOD (1889–1943), whose
Principles of Art (1938) championed the primacy of the imagination in
the creation of works of art. Here he opposed the psychological doctrines of I. A. Richards. But, like Richards, he greatly admired the
poetry of Eliot, and unlike most aestheticians his philosophic thought
was closely related to what was going on in the literature of his own
day. Collingwood's work in the thirties shows his increasing political
commitment to the Left position. By the time he wrote his *Autobiography* (1939) there is a harsh and violent strain in his writing, as when
he insists that the opposing philosophical school of 'realism' was
objectively pro-Fascist. Collingwood is a distinguished example of the
kind of philosopher whose writings appeal, as Berkeley's and Hume's
had done, to the educated person of literary and historical interests.
Since his time, most philosophy has tended to be more severely technical and deliberately self-restricted in scope.

Among the writers of the thirties WINSTON CHURCHILL (1874–1965) stands by himself, as he did at the time in politics. As a statesman he was widely feared and distrusted. And in the literary world he had long been treated as a figure of fun, or a charlatan. Herbert Read in *English Prose Style* (1928) placed a characteristic piece of Churchillian rhetoric beside words of naïve burning sincerity supposed to have been spoken by Vanzetti, a symbolic martyr of the Left. Read saw in Churchill's writing nothing but theatrical falsity. But theatricality was natural to Churchill, and so was archaism. In literature he was an antediluvian, the last Englishman who could use the word 'dauntless' in a serious context. His prose style derived from Macaulay, and like Macaulay he was a great journalist. Vividness and prompt wit are as typical of them both as their purple.

In 1940 Churchill was the right man at the right moment. Words were all the British had to fight with, and Churchill was accustomed to fighting with words. Life had always been a struggle for him, against physical inferiority, and his mother's neglect, and the oppressive image of his brilliant dead father. In his gloom and isolation he developed his private romanticism. And in 1940 his inner world of make-believe happened to coincide with reality. 'Whatever you may do,' he told the French generals, 'we shall fight on for ever and ever and ever.' It was then that Churchill was revealed as a fellow-countryman of William Blake, steering his furious course between the stars of God and the abysses of the Accuser. In Churchill's war-time speeches, made to the House of Commons and afterwards broadcast, English literature became a fighting weapon. The facts must not be idealized. Reynaud, the French Prime Minister, also made good speeches. They are forgotten, because France was defeated. Britain held out: but Britain had not been invaded. But this does not affect the place of Churchill in literature. Besides being himself a part of history, he was a notable historian. And in *My Early Life* (1930) he wrote one of the most charming of autobiographies.

The Second World War was in many ways a playback of the Great War. It was, of course, a period of great upheaval and disruption. But it was less traumatic spiritually than the Great War. It had been expected by most thinking people, and England survived it better than most of them had feared. The Second World War did not inflict the division between soldier and civilian which left such a bitter mark on Great War literature. There was no gap between the home front and the conscripted ex-civilians. Even after the 'finest hour' of 1940 England retained a very high degree of national unity during the second war. This was based largely on traditional patriotism, but also on the vague hopes of a better world. J. B. Priestley's popular war-time broadcasts reflected this hope. But somewhere about 1944 hopes for radical social change were to vanish. The Labour Government of 1945, which succeeded Churchill's, was very prosaic. It made valuable social reforms and effected the liberation of India; but it was a government of elderly men with little appeal to the idealism and imagination of youth. Yet there was no such spectacular disenchantment as in the years following the Great War. Disillusionment is only possible if there have been illusions, and by 1945 few intelligent men had any.

The 1940s were one of the worst periods of English literature. But perhaps it is remarkable that any literary life went on at all. No writer produced a work of art comparable in tragic power to Henry Moore's shelter drawings. The only partial exception is the fire-watching episode in Eliot's 'Little Gidding'. There were no 'war poets' as in 1914–18, because of the different character of the two wars. Poets killed in the war included Sidney Keyes (1922–43), the epitome of all the sensitive young men reading Yeats and Eliot and Rilke in translation; Alun Lewis (1915–44), a more original poet who followed the path of Hardy and Edward Thomas; and Keith Douglas (1920–44), who was more than the others to find his own voice and remain an active presence in the poetry of our own time. Among the civilians a baroque-decorative school flourished, in which 'apocalyptic' poets said nothing loudly and verbosely. Among these was Dylan Thomas, whose *Deaths and Entrances* (1946), though in a noisy ranting style, does convey something of London in the air-raids. But Thomas's best work was done elsewhere and deserves separate discussion. Of novels, Henry Green's *Caught* (1943), and Elizabeth Bowen's *The Heat of the Day* (1949), both catch, in different ways, the peculiar feeling of the time.

It was during the forties that the school of writers sometimes called 'Anglo-Oxford' began to come to public attention. These writers had in common the profession of some form of Christianity and some sort of connection with Oxford University: otherwise, the label is foolish. The first of these writers to become well known were Dorothy L. Sayers and C. S. Lewis. DOROTHY L. SAYERS (1893–1957) began with some excellent detective stories, which deteriorated when she fell in love with her aristocratic detective and wrote, in *Gaudy Night* (1935), the worst readable novel in the English language, with the exception of its successor, *Busman's Honeymoon* (1937). Her religious dramas, like her translation of Dante, are over-familiar in style. Dorothy Sayers, though not the least pretentious, is probably the weakest of these writers. C. S. LEWIS (1898–1963) excelled in many kinds—medieval scholarship, philology, science-fiction, religious apologetic, literary criticism, witty verse— without quite seeming a genius in any of them. His most lasting work may be in his stories for children. But his *Allegory of Love* (1936), a study of medieval literature, has been enjoyed by specialists and non-specialists alike. Both Dorothy Sayers and C. S. Lewis were agreed about the genius of CHARLES WILLIAMS (1886–1945), and it may have been mainly admiration for Williams that led T. S. Eliot, and the American Auden, to lend their support to 'Anglo-Oxford'. But William's cryptic poetry and unperformable plays are less attractive than his idiosyncratic history, *The Descent of the Dove* (1939), and his *Figure of Beatrice* (1943), a study of Dante. Williams might be called the iconographer of 'Anglo-Oxford'. Its really profound thinker may turn out to be Owen Barfield (b. 1898), the least discussed, but in some ways most interesting, of all these writers. No one who has read his *Poetic Diction* (1928), or his philosophical work *Saving the Appearances* (1957), can forget them. The most remarkable inventive achievement of this group was the sequence of stories called *The Lord of the Rings* (1954–5) by J. R. R. TOLKIEN (b. 1892). This strange book, at first merely the centre of a cult, was to become widely popular, in America as well as in England. It offers the strongest possible challenge to those who regard the work of writers like Joyce or Lawrence as what the twentieth century means by greatness. Tolkien has invented a complete imaginary world which finds its analogy, if anywhere, in *Beowulf* and Malory and the Sagas, in folk-tale and fairy-tale. Yet, despite the author's disclaimer, many readers have found it relevant to the spiritual struggles of our time. The writers labelled 'Anglo-Oxford' are all very different from one another. But they do seem to have this in common: they offer a challenging criticism of that unthinking loyalty to 'the modern world' which may be replacing for many contemporaries the more ancient loyalties to country or family or religious faith. In contrast, these writers like to evoke a more traditional, hierarchical order of values, in which the battle against what they see as evil draws on quasi-military virtues of discipline and obedience.

The best poet of the forties was DYLAN THOMAS (1914–53). His gifts were real, but very specialized. If de la Mare is the poet of children, and Auden the poet of undergraduates, Thomas is the poet of boys at puberty, the time when the youthful personality is invaded by exciting, frightening, incomprehensible forces. In his early poetry he created a verse-idiom in which to express this. A poem like 'The force that through the green fuse drives the flower' caught the attention of readers of poetry as no poem had done for years. As a poet, Thomas produced a few fine complete poems and many brilliant lines and passages. But even in his best work he is contorted and obscure, like his American equivalent Hart Crane, and, as with Crane, we sometimes wonder whether it is worth searching for his meaning. Thomas's peculiar style may owe something to his Welsh origin. His work cannot be fully understood without a knowledge of Wales. Behind his poetry lies Wales of the depression, culturally impoverished, and defaced by industrialism; but behind it lies also the beauty of Swansea Bay and the Gower Peninsula.

Thomas at first had only a coterie public. But in his later life he became a popular author. He is the Barrie of our time. His lilting poems about childhood, like 'Fern Hill', are much loved. His story 'A Child's Christmas in Wales' has come to rival Dickens's *Christmas Carol* in popularity. His radio play *Under Milk Wood* (1954) is the best known of his attempts to imagine a world that is purely good. It may have been the desperate need to recapture the enchantment of innocence that fostered the addiction to alcohol which was to kill him. Thomas appeared in many rôles: as a public personality and entertainer; as the 'Young Dog', gay and mischievous, delighting to tease his sophisticated patrons; as a drunken lout, indulging his vices and weaknesses. None of these are important in the Thomas of the best poems. We should hear less of the man and more of the poet. His moving poem 'Do not go gentle into that good night' shows that he was not written out as a poet in his last years. When we compare this poem with one by Graves, for example, or one by Auden, we see that Graves and Auden are real poets, but they seem to lack force in comparison with Thomas. Of all the poets after Eliot, none is his equal in poetic fire.

Two novelists of the time, JOYCE CARY (1888–1957) and Angus Wilson, revived hopes for a declining genre. Cary came from an upper-class background. He had several careers before he settled down to novel-writing. He had been a District Officer in Africa, an artist in Paris, a war correspondent in the Balkans. Cary's view of life was a sombre one. But there was a hard cheerfulness and buoyancy in his temperament which comes out in his work. Cary wrote in the tradition of Defoe, the impersonation by the author of an imaginary character. His most famous character, or 'humour', is the painter Gulley Jimson. With Kingsley Amis's 'James Dixon', and Muriel Spark's 'Jean Brodie', he is one of the few memorable humours of contemporary fiction. The title of the novel in which he appears, *The Horse's Mouth* (1944), is a pointer to Cary's general intentions. He was always asking what is the real thing, what is the truth about life. Cary had aspirations to be a philosophical novelist. He had carefully worked out his convictions about the qualities that are necessary to survive spiritually in a world of conflict. But, for a philosophical novelist, his mind was not sufficiently in contact with other minds. It seemed too closed. In his later novels Cary sought to give a broad encyclopaedic picture of the movement of English life. These novels raise doubts whether Cary, with all his devotion to his craft, was really a natural writer. He does not convey a spontaneous fusion of style and content, intuition and word. His imagination was primarily a visual one, and his attempts to make the reader see the picture led him into laboured conceits. His humour was sometimes heavy-handed. But, more than any other novelist of our time, Cary boldly confronted the traditional problems of the novelist. Not really 'intellectual' or 'modern', he was shrewd, intelligent, observant, and an excellent craftsman.

ANGUS WILSON (b. 1913) began as a short-story writer, but in *Hemlock and After* (1952) he established his place among the leading novelists of the fifties. This novel was one of the first English novels to tackle directly, without giving offence, the hitherto tabooed subject of homosexuality. But its central theme is recurrent in Wilson's work : the discovery, by a distinguished liberal humanist, of the forces of cruelty and violence within himself. In Wilson's hands the realistic tradition of the novel has become very brittle. *Hemlock and After* disconcerts us with its sudden changes of focus. Its characters seem to exist on very different planes. Some belong to a comic cartoon, especially the working-class characters, or the melodramatic villains. Others, like Bernard Sands, the hero, are more deeply studied, in the tradition of psychological fiction. All Wilson's books have this unevenness. Parts of them seem never to have left the scenario. Other parts are richer or denser. It is not clear whether this is because Wilson's essential talents are those of a short-story writer, or because the tradition in which he is writing has become uncertain of itself.

Of all the writers discussed in this chapter, the most controversial is GEORGE ORWELL (1903–50). Orwell, whose real name was Eric Blair, cannot be understood without reference to English class-structure. He had an upper-class education at Eton. But Eton was less important in forming him than 'St. Cyprian's', the preparatory school which Cyril Connolly has described in *Enemies of Promise* (1938) and Orwell himself in his devastating essay 'Such, Such Were the Joys'. Orwell took up a post as a colonial policeman in Burma. But in revulsion from imperialism he gave it up and plunged into the depths of poverty. He lived as a tramp, he worked as a dishwasher. He attempted to identify himself with the working class. At the same time, he never lost the class authority which he shared with other rebels like Keynes or J. B. S. Haldane. He was never completely *déclassé*. And, though he passionately disagreed with Kipling, he had a respect for Kipling's point of view. Like Kipling, he believed firmly that discipline, order, and patriotism were essential to national survival. So, though he was a left-wing author and involved in left-wing politics, he became the hammer of the Left. He assailed the Left orthodoxy of the day with even greater ferocity because its leaders were, like him, from upper-class and public-school backgrounds. Orwell's experiences in Spain, which he described in *Homage to Catalonia* (1938), were a turning-point in his life. From then on he saw completely through the lies of Stalin's propagandists. On domestic questions he was equally independent. In *The Road to Wigan Pier* (1937) he described the life of a depressed area in which he lived for a time, and drew social and political conclusions not to the taste of left-wing orthodoxy. So Orwell became an isolated figure: isolated socially, because though he kept his old school friends, he could not identify himself with the social class to which they belonged; isolated politically because though he despised the appeasing Conservative governments of the day, he could not identify himself with the 'Popular Front' promoted by the Stalinists.

It was the coming of war in 1939 that gave Orwell something to identify himself with. He was a patriot. And he realized that all his powers must be dedicated to ensuring the survival of England. Whatever the faults of England—and to Orwell they were many—England remained the symbol of everything he liked. Orwell was an old-fashioned man. He liked village life and country pleasures and old ways of doing things. His temperament was conservative. So he supported the war, and opposed the pacifist intellectuals of the time as fiercely as he opposed the Nazis.

As a writer, Orwell was primarily an essayist. His novels, as he admitted, are merely vehicles for his ideas. *Coming up for Air* (1939) is the best, because there Orwell virtually abandons the pretence that the hero is anything but a spokesman for himself, full of nostalgia for the England of his childhood, hating the new civilization of plastics and advertisers and synthetic foods that had displaced it. But Orwell's most memorable books are *Animal Farm* (1945) and *Nineteen Eighty-Four* (1949). With these he became an international writer. *Animal Farm*, like *Gulliver's Travels*, has become a children's classic, but like *Gulliver* it is meant for adults. It is a beast fable: it is also a withering satire on Stalin's dictatorship. The famous sentence, 'All animals are equal, but some animals are more equal than others', was added as an afterthought, but it sums up the mordant irony of the whole story. In *Nineteen Eighty-Four*, inspired by the Russian writer Zamyatin, Orwell wrote a terrible and distressing book. It is a despondent forecast, written by a dying man, of what will happen when totalitarianism is able to take over not only the body but the soul. *Nineteen Eighty-Four* has been much attacked on political grounds. When Orwell called the system which dominates his imaginary society 'Ingsoc', he was accused of playing into the hands of the enemies of socialism, and of surrendering to defeatism about the future. In fact Orwell had never believed in human perfectibility. But he went on believing in the possibility of change for the better. The one note of hope in *Nineteen Eighty-Four* is the song of a simple working woman, a 'prole'. The deeper theme of the book is not political but philosophical: *Nineteen Eighty-Four* should be related to Orwell's essay 'Politics and the English Language'. It is above all through linguistic manipulation that the rulers of Orwell's nightmare society effect their control of the mind. Orwell's lifelong preoccupation with the craft of writing is closely linked with his determination to defend telling the truth.

Epilogue: Literature Since 1950

EUROPE AFTER THE Second World War had come a long way from the serenity of *La Grande Jatte*. Its condition was epitomized, rather, by George Grosz's picture of *The Survivor* (1945), a haggard figure, hardly recognizable as human, stumbling, knife in teeth, among piled-up corpses. England, alone of the belligerent nations of Europe, did not experience such horrors. But she was materially and spiritually exhausted by her second Pyrrhic victory over Germany; and, if the destruction caused by the war was less complete and spectacular than in other European countries, so was the process of recovery. There was to be no 'economic miracle'. And the slow adjustment to England's changed place in the world was long hindered by lingering illusions. Perhaps only in the late sixties was it really accepted, emotionally, that England was no longer at the centre of world affairs, and was playing a comparatively minor rôle in the Russo-American conflict. The painful digestion of contemporary realities brought with it rumbles of resentment and a surge of nostalgia. The present of England seemed drab and the future dubious.

Yet the historian A. J. P. Taylor had some justification for saying that the English people had 'risen' after the Second World War. A better-fed and better-housed working class were to confront the age of austerity. The coherence and continuity of English life, its pervasive tolerance, its relative social peace, have proved their fitness to survive amid the unprecedented acceleration of change in the modern world. In the early fifties there was even a short-lived national euphoria, signalized by the Festival of Britain (1951) and the coronation of the young Queen Elizabeth II (1953). That mood was quickly to die out in the débâcle of the Suez war (1956). Yet it was the main achievement of the premiership of Harold Macmillan (1957–63) that the penultimate processes of Imperial dismantlement were carried out in a less traumatic atmosphere than might have been expected. The moment called for the policy of Bunyan's By-Ends, 'looking one way and rowing another', and Anthony Eden's successor showed himself better qualified for this feat of watermanship. In his day the English governing class drew heavily upon its traditional resources of blandness to temper the 'wind of change' to the shorn lambs of the middle classes and to reassure the working class that they had 'never had it so good'. Since his day this blandness seems to have vanished. If England in our time is not quite Yeats's Ireland of 'great hatred, little room', it seems to be a place with not much room and a good deal of dreary backbiting.

Literary periods are convenient for historians, but rarely coincide with reality. Jane Austen seems an odd figure in the Romantic period, and *Samson Agonistes* is out of place in an anthology of 'Restoration drama'. But, without too gross a distortion, three periods of English litreature can be distinguished in this century. The first, the age of Shaw, Wells, and Galsworthy, began about 1880 and faded out after the Great War. The second, beginning about 1910, came to an end some time in the forties. Perhaps 1943, the year that Eliot's *Four Quartets* were published as a whole, might be chosen as its terminus, for the influence of Eliot, both positive and by reaction, is so marked in this period that historians may well decide to call it after him. The third period, the one in which we now live, has not been dominated by a single figure. Few English critics believe that any great writer has emerged since 1950. This may be simply because no individual of transcendent gifts has happened to choose literature as a means of expression. That is the natural explanation. But it is interesting to reflect on the possibility that the *concept* of 'great writer' no longer applies in the modern world. However, neither of these explanations may prove necessary. Literary history abhors a vacuum, and it is quite likely that historians will discover (or postulate) a modern writer who overshadows his contemporaries as a Dryden or an Eliot seem in retrospect to have overshadowed theirs. But at the moment there is no obvious candidate. The institution of literature goes on; novels are published, plays are performed, critics air their views; even poetry survives, like some ancient tribal remnant in its tiny reservation. But there are few signs that readers, old or young, feel about the writers of our time what the boy Keats felt when he wrote the sonnet which begins 'Great spirits now on earth are sojourning'. That feeling was not unknown to the 1920s and thirties; but it seems to have vanished today. So it may be fitting to bestow on the present phase of literature only the impersonal title of the 'existentialist-democratic' period.

In modern times we normally look to the novel to provide the record and critique of moral and social changes. Those who are at home with the art of fiction as practised by Balzac and Stendhal, or by Scott and

Trollope, can still find anchor in the work of novelists of the older generation. But it is doubtful whether it will prove as durable as that of their masters. This is not only because their talent is inferior. It is largely because the institutional framework, the secure points of social reference, of the traditional novel are fast disappearing. The more solid modern English novelists seem to have found their creative theme in the two nations of England, not so much those distinguished by Disraeli, the rich and the poor—though this bifurcation is far from obsolete —as the more impalpable duality of 'we' and 'they'. Anthony Powell (b. 1905) and C. P. Snow (b. 1905) have been concerned with characters who (from the present point of view) count as 'they'. Powell writes of the traditional upper class, with a special interest in its rogues and oddities. Snow writes of the *novi homines* who have risen into the higher ranks of the Civil Service, or equivalent positions in an administrative-technological world. In contrast, J. B. Priestley (b. 1894) has concerned himself with 'us', the people outside the worlds described by Powell and Snow. In his journey from vaguely Left sentiment to a disgruntled populist conservatism Priestley has charted a representative intellectual history of our time.

The work of the novelists who first appeared in the fifties is distinguished from that of their predecessors by its lighter, looser structure, its disregard for the appearance of solidity, and its astringent coolness. The great writers' club (in Amis's phrase) had closed after the deaths of Joyce and Virginia Woolf in 1941, and it was not reopened. A businesslike intention to communicate with the reader replaced the pretentious internal wrestlings of the 'art-novels' which had fallen into disrepute. The best-selling *Lucky Jim* (1954), by Kingsley Amis (b. 1922), is typical. Predominantly an amusing farce which happened to catch the public's fancy, its main subject is the boorishness provoked by an insufferable sham culture in a provincial backwater; but it does not always manage to control the insurgence of deeper interests and problems. The frequent hostility which Amis has inspired is partly political in character. He has been a fierce opponent of the pro-Soviet Left: he may expose other insecurities besides those of his heroes. His stories of wartime Army life in *My Enemy's Enemy* (1962) explore human meanness and baseness with painfully sharp insight. Other stories show a more positive bent, an effort to recreate the idea of the gentleman in an age when this idea has lost its religious, social, and moral basis, to become the vaguely regretted anachronism that it is for the hero of Amis's *Take a Girl Like You* (1960). The work of John Wain (b. 1925), in *Hurry on Down* (1953) and its successors, reveals his preoccupation with what is enduringly English in a world of transient shams and illusions. His touch is less certain in his fiction than in his verse and criticism; but in his best writing he catches something of the blend of severity and tenderness that we associate with Chekhov. He is at the same time a humorist, and a harsh and sombre observer. The novels of Iris Murdoch (b. 1919) are distinctive and individual. For those who have read her, some everyday episodes, at once ominous and ludicrous, some queer tangles of human relationship, will always be coloured by memories of her novels. In her work from *Under the Net* (1954) onwards she has evolved, out of her Oxford philosophical training and her interest in French experimental fiction, a kind of story which might be called the dialectical romance. Her books have the same relation to feminine romantic fiction as Graham Greene's have to the thriller. She excels in the type of character who exemplifies Aristotle's dictum that thought of itself moves nothing. It is not true, as some have said, that her intellectuals are without ideas; but, though she is not a satirist, her best work is an exposure, which no satirist could improve on, of the shallowness and instability of much of our intellectual culture: its emotionality without deep feeling, its ingenuity without imagination, its intellectuality without seriousness.

We sometimes hear adverse criticism of the writers who are held to typify English literature since the fifties. They have been accused of a suffocating gentility. They have been ridiculed for their over-preoccupation with insular minutiae, such as the intricate sub-divisions of English class structure. They have been charged with complacent indifferences to the momentous events of a larger world. It is true that these writers have refrained from soliciting their imaginations to do justice to the appalling savageries, the vast impersonalities, the dizzying rapidities of the 'global village'. Much contemporary English writing does lie open to the charge made against Pasternak's *Dr. Zhivago* by some Communist critics, that the hero (and by implication the author) was an 'internal émigré'. But we cannot justly blame writers for remaining truthful to what actually does stimulate their thought and invention, and not what excited publicists think *ought* to inspire them. What is really disappointing about much present-day verse and fiction is that they do not take us out of ourselves. This is because the writer has not been taken out of himself; at the end we, and he, are the same worried sensualists that we were when we started.

Some readers who find the dominant school of fiction too insular and limited have turned to other writers who, in very different ways, have tried to broaden its range. The success of the four novels comprising the 'Alexandria Quartet' (1957–61) of Lawrence Durrell (b. 1912) suggests that there is a widespread hunger for flamboyant exoticism, both in locale and in *mores*, and for an ostentatious elaboration of technique. Durrell, a poet as well as a novelist, has not been afraid of the modern disparagement of 'fine writing'. His Alexandria, replete with atrocity, perversity, and abnormality, offers the most sensational alternative possible to the tepidity of English life and culture. But Durrell's eccentrics, unlike Proust's, remain in our memories as merely eccentrics; they do not send us back to everyday life with a heightened understanding of ourselves and the world. Moreover, we are not as shocked or thrilled as we ought to be: even if every strange incident or *trait de mœurs* is a direct transcription from life, his mode of writing inhibits belief in them. The poet and the fantasist in Durrell impede the novelist.

The work of William Golding (b. 1911) has also only an uneasy relationship to the central tradition of English fiction. He is a didactic writer, concerned, like the early Graham Greene, to expose the hollowness of Pelagian illusions about human nature; but, unlike Greene, his gift is less for realistic fiction than for the invention of a new kind of moral fable. *Pincher Martin* (1956) is a powerful study of human egocentricity. The anti-humanism of Golding sets him apart from most of the writers mentioned in this chapter. His best book, *Lord of the Flies* (1954), a sombre desert-island fable, is suffused with pessimism. It is the anti-humanist counterpart of a work like Albert Camus's *La Peste*. For many critics, Golding is the most interesting writer to emerge after the Second World War. But some have wondered if his preoccupation with stylized novelty of experiment is in excess of the moral substance of his work. It may be that a more profound study of 'the impulse to dominate', which has nearly wrecked our world already, and may one day succeed in doing so entirely, is to be found in the *Eustace and Hilda* trilogy (1944–7) of L. P. Hartley (b. 1895), which uses more traditional methods of character-study.

More promise for the future of English fiction may be seen in the rise of a number of writers qualified to treat English working-class life from within. The working class had hitherto mainly appeared in literature as comic relief, or propaganda figures, or homosexual delinquents—the latter being the only types, apparently, with whom middle-class novelists were acquainted. But in recent years several writers of talent, coming from that class, have shown themselves the successors of Lawrence in achieving a humane inward treatment of people who were once 'submerged'. *Saturday Night and Sunday Morning* (1958), by Alan Sillitoe (b. 1928), is memorable; and with another of these writers we may speak of genius rather than talent. *This Sporting Life* (1960), by David Storey (b. 1933), has claims to be the most astonishing novel of our time. Dealing with a professional rugby footballer, it sends us back for comparison to Arnold Bennett's story 'The Matador of the Five Towns'; but Storey's writing has a power and a radiance Bennett never achieved, and he has been able to invest a plain story of rather inarticulate people with tragic dignity. He has succeeded, where most naturalistic writers have failed, in keeping his language 'level with life' without the surrender of his own controlling intelligence and judgement.

But the prevailing mood in literature today perhaps favours the analytical rather than the creative mind. It may be significant that the nostalgia and the turning-inward of imaginative literature have been accompanied by considerable activity in criticism, literary, social, and cultural. We should note here the work of Raymond Williams (b. 1921); and of Richard Hoggart (b. 1918), who continued that study of the sociology of popular literature pioneered by Q. D. Leavis in *Fiction and the Reading Public* (1932). This work shows an increased concern about the basis of humane culture in a democracy, and the social and political implications of that tendency (so marked since Arnold) to go to litera- ture for what men once sought in religion. The artless plays of Arnold Wesker (b. 1932) may also have contributed to the awakening of a keener social consciousness. In literary criticism, the work of F. R. Leavis and his associates at Cambridge in the journal *Scrutiny* (1932– 53) stands unsurpassed for its sustained incisiveness and rigour; but *Essays in Criticism*, started in 1951 by F. W. Bateson at Oxford, has also done much, with its own more urbane tone and accent, to bring together an intellectual community in which Bateson has combined the Socratic rôles of the gadfly and the midwife. Such critics are distin- guished by their pressing concern for high standards in an age when the study of literature is not only a joy, or a discipline, but a *moyen de parvenir*.

English drama since the twenties long seemed a backwater. After Shaw's heyday the separation between the theatre and literature, which he had tried to abolish, continued in the work of a dramatist like Terence Rattigan (b. 1911). In plays like *The Browning Version* (1948) Rattigan showed a technical accomplishment not bettered by any playwright of his time; but rarely did he offer anything radically disturbing to the tastes and convictions of the West End playgoer. The literary drama, in its own way, seemed equally unvital. Eliot's plays have their author's distinction, but for many admirers they are the most dispensable part of his work; the Auden/Isherwood propaganda plays of the thirties now look like coterie charades; and the poetic drama of Christopher Fry (b. 1907), for which great claims were made in the forties, appears to have been a false dawn.

A revival in English drama has been seen by some critics as beginning with *Look Back in Anger* (produced 1956) by John Osborne (b. 1929). This play, together with *The Entertainer* (1959), was readily related, at the time, to social and political topicalities, the unease, discontent, and frustration of English society in the backwash of the Suez war. The ranting *déclassé* 'Jimmy Porter' became its spokesman, just as the Byronic hero, or Hamlet, or Marlowe's Dr. Faustus, had been for similar moods in theirs. It seemed natural to relate the vogue of 'anger' to the emergence of a new educated class which felt itself denied the opportunities and privileges of the old. The preoccupations of Osborne were assimilated to those of Amis or Wain, or those of Wesker and Raymond Williams. But in the light of Osborne's later work it would seem that his drama, though it has political implications, is really less political than was thought. His gloomy, hate-ridden plays, like Strindberg's or Edward Albee's, are rooted in domestic obsessions. He may be contrasted with his remarkable contemporary John Arden (b. 1930), of *Serjeant Musgrave's Dance* (1959), in that his plays are essentially unliterary. They illustrate the recent phenomenon which John Wain has noted, the taking-over of drama by the actors. Drama written by actors has not always, of course, been unliterary. Shakespeare and Molière were actors; and their plays need to be performed to have their full effect. But in our time the distinction between plays for reading and plays for acting is much greater; and Osborne remains on the actor's side of the divide.

The work of Harold Pinter (b. 1930) presents many problems. When we question the arbitrariness of the events in a play like *The Homecoming* (1965), the things that in real life would be disgusting or shocking or inhuman, but there seem merely inexplicable, we wonder if our questions are relevant. Pinter's art resists the application of normal criteria of reason and purpose. It is anti-humanist, with its situations which seem like happenings on a street corner upon which we have come by chance; its dialogue, banal or coarse, in which through the wonderfully caught inconsequence of ordinary speech there filter sinister overtones of chaos and insanity; its characters, in whom the capacity for moral, civil, or even intelligible behaviour seems numbed. Pinter has some affinities with Samuel Beckett (b. 1906), the modern dramatist who divides with Bertolt Brecht (1898–1956) the homage of the European theatre-public. Beckett is for the modern generation what Maurice Maeterlinck was for their Edwardian forefathers; whimsical squalor is more to our taste than whimsical dreaminess. In *Waiting for Godot* (1952; English translation 1954), and perhaps in that play alone, he has created a work of art. Whatever his debt to Joyce, and to *Sweeney Agonistes*, he has given his own distinctive interpretation to the ancient rôle of the clown. His German rival Brecht has revived another old genre, the Morality play. Brecht's theory of drama lays down that the playwright should completely control the responses of the audience. Whether this is the case in his most powerful work, such as *Mother Courage*, is doubtful: but his didactic aim is certain. Pinter's work, like

Beckett's, is more puzzling. But is it unfair to condemn it, as some have done, because it asks us to see life as inconsequent to the point of insanity. It is perfectly legitimate to dramatize mental disorientation. The artist has the right to explore all human possibilities, though obviously the public may ignore such work if it does not interest them.

Much poetry in the 1950s was written in conscious revulsion from the extravagant postures and irrationalities of the previous decade. Dylan Thomas (d. 1953) was perhaps the last to adopt the great-poet manner. Poets like Kathleen Raine (b. 1908) and Vernon Watkins (1906–67) still followed the way of Yeats, hieratic and hermetic, but their verse is quiet and inward-looking, not vociferous. It was characteristic of the fifties that the nostalgic verse of John Betjeman (b. 1906) should have been so popular. Betjeman's poetry is rooted in traditional Victorian styles, but he handles them with an arch sentiment and irony that belong to our own time. His poem on the death of George V (1936), with its touch of mockery and its undertone of genuine piety, is a good example of his characteristic tone. Equally nostalgic, but more gifted as a poet, more sensitive in his verse-movement, and fresher in his diction, is Philip Larkin (b. 1922). Larkin's work is small in quantity and narrow in range; but to discuss it is to escape from the world of literary fashions: we talk about poems, not trends. A poem like 'The Whitsun Weddings' has a depth of feeling which convinces us that the poet in Larkin is not confined to his well-known half-comic *persona* in 'Church Going', taking off his bicycle-clips with 'awkward reverence' in the unfamiliar surroundings of a church. His best poems find their places on that short list of the best poems of our time, which might also include Ted Hughes's 'Pike', Thom Gunn's 'In Santa Maria del Popolo', F. T. Prince's translations from St. John of the Cross, Edwin Muir's 'The Horses', and John Wain's 'Anecdote of 2 a.m.'. Such poems come unbidden to the mind; they take us away from ourselves and the poets, into a world where the imagination is stirred and the emotions freed. Any good anthology of this period would also find room for some poems by Donald Davie (b. 1922), whose 'Remembering the Thirties' is a good example of the dry, cool, yet not unfeeling quality of his verse; and for work of D. J. Enright (b. 1920), whose colloquial wry asides have given many readers a similar pleasure to that which Louis MacNeice's early work gave their predecessors. The most remarkable of recent poets is Ted Hughes (b. 1930). His best work glows with a primitive intensity of response to the life of animals as the reflection of the life of God. It is sometimes nervously tensed, as if to stun the reader into submission; but it is more effective when it is more relaxed, observation rather than insistence. Hughes's mature work, as in the volume called *Wodwo* (1967), shows a sensitive delicacy as well as a muscular strength. What is more disquieting is his habit, which has grown, of resorting to an unparalleled violence of expression without creating a situation to explain it. But since Dylan Thomas the language has had no poet of such fire and force.

The position of poetry in modern England is not exhilarating. The only use of poems seems to be to fill up columns in magazines; they are reviewed and read only by poets, if at all; they are spoken to jazz. But to say that poetry has declined is like saying—as many people do—that Christianity has declined. Certainly there are fewer nominal Christians than ever before, just as there are fewer nominal readers of poetry; but what does that prove? Poetry remains the most intimate, reflective, and delicate means of expressing the spiritual life of the individual and the nation.

The future of English poetry, and of English literature in general, is bound up with the future of England and the English people. How hopeful is that future? Shaw's Caesar was ready to destroy the past and build the future with its ruins. Orwell's Winston Smith refused to drink a toast to the future and insisted on drinking to the past. Many Englishmen today sympathize with Orwell's attitude rather than with Shaw's. Present-day literature is not very exciting, or very promising. The twentieth century may not be a great age of literature, in England or anywhere else. Our age may be remembered rather as an age of science and technology. Some have even thought that literature will become obsolete. But this is unlikely: the power of words will surely always remain, because only words can command thoughts. Television will no more supersede literature than the films did. And it should be remembered that there have been dull periods before in English history, times of intellectual and imaginative stagnation which tend to occur, for some reason, in the sixties and seventies of each century. (America was lost in one of them.) According to precedent, there should be a lively period of literature in the near future (1980–2030)—if there is any future.

Such concerns may seem very marginal, in days when the national attention is more than ever fixed on England's need to secure a firm economic base. But once in a while we may look beyond practical exigencies and speculate on England's spiritual contribution to the future of mankind. We may turn our thoughts to other times in history when England has played a unique part: to seventh-century Northumbria, keeping alive the light of civilization in a dark time; to the age of English Gothic, not so wonderful as French Gothic, but with its own unique beauty; to the seventeenth century, when fundamental issues of religion and justice were discussed far and wide in the most literate society of Europe; to the eighteenth century, when England was the envy of Europe for domestic tolerance and sanity; to the nineteenth century, when England was the pioneer industrial nation and the work-shop of the world. No one can say what new contribution to the life of the spirit may be yet to come from the vigour, inventiveness, and clemency of the English people at their best. But sceptics would be unwise to predict that there will be none. 'A great poem,' said Hopkins, 'is like a great battle won by England'; and we can be moved by his words, even if the only battles we now want England to win are victories of the spirit.

A Select Reading List

Dates given for plays are of first production; for other works, of first publication, whether in England or America.

(D = drama, F = fiction, P = prose non-fiction, V = verse)

1900 JOSEPH CONRAD, *Lord Jim* F
1901 RUDYARD KIPLING, *Kim* F
1902 WALTER DE LA MARE, *Songs of Childhood* V
1903 SAMUEL BUTLER, *The Way of All Flesh* (posth.) F
      BERNARD SHAW, *Man and Superman* D
1904 J. M. BARRIE, *Peter Pan* D
      CONRAD, *Nostromo* F
      HENRY JAMES, *The Golden Bowl* F
1906 JOHN GALSWORTHY, *The Man of Property* F
1907 CONRAD, *The Secret Agent* F
      J. M. SYNGE, *The Playboy of the Western World* D
1908 HILAIRE BELLOC, *Mr. Clutterbuck's Election* F
      ARNOLD BENNETT, *The Old Wives' Tale* F
      G. K. CHESTERTON, *The Man who was Thursday* F
      KENNETH GRAHAME, *The Wind in the Willows* F
1909 H. G. WELLS, *Tono-Bungay* F
1910 E. M. FORSTER, *Howards End* F
1911 MAX BEERBOHM, *Zuleika Dobson* F
      CONRAD, *Under Western Eyes* F
1912 SHAW, *Pygmalion* D
1913 D. H. LAWRENCE, *Sons and Lovers* F
1914 JAMES JOYCE, *Dubliners* F
1915 LAWRENCE, *The Rainbow* F
1916 JOYCE, *A Portrait of the Artist as a Young Man* F
1917 T. S. ELIOT, *Prufrock and Other Observations* V
      W. B. YEATS, *The Wild Swans at Coole* V

1918   G. M. HOPKINS, *Poems* (posth.)   V
       LYTTON STRACHEY, *Eminent Victorians*   P
1919   THOMAS HARDY, *Moments of Vision*   V
1920   ELIOT, *The Sacred Wood*   P
       LAWRENCE, *Women in Love*   F
       WELLS, *The Outline of History*   P
1921   ALDOUS HUXLEY, *Crome Yellow*   F
       SHAW, *Back to Methuselah*   D
1922   ELIOT, *The Waste Land*   V
       A. E. HOUSMAN, *Last Poems*   V
       JOYCE, *Ulysses*   F
1924   FORSTER, *A Passage to India*   F
       I. A. RICHARDS, *Principles of Literary Criticism*   P
       SHAW, *St. Joan*   D
       P. G. WODEHOUSE, *The Inimitable Jeeves*   F
1925   SEAN O'CASEY, *Juno and the Paycock*   D
       VIRGINIA WOOLF, *The Common Reader*   P
       YEATS, *A Vision*   P
1926   EZRA POUND, *Personae*   V
1927   V. WOOLF, *To the Lighthouse*   F
1928   T. F. POWYS, *Mr. Weston's Good Wine*   F
       EVELYN WAUGH, *Decline and Fall*   F
       YEATS, *The Tower*   V
1929   ROBERT GRAVES, *Good-bye to All That*   P
       J. B. PRIESTLEY, *The Good Companions*   F
1930   W. H. AUDEN, *Poems*   V
       NOEL COWARD, *Private Lives*   D
       WILLIAM EMPSON, *Seven Types of Ambiguity*   P
       G. WILSON KNIGHT, *The Wheel of Fire*   P
       W. SOMERSET MAUGHAM, *Cakes and Ale*   F
       SIEGFRIED SASSOON, *Memoirs of an Infantry Officer*   P
1931   V. WOOLF, *The Waves*   F
1932   AUDEN, *The Orators*   V
       ELIOT, *Sweeney Agonistes*   D
       HUXLEY, *Brave New World*   F
       LAWRENCE, *Letters* (posth.)   P
1934   YEATS, *Collected Plays*   D
1935   IVY COMPTON-BURNETT, *A House and its Head*   F
       ELIOT, *Murder in the Cathedral*   D
       HOPKINS, *Letters to Robert Bridges* (posth.)   P
       CHRISTOPHER ISHERWOOD, *Mr. Norris Changes Trains*   F
1936   C. S. LEWIS, *The Allegory of Love*   P
       DYLAN THOMAS, *Twenty-five Poems*   V

1938 MAUGHAM, *The Summing-Up* P
      GEORGE ORWELL, *Homage to Catalonia* P
1939 R. G. COLLINGWOOD, *An Autobiography* P
      JOYCE, *Finnegans Wake* F
1940 GRAHAM GREENE, *The Power and the Glory* F
      ARTHUR KOESTLER, *Darkness at Noon* F
1941 WINSTON CHURCHILL, *Into Battle* P
1943 ELIOT, *Four Quartets* V
      HENRY GREEN, *Caught* F
      L. H. MYERS, *The Near and the Far* F
1944 JOYCE CARY, *The Horse's Mouth* F
      L. P. HARTLEY, *The Shrimp and the Anemone* F
1945 ORWELL, *Animal Farm* F
1948 GRAVES, *The White Goddess* P
      F. R. LEAVIS, *The Great Tradition* P
1949 ELIZABETH BOWEN, *The Heat of the Day* F
      ORWELL, *Nineteen Eighty-Four* F
      POUND, *The Pisan Cantos* V
      WAUGH, *The Loved One* F
1950 ELIOT, *The Cocktail Party* D
1951 ANTHONY POWELL, *A Question of Upbringing* F
      C. P. SNOW, *The Masters* F
      STEPHEN SPENDER, *World Within World* P
1952 ANGUS WILSON, *Hemlock and After* F
1953 JOHN WAIN, *Hurry on Down* F
1954 KINGSLEY AMIS, *Lucky Jim* F
      DONALD DAVIE, *Brides of Reason* V
      WILLIAM GOLDING, *Lord of the Flies* F
      EDWIN MUIR, *An Autobiography* P
      IRIS MURDOCH, *Under the Net* F
      J. R. R. TOLKIEN, *The Lord of the Rings* (1954–5) F
1955 PHILIP LARKIN, *The Less Deceived* V
1956 GOLDING, *Pincher Martin* F
      JOHN OSBORNE, *Look Back in Anger* D
      POUND, *The Women of Trachis* D
1957 TED HUGHES, *The Hawk in the Rain* V
1958 I. MURDOCH, *The Bell* F
      ALAN SILLITOE, *Saturday Night and Sunday Morning* F
1959 JOHN ARDEN, *Serjeant Musgrave's Dance* D
1960 AMIS, *Take a Girl Like You* F
      HAROLD PINTER, *The Caretaker* D
      DAVID STOREY, *This Sporting Life* F

1961   EMPSON, *Milton's God*   P
       WAIN, *Weep Before God*   V
1963   F. T. PRINCE, *The Doors of Stone*   V
       STOREY, *Radcliffe*   F
1964   GOLDING, *The Spire*   F
       LARKIN, *The Whitsun Weddings*   V
       PINTER, *The Homecoming*   D
1967   HUGHES, *Wodwo*   V
1974   TOM STOPPARD, *Travesties*   D
1975   LARKIN, *High Windows*   V
1977   HUGHES, *Gaudete*   V

Index

Index